Prehistory Papers II

Cross-disciplinary Studies Into our Past

Paul Dunbavin

ISBN: 978-0-9525029-5-1

British Library Cataloguing in Publication Data
A catalogue record for this book is available from the British Library

ISBN: 978-0-9525029-5-1

BY THE SAME AUTHOR

Atlantis of the West
Picts & Ancient Britons
Under Ancient Skies
Towers of Atlantis
Prehistory Papers

CONTENTS

PREFACE

In an article within a millennium edition of the journal *Nature*, entitled *Decline of the Generalist,* physicist Frederick Seitz bemoaned the increasing specialisation of academic studies.[1] He highlighted that few academics under the age of fifty showed any interest at all in research outside their own specialist field; and that this was particularly prevalent in the humanities. This is indeed a major failing within the academic system, whereby a specialist qualification is deemed to be a gateway to publication on any other subject you may wish.

The present author is a generalist. Now what does that mean exactly? It implies someone with broad general knowledge, researching *across* academic boundaries – a "jack-of-all-trades; master of none" to use an old saying. Whether or not you consider that to be a derogatory classification, or an advantage, probably defines where you sit within that debate.

There has always been a huge educational divide between arts and sciences; students are forced to choose their path at an early age. Most will likely know which subjects are their best, but a few are forced to drop a subject that they like, simply because it does not fit the curriculum of their institution. The school won't let you take both history *and* physics, because the lessons are scheduled at the same time!

Seitz failed to appreciate that it is the academic system itself that drives increasing specialisation. He suggested that the universities should remedy this decline in general knowledge by recognizing that 'elite' students could absorb a more diverse spectrum of studies. I remember smiling at this suggestion back in 2000. Who will give the student any points should he fail his physics exam because he has been spending too much time reading history? How then will he ever join the 'elite'?

Students are also deterred from expressing original ideas as their tutors will reward only the required text-book answer. Only when they move on to PhD level are they expected to produce novel research, by which time the creativity has likely been squeezed out of them. In the course of my own cross-disciplinary research I have often spent valuable time reading theses that held little original content. Once beyond the graduation barrier it's back to having their homework marked again. Should the alumnus attempt to publish a new theory then it must first negotiate the barrier of a specialist referee; a senior academic who will recoil at anything that doesn't fit their own narrow world view. Thus textbook knowledge is converted into unchallengeable dogma; eminent consensus becomes fact.

This problem is again particularly acute in the humanities, where consensus is based on the opinions of eminent authorities, citing earlier generations of same. In the sciences a referee should check the data and mathematics – and if that be sound – then a paper may find its rightful place in publication. In the humanities the referee sits like an infallible magistrate, censoring any author who does not adhere to the specialist terms and received wisdom. This problem of 'text-book inertia' also extends to the semi-sciences, such as archaeology or geology, where field data and cumulative expert opinion must come together. Thus many specialist essays become tedious lists of references and jargon, opaque to the general reader – or indeed to specialists in other fields.

The next challenge lies in the lack of a true cross-disciplinary journal in which to publish the work of the generalist. There are no interdisciplinary studies departments in any university and no generalist professors able to give an unbiased review across a diverse range of subjects. Refereed journals are based on the defined academic disciplines, each paper considered only by a specialist in that field, unable to see beyond. The expert referee will expect the author to know every authority in their own subject – but it is unreasonable to expect the cross-disciplinary researcher (the generalist) to read *every* paper in *every* subject.

I remember, back in the 1980s and 90s being shocked by the negativity of academic peer-review compared to the constructive quality-assurance reviews that I was accustomed-to in private industry. I was also surprised by the arrogance and poor manners displayed by some referees; and by their lack of imagination.

While on the issue of 'elites': the cross-disciplinary generalist will also encounter the real and unpleasant impediments of academic snobbery. There is a perception that academically qualified persons are a cut above the general population. To quote my own grand-nephew, a late-starting student, "you think when you go to university (that) you will be among intelligent people – but you're not"! A graduate at whatever level of accomplishment remains a highly trained specialist. They may be proficient within their chosen field but beyond its bounds they possess no more competence than their taxi driver; yet would the taxi driver's research be published?

As Nils Holm explained in his study of Intelligence Quotient, the median IQ score of 100 is intended to be the average of the general population; whereas the mean for a random sample of university students was around 125. The level deemed 'highly intelligent' would be above 147, however Holm measured only a single academic who reached 149 and none achieved above that.[2] As he comments: "*a university student with an IQ of 125 becomes a professor with an IQ of 125*". He further adds "*Wherever the brightest people on this planet go, it's not research and education…there are no more high-IQ people among academics than in the general population*".

I can add my own experience when (briefly) I was Mensa loc-sec in Aberdeen. We held a few regional tests because the locals were reluctant to travel down to England. I cannot remember an academic who achieved 148. I do recall a motor mechanic, oil-rig workers and a wealthy housewife (or homemaker if you prefer) who could converse on any subject from science to Liverpool football club! Generalists are *not* in decline; they are simply *not* academics.

A final obstacle is economic. Specialist journals are often *subscription-based* or are paywalled online. A cross disciplinary investigator must pay multiple subscriptions to view some new research papers. Alternatively, potential readers are invited to gain access "through their institution". There seems to be a premise by the editors that only university students or graduates will be interested in reading research papers or are capable of understanding them. Perhaps they just want to ensure that taxi drivers don't get hold of them!

Fortunately, since 2000 when Seitz wrote his *Nature* article the internet has grown exponentially and it allows us to bypass the exclusive club of universities and elite academics and put out research for anyone who dares to cite it. True, on the internet it may sit alongside much twaddle and fake-news, but at least it is there in print to be found by the most thorough researchers. The problem is that university scholars tend only to read the journals and papers in their own specialist field. Many fear that they may themselves be censured should they cite or publish research that has not been filtered through the recognised channels. To quote Anthony Durham: "*People may think (it) is intellectually second-rate…or sheer nuttery*".[3] If the specialists fail to study and cite more widely then the fault lies with them, not the with generalists.

This is Volume II of Prehistory Papers. As with the first volume it provides a permanent citation-repository, with an ISBN, for the author's cross-disciplinary articles, lest they disappear at some point from their original ephemeral websites. The articles cross a range of subjects: *ancient history, mythology, archaeology, genetics, sea-levels, climatology, Egyptology, astronomy, calendars, geophysics, linguistics* and others. The format and content is preserved as closely as possible to the original online published format. The articles may cite a variety of sources, from the omnipotent *Nature* to non-academic websites, so long as they offer sound and original contributions. Correctly, they are *articles*, rather than academic papers; specialist terminology is avoided so that they are comprehensible to the general reader, or to researchers of a different discipline.

Note that all grammar herein is British English, be it correctly applied or not, despite the attempts of Microsoft to force us all to use Americanisations – or should that be Americanizations?

---

[1] Seitz, F. *Nature*, Vol 403, 3 February 2000, p 483. www.nature.com

[2] http://t3x.org/iq/whatnow.html

[3] Anthony Durham & Michael Goormachtigh
www.proto-english.org/galatians.pdf

1

Supernova Ejecta and the Dangers to Earth

Summary: *As discussed in an earlier article 'Dangers to Earth from Ancient Supernovas' the risk of catastrophic collision with a comet or asteroid comes not just from objects orbiting our sun. There are other forces that may reach us from the galaxy or perhaps from the wider cosmos. While astronomers typically focus upon the objects that they can detect, optically or by any other method, the real danger may be from forces that we are unable to see or predict. In this article the focus should fall not on the stellar outbursts themselves rather upon their wider effects and the debris that they eject; and how these events could have caused catastrophic phenomena in Earth prehistory.*

It is not unreasonable to assume, given the advance of science and mensuration, that a day will arrive when astronomers can map every tiny asteroid and comet that orbits the sun, right out to the limits of the Oort cloud; and with the aid of supercomputers to predict their orbits far into the future. Those that might one day pose a threat could be watched and given a gentle 'nudge' to change their orbit and we may think ourselves safe again. The 'Domesday comet' is probably already on its way and will one day reach us. Perhaps in the meantime we may ponder how to divert it. But what about those visitors on a hyperbolic trajectory like *Oumuamua* and comet *Borisov* that originate from beyond our solar system?

When I first wrote about extra-solar comets and oblique impacts in the early 1990s, the suggestion that comets might strike the Earth was still a toxic subject – until the impact of comet Shoemaker-Levy-9 on Jupiter was witnessed on our TV screens. For most of the era of telescopic astronomy, keen amateur observers discovered solar asteroids and comets only when they passed close enough to be seen as tiny objects moving against the stellar background. There was what Stefan Michalowski called the 'giggle factor' attached to the possibility of impacts. [1] Eugene Shoemaker declared that the 'giggle factor' was gone when we witnessed a comet strike giant Jupiter. Sadly, denial has not gone away, because there remain other unseen dangers that could harm our planet or have done so in the past. As astronomers probe the universe in new ways they discover many new phenomena: quasars, pulsars, dark-matter halos, rogue planets, gamma-ray bursts, gravitational waves; all unheard of half a century ago. What next?

Catastrophism in Earth history?

Many enigmas and possible catastrophic episodes may be cited during human prehistory that demand an explanation as to what could have caused them. The confirmation that an asteroid strike in Yucatan caused the ancient demise of the dinosaurs has set the norm and any suggestion of catastrophic phenomena in more recent Earth history founders on the reply: where is the crater? Even the colossal asteroid impacts that cause mass extinctions would not have sufficient kinetic energy to appreciably affect the Earth's axis or its orbit. This has long been sufficient for mainstream science to dismiss the idea of changes to Earth's obliquity and pole shifts during recent prehistory as pseudo-science. This has now become a serious blind spot in our understanding of the past.

Gradualist geology and climate science cannot explain the abrupt transitions between glacial periods, and at the end of the Ice Age; or the sharp transitions between stable climate regimes that have occurred during the Holocene. It cannot explain the rapid changes of sea level: the raised beaches and submerged forests that have transpired over the same period. It could not explain the references to astronomical phenomena described in various religious and mythological sources that suggest ancient pole shifts and axis tilts. Gradualist geology could not explain a possible change to the length of day since the earliest calendars. It could not explain climate and sea-level events, such as Joseph's famine, or Atlantis – or Noah's Flood. These examples from human prehistory demand a source of *high-energy* catastrophic events that do not leave an obvious impact crater. They were *survivable* events (i.e. they were not followed by a mass extinction) yet they possessed sufficient energy to have reset the rotation and climate of the Earth. Here are just a few suggestions based on the latest astronomy and physics.

Hyperbolic Exocomets

The appearance of comet *Oumuamua* passing close to us on its hyperbolic trajectory in 2017 has opened minds. Just two years later comet *2I/2019 Borisov* was observed with an even higher excess velocity. With two such discoveries within just two years we have to wonder how many earlier examples could have been missed. [*see note 1*] Astronomers have long been aware of hyperbolic comets with a small excess velocity; but these could be explained as solar comets ejected by a close encounter with one of the planets, only to fall back millions of years later. [2]

Oumuamua was a tiny object unnoticed until it was already on its way out of the solar system, most likely an asteroid ejected from its own star system. Its elongated shape (at most 1000 x 100 m) suggests that it is a fragment of a larger planetesimal torn-apart by whatever event projected it into interstellar space. Comet Borisov was somewhat larger and was enveloped in a coma more closely resembling a solar comet – apart from its excess velocity.

Just recently (2022) I have noted the possibility of impacts by exocomets mentioned by one of the 'television academics', together with another guest who ventured the possibility of oblique 'bouncing' impacts that would leave little trace on the Earth's surface. Such discussion could never have happened in earlier decades. When first I explored such matters in *The Atlantis Researches* back in the 1990s the concept of impact events was still derided as mere pseudo-science; one simply could not mention such things and be taken seriously.

Supernovas and Remnants

Astronomers regularly observe supernovas in distant galaxies although none have been observed in our own galaxy in the era of telescopic astronomy. An earlier article *Dangers to Earth from Ancient Supernovas* examined the question of what happens to the cloud of smaller bodies that must be orbiting a massive star before it goes nova. [3] These may comprise a range from planetesimal-sized objects down to meteorites small enough to hold in your hand. Pieces of the exploding star's iron and silicon core might also be flung-out by the rapid spin-up of a supernova as it collapses. If these are propelled-away rapidly enough then their kinetic energy would exceed any threat from a solar asteroid. By the time the expanding shell of high-energy meteors reached us it would be so dispersed that they would be millions of kilometres apart. They should arrive with about the same regularity as we observe local supernovae (so about every few hundred years) with impacts being even less frequent. We should only detect such meteors during the brief few days when the shell of solid ejecta passes rapidly through the solar neighbourhood.

Around every giant star there must be a region where planetesimals and asteroids orbit in a kind of perverse 'Goldilocks zone'. The lifetime of a supergiant star is just a few million years; not long enough for planets to coalesce. Before it explodes the star must pass through an expansive Wolf-Rayet phase that would envelop the planetesimals in its gas cloud. Close-in to the final supernova explosion the asteroids would be reduced to dust to become part of the visible remnant, eventually to cool and merge with the interstellar medium. Further out, the expanding shock wave would pass by the asteroids leaving them battered but still in orbit about the collapsed star. Between these two extremes there must lie a zone where the planetesimals are disrupted yet are not reduced completely to dust; fragments of an optimal size would accelerated away by the wind of the supernova.

Astronomers observe supernova remnants expanding at velocities of 1500 km/s (*Crab Nebula*) and even 13800 km/s (*Cassiopeia A*) Compare these to the relatively sedate orbital velocity of Halley's Comet at 55 km/sec or even the unbound Oumuamua at 87.3 km/sec.

One will often see, discussed in various astrophysical papers, the explanation that visible supernova remnants fade as they cool and expand until their density diminishes to that of the interstellar medium. This really amounts to a near-perfect vacuum colliding with an even more perfect vacuum; a strange concept! The meteorites that regularly strike the Earth have orbited in the solar wind since the formation of the solar system and have not been halted. If a supernova remnant contains swept-up solid ejecta then, at the hyper-velocities considered, there is nothing in the interstellar medium that could prevent the shells of meteors from expanding long after the visible nebula has faded.

Supernovae are not the only potential source of hypervelocity comets and asteroids that could reach the solar neighbourhood. Since the 1950s when Hoyle first proposed the theory of nuclear synthesis in stars the study of stellar collapse has been further refined. Physicists now recognise that even the high densities of a supernova core-collapse are insufficient to explain the abundance of the r- s- and p-process elements heavier than iron and nickel, such as gold, platinum and uranium. To form these heavy nuclei requires the high densities of a neutron star merger – themselves already collapsed supernova remnants. By inference, the presence of these heavy elements on Earth mandates that the primaeval solar nebula must have been preceded by a neutron-star merger.

Gamma Ray Bursts

Discovered accidentally in the 1960s by Vela satellites monitoring for nuclear tests, these were soon recognised as cosmic in origin; the product of explosions in distant galaxies. Two classes of gamma ray sources are now recognised: *long bursts* caused by implosion (hypernova) of high-mass luminous stars; and the *short bursts* attributed to the merger of neutron stars. Such collapses emit polar jets as the particles and radiation are channelled by the magnetic fields. The only reason we observe so many is that their magnitude is so bright that they are visible from the edge of the universe.

Gamma ray bursts are statistically rare, loosely estimated at a few per million-years in any galaxy; but consider that there must be 180 times this estimate for events where the polar 'beam' is not pointed in our direction. Some theories require that the remnant left behind would be a magnetar – a fast-spinning neutron star. Some theories even suggest that the Cambrian extinction some 488 million years ago was caused by a gamma ray burst in the solar neighbourhood. However, we need not dwell on the causal mechanism of such events (which is after-all only informed speculation by astrophysicists) rather to consider their solid ejecta and gravitational waves.

FBOTs

In 2018 astronomers discovered evidence in distant galaxies for a new class of supernova explosion. These have been termed Fast Blue Optical Transients (or FBOTs). Some have been given convenient nicknames; one explosion, known as "the Cow" was observed to be 10-times more powerful than any previously known supernova. [4] Another named "Koala" was almost as bright as a gamma-ray burst. [5] However, while gamma ray bursts may eject just a small mass of high-energy particles and radiation along the polar beams, the FBOTs may launch as much as 10% of our Sun's mass at relativistic speeds approaching even the speed of light.

Unlike a gamma-ray burst, the material ejected by an FBOT leaves the star in all directions. The name derives from the characteristic that the bright flash fades much more quickly than a normal supernova and they are hotter – the high temperature giving them their blue tint. Astronomers theorise that this new class of supernova needs a different mechanism to explain them. One suggestion is a black hole absorbing a white dwarf or a neutron star which then fades rapidly as the remnant falls within the event horizon; alternatively they may be examples of a core collapse producing a black hole, but in this case the polar 'beam' of gamma rays is not pointed directly at us.

The focus here has to be on the material expelled by the FBOT at relativistic speeds. Again, such ejecta must comprise small solid bodies, not just streams of hot gas. We may only speculate that the remnant, if we could observe one, would also fade more rapidly that any known remnant nebula. If such explosions can be observed in distant galaxies then it follows that they must have occurred in the Milky Way galaxy and their nebulae have long ago dispersed and faded – *but their shell of ejected meteors, travelling at relativistic speeds, continue to expand.*

If the supernova creates a central collapsar then its gravity may be enough to pull-back and retain much of the ejecta within the expanding remnant, but not when the parent star has been completely disrupted as in a Type I supernova. Ironically, the least powerful and most common class of supernova may present the greatest danger to us – and once the gaseous remnant has dispersed – totally undetectable by astronomers.

Unnovas

Another phenomenon related to the fast stars and FBOTs is the Unnova, sometimes misleadingly called a failed supernova. These are very far from failures; they are examples of the most massive stars (yellow hyper-giants of 20-60 solar masses) that try to explode by core-collapse but are too massive and are rotating relatively slowly, such that their light, or anything else, cannot escape from the event horizon. To our eyes the collapsing star would simply pop-out of existence. There are candidate stars that may be examples of this phenomenon; N6946-BH1 was observed to brighten and fade in 2009. The search for such stars has only come to the fore since the millennium as astronomers had been unable to find supernova remnants formed by the most massive supergiants.

Once again, we should expect that meteors and comets in just the right orbit might be whipped around such a collapsing star and thus be accelerated into the galaxy at relativistic velocities. This is really no different from the way that hyperbolic solar comets are ejected from our own solar system by close passage to Jupiter or Saturn – except that the velocities are so much higher.

We may have an example in one of our galactic neighbours: Cassiopeia A that exploded unnoticed in the mid-seventeenth century. Here astronomers observe not only the rapid expansion of the remnant at 21.6 million km/h, but also a region that is falling back at an equally impressive velocity of 6.9 million km/h; perhaps an indicator that it is under the intense gravitational pull of an invisible former companion star. [6]

Consider for a moment how long it might take for supernova ejecta to reach us. To take again the example of Cassiopeia A; if an ejected meteor were travelling at the observed rate of expansion, then at its distance of 10,000 light years it should reach us about 220,000 years from now. The immediate danger would therefore come from a similar supernova that exploded at this distance two hundred and twenty thousand years ago and whose ejecta would only now be reaching us. Of course, the fast meteors and exocomets could approach from various distances and velocities; and from any direction. There is little or no prospect of predicting such arrivals until humans become capable of interstellar travel.

Rogue Stars and Planets

Other possibilities exist for sources of high-energy ejecta that could reach Earth. At the centre of our galaxy lies a supermassive black hole of 4 million solar masses called Sagittarius A-Star. We have all seen the excellent animations of the closest stars as they are observed to swing around it at velocities so fast that that they can be measured.

In 2014 Sgr A* was observed to tear apart a gas cloud surrounding a small star. However, recent analysis would suggest that less than 1% of the matter orbiting around the black hole actually falls within its event horizon; the rest is ejected into the galaxy. [7]

One such fast-star S5-HVs1 was observed to be leaving the galaxy at a velocity of 1700 km/sec. Its track indicates that it has survived a close encounter with Sagittarius A-star. Again we should ask: how many smaller unseen rogue planets, comets and meteors are passing by us at comparable velocities? Answer: there could be billions. No longer is it mere science fiction.

Tektites

Should one of the hypervelocity fragments from an ancient supernova strike the Earth then what kind of physical evidence might we expect it to leave behind? Certainly not a crater, any more than you would expect a bullet from a gun to leave a crater in soft material. However the science of bolide ballistics does give us useful analogies. Most likely they would drill a hole deep into the mantle before being dissolved, or perhaps a ricochet scar from an oblique impact. The most likely hard evidence would be a strewn field of micro-tektites (impact glass) around the point of entry. We are considering here a football-sized body, or even smaller, travelling so fast that that they could penetrate to the mantle. We should expect the impact site to be inconspicuous and disguised by infill or volcanic extrusions. [8]

Prime locations to search for hard evidence would be the smallest tektite fields that are not associated with any known crater; and always bear in mind that three-quarters of all impacts must occur in the ocean leaving even less accessible evidence. It may be easier to find one on the Moon, where there has been less geology to conceal them. We shall see. Very little physical evidence would remain on the Earth's surface after a few hundred years but we may still detect short-lived radioactive isotopes that were synthesised in the parent supernova.

Next Page:

Tektite Strewn Fields. Most of the largest are millions of years old are linked to ancient craters. Examples of Holocene age are likely to be microtektite sites, too small to show on a large-scale map.

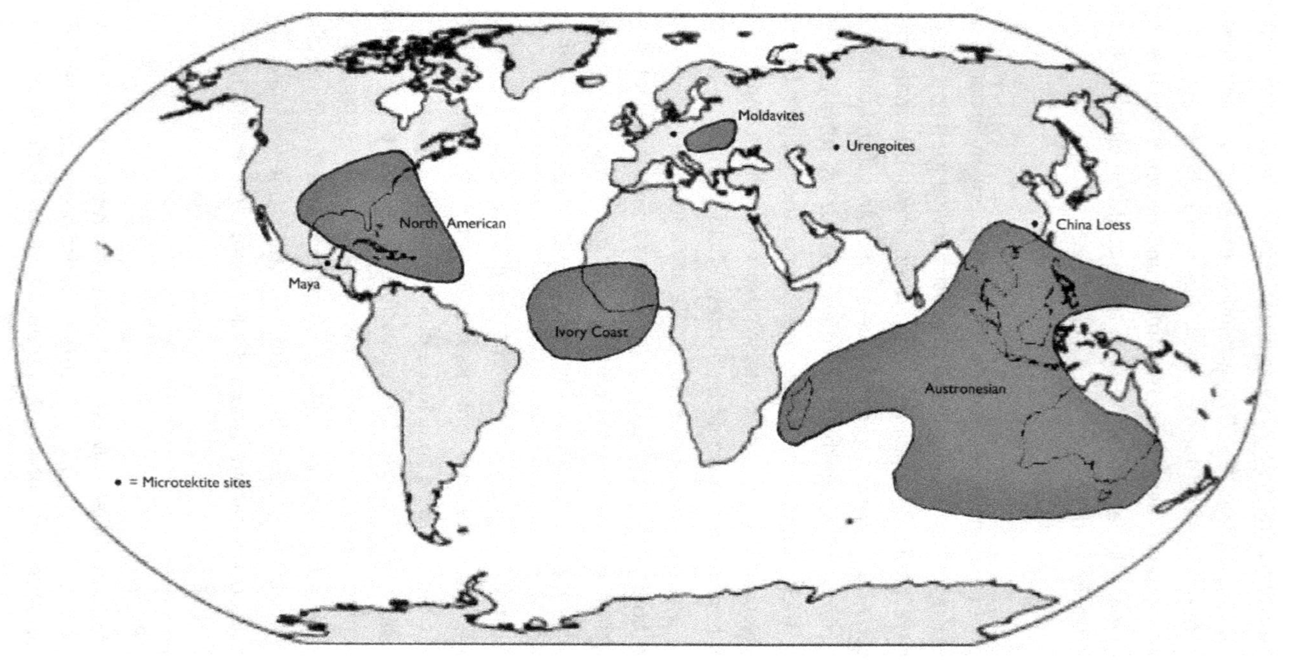
Moldavites
• Urengoites
North American
China Loess
Maya
Ivory Coast
Austronesian
• = Microtektite sites

New Physics

If you wish then you can look into the more speculative and exotic phenomena that many astronomers and physicists now consider possible.

Gravitational Waves

Long theorized, but first detected in 2015, these are thought to be produced by the mergers of massive objects such as neutron stars and black holes. They must also occur when stars fall into Sagittarius A-star and when galaxies and supermassive black holes merge: a frightful concept! All the events so-far detected by the most sensitive gravitational wave detectors on earth result from mergers of collapsed stars in distant galaxies. Typically the amplitude of the waves is less than the width of a human hair and would go unnoticed – each of us has probably experienced numerous gravitational waves during our lifetime; it is no different to the radio waves and neutrinos that pass through us all the time.

A gravitational wave is a stretching and squeezing of the space-time fabric produced by high gravity events. Atoms and particles, as well as planets (which are merely large groups of atoms for this example) would alternately stretch and squeeze according to the wavelength. It is important to visualise that it is the spacetime structure that deforms not the matter that occupies it. Precisely what we would feel from a gravitational wave that originated much closer to us could only be speculation and imagination at this point.

Whatever else, the gravitational wave has a *point of origin* and a *direction*. It carries energy and it should affect the Earth in the same way as any other impulse. It would act to change the angular momentum of the planet, resulting in a nutation of the axis and could even alter the length of day. A change to the shape of the Earth (the squeezing and pulling) must also trigger a wobble and a pole shift. The real difference however, between this and the impulse delivered by an impact event, is that it should leave no crater or any other hard evidence on the surface.

A gravitational wave would not have to be spectacular to cause geological effects; a variation of perhaps a few millimetres might be enough to trigger worldwide earthquakes and flows of magma in the core and mantle, thus altering the shape of the geoid and its rotational balance. The rest is then just known geophysics.

Once again, it is important to appreciate that although physicists may talk as if they know what is going-on, they don't! No-one really understands gravity!

Mini-black-holes

The only known process by which a black hole could be created is by the gravitational collapse of a massive star at the end of its life, such that the core falls within its event horizon and the required escape velocity exceeds the speed of light. To form a stellar black hole, the collapsed core must be of a minimum of about 2 solar masses, commencing from a supergiant of 25+ solar masses, The resultant black hole would occupy a diameter of about 25 km. However, there is no minimum size limit so long as the required density could be achieved.

Scientists such as Jakub Scholtz and James Unwin propose that in the extreme conditions of the early universe, local unevenness could have created conditions where matter was clumped sufficiently for mini black holes to form. They suggest that the as yet unobserved Planet 9 could be a primordial black hole about the diameter of a tennis ball. [9] Some primordial black holes might be no bigger than fundamental particles. Once in existence, these would behave like any other massive object subject to gravity as the universe expanded; most falling into supermassive black holes and stars or orbiting them. This raises the obvious question why are there not one or two orbiting the sun; are they the missing 'dark matter', etc.

Popular science-fiction would give us the notion that we would be sucked into such a black hole, but this is erroneous; from distance they would represent no more danger than a rock of similar mass. However, there is always the possibility that a close fly-by could produce tidal effects in the oceans and crust; and resultant catastrophism as has been proposed by other authors. The mini-black-hole theory is not one that that I favour but is listed here for completeness.

Gravity Leaks?

What is gravity? If you know then please tell the physicists. Modern astrophysicists can tell you how it behaves, building upon Einstein's relativity; they can even suggest that the newly-confirmed Higgs Boson confers mass; and it is the mass (whatever that is) that bends the space-time fabric; but this merely transfers the problem to a deeper level of unknown.

A stellar cast of physicists at LIGO sought to use gravitational waves as a way to probe whether gravity was 'leaking' from our universe into an adjacent parallel universe. They seem to be convinced that it does not; but what about gravity leaking into our universe from an adjacent one?

This conundrum derives from the multiverse theory, whereby an infinite series of parallel universes or 'branes' must exist in parallel, splitting-off at quantum level. These other universes would be 'stacked' adjacent to our own in a fourth dimension, each a Planck distance apart – rather like two-dimensional sheets of paper stacked in the third dimension. Gravity obeys an inverse square law; that is to say, it's strength is inversely proportional to the square of the distance from the source. Therefore it is reasonable to suggest that its influence in the higher dimensions would obey the same law. The gravity that we experience is therefore just a fraction of the total force, which could explain why it is so weak compared to the other fundamental forces.

This raises the possibility that the Earth may pass close to a source of mass (a planet or star) lying in an 'adjacent' universe and if it be close enough then its gravity would be felt in our own. These are the science fiction 'gravity anomalies' that you may see on an episode of *Star Trek* – gravitational pull emanating apparently from nowhere! Indeed it is such a difficult concept that there is not even adequate language to describe it.

All we really need to consider is that the gravitational effect of a mass in an adjacent universe should be similar to gravity from a mass in our own universe. However, such physics as is published would suggest that the body must approach extremely close – almost passing through us – in the higher dimension in order for us to experience its effects. Perhaps we should not worry about this idea until a physicist can explain what dark matter is and where it is.

Conclusions

If we observe exocomets then there must also be many more smaller exo-meteors. If we can watch high-energy phenomena occurring in distant galaxies then they must also occur in our own galaxy. Because we only see the rare phenomena during our short human timeframe we fail to perceive the long-term threat that they pose. It is rather like building your house close to a volcano and relying on the security that it has never erupted in your lifetime. We cannot do much about the future, but we can at least recognise the effect they might have had in the past and consider their effect on recent geology and human prehistory.

It is unfortunate that so much discussion of catastrophism in prehistory during the twentieth century was so unempirical that it could be easily demolished by scientists. This has led to a neglect and unwillingness by mainstream geologists to consider the question for fear of professional ridicule. It is a subject that must be considered. All of the phenomena suggested above could cause cataclysmic episodes on the Earth and yet they would not leave any hard evidence on the surface.

Let me pose you a troubling series of questions. How do you know that there is not a dark collapsar lurking, a few thousand light-years from earth, that 'exploded' millennia ago and sent a shell of meteors in our direction at unthinkable velocity? Is there a dark star awaiting discovery in our galactic locality, of just the right mass that may collapse further and send a gravitational wave in our direction disturbing our stable rotation as it passes through us? What would that feel like and what might its geological effects be? Is there a planet in an adjacent parallel universe that may pass close-enough in a higher dimension for its gravity to leak into our own? Are you waiting for a recognised 'expert' or professor to tell you whether such concepts are real or pseudo-science? Another definition of pseudo-science might be science that your expert has not yet thought of, or perhaps fears to mention lest their papers be rejected. Beware the giggle factor!

Note 1: *As this article was in preparation, evidence was released that a 0.45m diameter meteor estimated to be travelling at 210,000 km/h (58.33 km/sec) broke apart in the atmosphere over New Guinea in 2014. This discovery actually predated Oumuamua but was awaiting conclusive verification of the data. As may be noted from the above discussion this velocity is still far below the maximum that could be generated by stellar phenomena, but well above the commonly observed velocities for meteorites of solar system origin. The authors suggest that the bolide came from the inner part of a planetary system in the disk of the Milky Way galaxy.* [10]

Relevant Hyperlinks

https://solarsystem.nasa.gov/asteroids-comets-and-meteors/comets/2I-Borisov/in-depth/
https://articles.adsabs.harvard.edu/cgi-bin/nph-iarticle_query?1991JBAA..101..119H&defaultprint=YES&filetype=.pdf
https://arxiv.org/abs/2201.08911
https://www.thoughtco.com/eye-of-the-sahara-4164093
https://astrobites.org/2011/10/24/the-case-of-the-disappearing-star-un-novae-and-ultra-long-gamma-ray-transients/
https://en.wikipedia.org/wiki/N6946-BH1#/media/File:PIA21467.jpg
https://en.wikipedia.org/wiki/Failed_supernova
https://hubblesite.org/contents/media/images/2017/19/4039-Image.html?news=true
https://www.nasa.gov/mission_pages/chandra/multimedia/black-hole-SagittariusA.html
https://en.wikipedia.org/wiki/File:SgrA2018.gif
https://www.universeguide.com/fact/hypervelocitystars
http://www.sci-news.com/astronomy/s5-hvs1-hypervelocity-star-07799.html
https://geologyscience.com/gallery/eye-of-the-sahara-or-richat-structure/
https://www.scientificamerican.com/gallery/the-smallest-known-black-hole/
https://arxiv.org/abs/1811.00364
https://www.forbes.com/sites/startswithabang/2019/03/15/this-is-why-the-multiverse-must-exist/?sh=15cca9566d08
https://public.nrao.edu/gallery/category/supernova-explosions-and-supernova-remnants/

https://www.space.com/38471-gravitational-waves-neutron-star-crashes-discovery-explained.html

https://www.sciencedirect.com/science/article/pii/S0016703718301236

https://public.nrao.edu/gallery/category/supernova-explosions-and-supernova-remnants/

https://ntrs.nasa.gov/api/citations/19980007188/downloads/19980007188.pdf

https://www.iac.es/en/outreach/news/astronomers-discover-first-supernova-explosion-wolf-rayet-star

References

1 *'Giggle factor' is no laughing matter to scientists, Posted 3/11/2003 8:53 PM, by Eric J. Lyman, Special for USA TODAY.*

2 *Hughes, D.W. (1991) On Hyperbolic Comets, J. Br. Astron. Soc.* ***101****, 2, 1991*

3 *Dunbavin, Paul (2020) Dangers to Earth from Ancient Supernovas, in Prehistory Papers, pp 1-12, Third Millennium Publishing, Beverley, ISBN: 978-0-9525029-4-4*

4 *Swift spectra of AT2018cow: A White Dwarf Tidal Disruption Event? https://arxiv.org/abs/1808.08492*

5 *Ho, Anna Y. Q. et al (2020) The Koala: A Fast Blue Optical Transient with Luminous Radio Emission from a Starburst Dwarf Galaxy at<i>z</i>= 0.27, The Astrophysical Journal, 859, 1 https://iopscience.iop.org/article/10.3847/1538-4357/ab8bcf*

6 *Vink, J. et al (2022) The forward and reverse shock dynamics of Cassiopeia A https://arxiv.org/abs/2201.08911*

7 *Wang, Q.D. et al (2013) Dissecting X-ray-emitting Gas around the Center of our Galaxy, arXiv:1307.5845 [astro-ph.HE] or arXiv:1307.5845v2 [astro-ph.HE] https://doi.org/10.48550/arXiv.1307.5845Rogue stars (Wang?) https://arxiv.org/pdf/1307.5845.pdf*

8 *Petersen, Carolyn Collins. "What Is the Eye of the Sahara?" ThoughtCo, Aug. 27, 2020, thoughtco.com/eye-of-the-sahara-4164093.*

9 *Scholz, Jakob and Unwin, James (2019). What if Planet 9 is a primordial Black Hole? https://arxiv.org/pdf/1909.11090.pdf*

10 *Amir Siraj, Abraham Loeb, The 2019 Discovery of a Meteor of Interstellar Origin https://arxiv.org/abs/1904.07224*

2

Stonehenge Blindness

Summary:
Two papers published in recent academic media reveal a transformation in the attitude of archaeologists towards the concept of astronomical alignments at Stonehenge and other Neolithic monuments. It may be worthwhile to look back at why it has taken them so long to reach this consensus. Part of the problem lies in the theological divide that persisted for half a century between field archaeologists and archaeoastronomers; but also, the dogma about 'Iron Age Celts' which held that there could be no connection between the Druid astronomy described in classical sources and the earlier 'pre-Celts'. Now that DNA science has removed this artificial barrier we may see that Neolithic people were far more competent astronomers than was previously supposed.

In a review of the "*Pathways to the Cosmos*" conference held at Dublin Castle in September 2018 Liz Henty makes some perhaps surprising comments. [1] She notes that this is the first such conference where archaeologists and archaeoastronomers have combined to broadly agree that some Neolithic monuments in Britain and Ireland were astronomically aligned. She comments:

> *...it has healed the long divide created when archaeoastronomers and archaeologists went their separate ways in the 1970s over arguments about Alexander Thom's megalithic science (see for example Thom 1967), each dismissive of the other.*

So, in theory at least, we can now write about astronomical alignments at Neolithic monuments without fear of the ridicule that has transpired over the last fifty years. As the conference took place in Ireland it focused on the more distinct evidence of alignments at the 'passage graves' rather than the stone circles, where more subjective interpretation is necessary; but the prominent names of modern archaeology made their contributions.

Also, in 2022, another article/paper by the archaeologist Timothy Darvill in the journal *Antiquity* was widely reported by the popular press. Writing on the history of interpretation of astronomical alignments at Stonehenge he exposes some of the prejudicial attitudes that have held back progress for so long. [2] He sets out in some detail the astronomical alignments of the extant Sarsen circle (the final Phase 3 of the monument). Most of his content is unquestionable and highlights the ability of the ancient surveyors. The concern is that from the secondary reports in some of the popular media one might gain the impression that he was the first ever to suggest such alignments. After summarising the earlier work of Lockyer, Hawkins and Thom, he comments:

> *These and many other interpretations, however, are all unsatisfactory, as they often use non-contemporaneous elements of the monument, reference astronomical alignments that do not withstand close scrutiny (Ruggles 1997: 203) or perpetuate the discredited idea of a 'Celtic Calendar' (Hutton 1996: 408–11).*

Darvill concludes, from the Sarsen layout, that Stonehenge embodied a solar calendar and remarks on the later phases of reconstruction at the site:

> *...its uses from Stage 2 onwards, providing a secure cosmologically referenced framework for the observance of festivals, ceremonies and rituals that were the reason for the monument's construction. The selection of the existing Stage 1 earthwork enclosure, which had formerly been used as a cemetery, as the site for this innovative development elicits no surprise.*

The work of earlier theorists that led up to the 'great divide' must be appreciated before this debate can be fully understood.

Firstly, to summarise current thinking about the chronology of Stonehenge the earliest phase of construction is dated to around 3000 BC with the building of the circular henge and ditch. The four Station Stones also date from this early phase. Phase 2 is dated from around 2700 BC when the monument was redesigned, to incorporate the Bluestones transported from the Preseli mountains. The monument was completed during phase 3 concluding around 1500 BC when the great sarsen circle that we see today was constructed. Although archaeologists now acknowledge as many as six stages, this convenient nomenclature remains in common use.

The antiquarian John Aubrey in 1666 first noticed the ring of 56 equally spaced chalk-filled depressions around the outer bank. [3] Archaeological excavation has determined that the Aubrey Holes date from Phase 1 of the monument. Opinion is that they were probably not post holes but perhaps re-used to hold cremated remains. One may speculate that they marked locations where a priest or a temporary structure would stand during a ceremony, or perhaps from where an observation was made. The important point is that there are 56 holes and that number is not random chance.

Around the main sarsen circle, dated to the final phase of the monument, are the rings of 29 "Z" holes and the 30 "Y" holes. The earlier circle of 56 pits, whatever their original purpose, were allowed to fall into disuse and grass grew over them.

Various suggestions of astronomical influence at stone circles have been advanced over the years, such as that of Rev. Gidley in the nineteenth century (*see Note 1 below*). [4] and of course the supposed links to the Druids suggested by Aubrey and Stukeley, so disparaged by later archaeologists. I shall not probe the older references here, except to quote Piggott's dismissive summary (1968 p 136) [5]

> *The association of the monument and the priesthood has become so established...that it is too often forgotten that its origins lie no earlier than the seventeenth century, and that when Aubrey's suggestion was printed by Gibson in 1695 it was merely one among many alternative views...*

Astronomical alignment theories were not widely taken-up until Gerald Hawkins and his 1965 book *Stonehenge Decoded* caught popular interest. [6] In the 1960's, books of science aimed at the popular market were much less common and so could provoke controversy when well-promoted by their publishers; much more so than in the internet era when new ideas can escape more easily.

It was Hawkins' theory that Stonehenge and other circles were observatories to forecast eclipses. This concept was marketed to capture popular interest – to the disapproval of the professional archaeologists. He would refer to Stonehenge as a stone age computer for predicting eclipses and his use of printouts from 1960s mainframe computers would help to confer credibility on his theory.

Another landmark would be the publication in 1967 by Professor Alexander Thom of his thirty years of detailed surveys at stone circles. [7] Hawkins also drew on some of Thom's earlier work. [8] While contemporary archaeologists were quite open to the idea of crude horizon alignments for religious ritual they would baulk at the suggestion of ancient science. Thom's surveys also introduced the concept of a 'megalithic yard' and other standard units of measure. These ideas were easier to grasp than his astronomy and thereby easier to criticise. Once the various critics could unpick one part of his theory it could be used to discredit the remainder.

A short but still excellent booklet on Stonehenge archaeoastronomy from the same era is that by C.A. Newham, dating from 1972; although it follows the pre-radiocarbon dating assumptions it contains numerous diagrams illustrating the alignments. [9] His personal correspondence with Hawkins was cited in *Stonehenge Decoded* and his astronomy also influenced later archaeoastronomers. Newham interpreted the rings of Y and Z pits as marking the 59 days of two lunar months (29+30).

On the matter of the 56 Aubrey Holes, Newham asked: why 56 holes? His suggestion was that:

> *...56 is almost three times the years taken to complete the retrograde nodal cycle of the moon (3 x 18.61 = 55.83)*

This numerical coincidence was employed by Hawkins and Hoyle in support of their own theories that Stonehenge was a practical eclipse observatory (eclipses occur when sun and moon meet at the nodes). Now there is nothing wrong with this astronomy; Newham himself never refers to eclipses beyond his simple comment. Moreover, there is no mention in the surviving classical references to suggest that the stone circle builders concerned themselves with eclipses. Newham and those who cited him were prevented by contemporary dogma from making any link between the astronomy of the Stonehenge builders and that of the later 'Celtic' Druids.

The eminent astrophysicist Sir Fred Hoyle would follow the same route as Hawkins in trying to show that the 56 Aubrey holes were a device to predict the chances of an eclipse. [10] His theory would have the ancients rolling a boulder from one Aubrey marker to the next every 6.5 days to record precisely where they were in the nodal cycle. One wonders what might transpire if the astronomer-priest forgot to move the stone? Perhaps he would be consigned to the wicker man. Hoyle's eminence in other fields (he originated the theory of nucleosynthesis in stars) allowed him to easily gain publication of a book on subjects he knew little about. His numerous equations and emphasis on ancient 'pure' science only added to the scepticism of the archaeologists and it is perhaps understandable that they stood back from it all. The complex eclipse prediction theories would lead everyone in the wrong direction.

Druids and 'Celts'

As an indicator of how attitudes to stone circles and the Druids were perceived in the 1960s we need look no further than the summary included in the *Stonehenge Official Handbook* by archaeologist R.S. Newall, as published by HMSO. [11] This booklet was on sale to visitors between 1959 and the 1990s. In the opening paragraph we find:

> *The average visitor to Stonehenge will in all likelihood have been taught that Stonehenge was built by the Druids. You can clear your mind of this statement…*
> *The ancient Druids had no connection with Stonehenge or any other monument of the Bronze Age or, indeed of any earlier period in the British Isles. No doubt they pretended that they had, or even that they built it. They were a class of people who no doubt had a good deal of knowledge, they came to Britain during the early Iron Age invasions in about the third century before Christ.*

So, there you have it, articulated as 'official' government science. Where did the author obtain this disparaging view of Druids and the archaeological dogma that he summarises? The scepticism stems from the 1950s excavations of Stuart Piggott and the earlier generation of archaeologists such as Atkinson, back in the era when the stone circles were dated via pottery cross-dating. Stonehenge was then perceived as contemporary with Mycenaean Greece. The primitive Britons (the pre-Celts) supposedly remained in the stone age while the eastern Mediterranean had advanced to using bronze. Even when radiocarbon dating and tree-ring calibration revised the date of the monuments to a thousand years earlier, the dogma about an Iron Age invasion of 'Celts' persisted. This artificial divide stretches back to nineteenth century scholarship; it would endure until the early twenty-first century when DNA studies began to show that there never was a distinct Celtic race nor an Iron Age invasion. These false doctrines would forbid any comparison of Neolithic astronomical alignments with the Druid astronomy that we find in Greek, Roman and other historical sources.

DNA studies now suggest that the substantial immigration of British population actually took place during the early neolithic and again in the later neolithic. [12] Once you disprove the idea of an invading 'Celtic' race then you must at the same time invalidate the concept of pre-Celts. We may now consider an uninterrupted evolution of people and culture from the era when the stone circles were built, right through to the Roman invasions.

One contributor who could never be accused of Stonehenge blindness was the late Euan MacKie. As an archaeologist of note his views were influenced by ideas wider than just field excavations. He was not afraid to cite the archaeoastronomers, or even occasionally the adherents of Velikovsky and Ley Lines. In one of his later papers are a few pointed remarks about his fellow archaeologists. [13] Some are worthy of quote in this context:

> *Thom's work, which is now rarely considered in publications, and his conclusions are generally thought too weighty for the evidence he assembled.*

He was also not afraid to criticise his own over-enthusiasm for the concept of stone age science:

> *The author also has to take some of the blame; the title of his book—Science and Society in Prehistoric Britain (MacKie 1977)—obviously perpetuated the myth and was ill chosen.* [14]

> *...the underlying reason for the doubts about Thom's accurate long alignment hypothesis seems to have been forgotten, and Clive Ruggles, Gordon Barclay, and Mike Pitts, for example, continue to criticize this and related concepts...*

> *...the author had already, several years earlier, abandoned as misguided the idea of "prehistoric science" and admitted that the possible parallel drawn with the Maya in 1977 had gone too far (MacKie 1977:341, including footnotes 2 and 3).*

Although MacKie may have ventured too far in daring to actually publish the parallel with Mayan astronomy in 1977 the comparison itself is not outrageous.

As a professional archaeologist who has been actively involved in this field since 1969 (and who trained in the late 1950s), I remain convinced that precision alignments exist, that this existence (pace Ruggles) has been confirmed by several objective and convincing fieldwork tests, and that there is other quite independent archaeological evidence for the presence in Neolithic times (broadly the 5th and 4th millennia BCE) of an elite class with advanced astronomical and geometrical and measuring skills.

And touching upon the subject of Druids:

...the time gap between our hypothetical prehistoric priesthood and the well-described orders of Druids in the Iron Age has been reduced to not much more than a thousand years. Classical sources from several centuries BCE tell us that the Druids had extensive knowledge of cosmology and astronomy, and it now seems to the author even more likely that this priestly class was directly descended from the European Neolithic orders...

Note that MacKie, writing this in 2006 still did not dare to make the direct link to 'Celtic' Druids as the guardians of the ancient knowledge, due to the entrenched dogma about invading Celts that was so difficult to overcome.

The archaeologists, whom MacKie would politely criticise, were the 'establishment' of his day who were deemed somehow qualified to define what should be considered orthodox prehistory and what should not, by virtue of their skill to classify the artefacts that survive in the ground. The primitive Britons were only allowed to scatter bones and pottery around; these were the 'beaker folk' and the 'Rinyo-Clacton-ware folk', etc – not real, thinking, people!

It is troubling therefore to find a modern archaeologist such as Darvill still considering the builders of Stonehenge as perhaps influenced by the solar calendars of Egypt. To quote again:

Archaeologically, the question is whether the Egyptian Civil Calendar, or a variation thereof, could have been known to communities living in southern Britain in the mid-third millennium BC, and adopted by them. Barely a century ago, the answer would have been resoundingly affirmative (e.g., Childe 1929). As diffusionist models crumbled and connections between the Mediterranean world and Northern Europe were systematically uncoupled to emphasise autonomous local development (Renfrew 1973: 84–108), such thinking became deeply unfashionable. Now, however, the pendulum of interpretation is swinging back in favour of long-distance contacts ...

This prompted an amusing headline in a British newspaper:: "*Mystery of Stonehenge 'solved' as ancient Egyptians used it for solar calendar, expert claims*". Probably not quite what the author intended! It seems modern archaeologists still cannot bring themselves to utter the words 'Stonehenge' and 'Druid' in the same context. Among the Neolithic British and Irish were the forbears of Newton, Halley, Hoyle and James Clerk Maxwell; they possessed their own astronomers every bit as capable as those in Babylon or Egypt.

Naked-Eye Astronomy

Those who take little interest in astronomy often fail to appreciate that observation of the night sky is *not* difficult. To give a real example: every year around 20-21 March at the spring equinox, the sun rises behind a terraced house opposite my own and around 6 AM it shines through a window down a long corridor and illuminates a painting on the far wall. Pure coincidence! It will do exactly the same thing next year. All I would need to do to calculate the number of days in the solar year is to mark-off the days, Robinson Crusoe style, until the same alignment comes round again. It's not rocket science. Perhaps I should call the neighbours in for a breakfast party and make it a 'Festival of Apollo'!

These simple personal observations of the sky are one reason why I recoil at academic suggestions that ancient astronomer-priests, druids, or call-them-what-you-like, needed to build grandiose stone monuments solely to define the annual calendar and its ritual observances. An architectural comparison with the east-west alignment of the medieval cathedrals, or the oculus of the Roman Pantheon would be a much better analogy.

Ancient people could easily discover and rediscover solar alignments quite by chance as pointers to seasonal events. Long before the advent of farming the hunter gatherer needed to be ready for the migrations of wild animals and seasonal vegetation. They would then, for practical reasons, need to divide the year into smaller units. The recurrence of the lunar phases is an obvious sub-division. Does it really matter that the periods of sun and moon are not commensurate? For practical purposes, no. Why should it have concerned ancient people? It is just another fact of nature. The moon wanders through the Julio-Gregorian calendar and we schedule its phases easily enough. Why did archaeologists ever deny that stone age people were capable of practical forward planning? In the ancient calendars of India, the months of the year are determined not by the phase of the moon rather by its location. The zodiacal 'constellations' through which the moon passes hold more importance than its phase. The sky is no mystery for the diligent naked-eye astronomer. Every modern amateur astronomer knows which constellation will be visible in the south at a particular season. Even at the age of eight I recall waiting for a fine summer night so that I could see *Antares*; and that it was only possible to view *Fomalhaut* just above the southern horizon on a few clear nights in September. [*Note 2] It is then a simple matter to align two wooden posts as a reminder where to look next year, or to align two stones so that their children and grandchildren don't have to think it all out again. Why has it been so difficult for archaeologists to admit that ancient druids and shamans could have preserved such basic calendrical knowledge?

Once we remove the artificial barriers then we have all the information that we need from the ancient literary sources to work-out what our ancestors were actually doing. *The information has always been there*, except that the archaeologists would dismiss any historical sources that did not fit their preconceptions.

The Historical References

The first piece of testimony to consider is the quotation of **Hecataeus** (c.330 BC) as paraphrased by Diodorus Siculus, which describes the festivals of the *Hyperboreans* on *'an island beyond the Celts'*. [*Diodorus Siculus, II, 47*] This large island, beyond the Celts, could only refer-to either Britain or Ireland. There are no others. Diodorus describes a '*magnificent sacred precinct of Apollo*' and a '*temple of the spheres*'; he tells us that the priests, the *Boreadae*, understood the nineteen-year cycle of Meton and that the god Apollo (a solar deity) visited the island every nineteen years.

However, it is anomalous that while the Meton cycle is a repeating lunisolar cycle (235 lunar months equate closely to 19 solar years) it is described rather as: '*the period in which the return of the stars to the same place in the heavens is accomplished*'. This does not define the Meton cycle. Rather than a calendar cycle it would seem to be describing the orbit of a superior planet around the zodiac.

Even Gerald Hawkins quoted Diodorus Siculus for his book *Stonehenge Decoded* back in the 1960s, in support of his eclipse theories (page 165). However, nothing in the passage actually suggests eclipses. For Hawkins the spherical temple was a clear reference to Stonehenge or one of the other stone circles.

The Hyperboreans have long been derided by classical scholars as purely mythical, citing earlier authorities who sought to relegate them to the frozen north, or beyond the Urals where they could safely be ignored. It simply was not convenient for archaeologists to find Hyperboreans among the stone-age Britons; and of course, the Boreadae could not be equated with the Druids because the stone circles long predated the supposed Celtic invasions. These artificial barriers are now lifted.

Herodotus (c.450 BC) preserves that the Hyperboreans maintained contact since the most ancient times with the priests of Apollo in Athens and Delos, sending two girls and their attendants with offerings via the Adriatic Sea – thus giving us a further clue whence they came. [*Herodotus IV, 33*] These visitors arrived *from the northwest,* whereas visitors from 'Scythia' or central Asia would have arrived via the Black Sea.

As a parallel aside, genealogists note the presence of the E3b gene in the North Wales region of Abergele and the Great Orme copper mines, which find their closest equivalent in populations around Greece and the Aegean coast of Turkey, but strongest in Albania and the Adriatic islands. [15] This may offer confirmation that Bronze Age colonists voyaged from Greece to North Wales in the Late Neolithic, probably seeking tin and copper. In the later Iron Age and Roman times, the Island of Anglesey was the cult centre of the Druids. [*Tacitus Annals, XIV, 30*] The importance of this connection has always been denied because most of the Roman accounts describe only the Druids of Gaul. Archaeologists therefore maintained that Druidism came into Britain along with the supposed invasion of Iron Age Celts, ignoring the very clear statement by **Julius Caesar** that the druidic system originated in Britain and was only later introduced into Gaul. [*Gallic War VI, 13*] Now that DNA evidence has removed the Celtic-invasion fallacy, we may see more clearly that the British Druids were a local evolution from a much older shamanist priesthood.

Another valuable clue offered by Caesar, citing lost literary sources, was that the gods of the Celts (specifically of the Gauls) were essentially the same deities as those worshipped by the Greeks and Romans. [*Gallic War VI, 17*] Again, this valuable remark has always been dismissed by archaeologists because it did not fit their orthodox view of barbarian Celts and pre-Celts.

The Roman author **Pomponius Mela** [*De Chorographica, III, 2, 18-19*] informs us that the Druids possessed extraordinary astronomical wisdom, notwithstanding the undoubted cruelty of some of their ceremonies. He says that they claimed, "*to know the size and shape of the world and the motion of the stars and the heavens*". They were forbidden to commit this knowledge to writing.

From the Roman encyclopaedist **Pliny**, we gain the further insight that the Druids used a lunar calendar and also used the moon to map time in longer 30-year 'ages' or *saeculi*. [*Natural History XVI, 250*] **Plutarch** provides the extra data that Britons in the Western Isles would wait thirty years for Saturn to return to Taurus, in order to schedule sea voyages to the ancient oracle of Cronus. [*The Face in the Moon, 941*] These two historical references together confirm that the Britons were carefully observing the 30-year geocentric orbit of Saturn – and they were doing-so as far back in prehistory as you wish to place the era of Cronus and the other Titans. In 30 solar years Saturn makes 29 geocentric orbits in our sky, thus "returning to the same place in the heavens". Plutarch's evidence gives us the further clue that the starting point for each 30-year cycle was the constellation Taurus.

29 Saturn orbits	**= 29 x 378.09292**	**= 10964.694 days**	**= 30.02 solar years**

The link between Saturn and the Moon is also evident at Stonehenge. We may see that 56 synodic periods of Saturn equate to 717 lunar months.

717 lunar months	**= 717 x 29.530598**	**= 21173.43 days**	**= 57.97 solar years**
56 synodic periods	**= 56 x 378.09292**	**= 21173.2 days**	**(approx. 58 years)**

After 59 years and 57 synodic orbits a solar correspondence occurs. Saturn returns to its starting point precisely two days later in the solar year.

59 solar years	**= 59 x 365.2422**	**= 21549.29 days**
57 synodic periods	**= 57 x 378.09292**	**= 21551.29 days**

These astronomical correspondences when meshed with the lunisolar cycle could therefore be used to refine the calendar to an accuracy that would not be achieved again until the Gregorian reform.

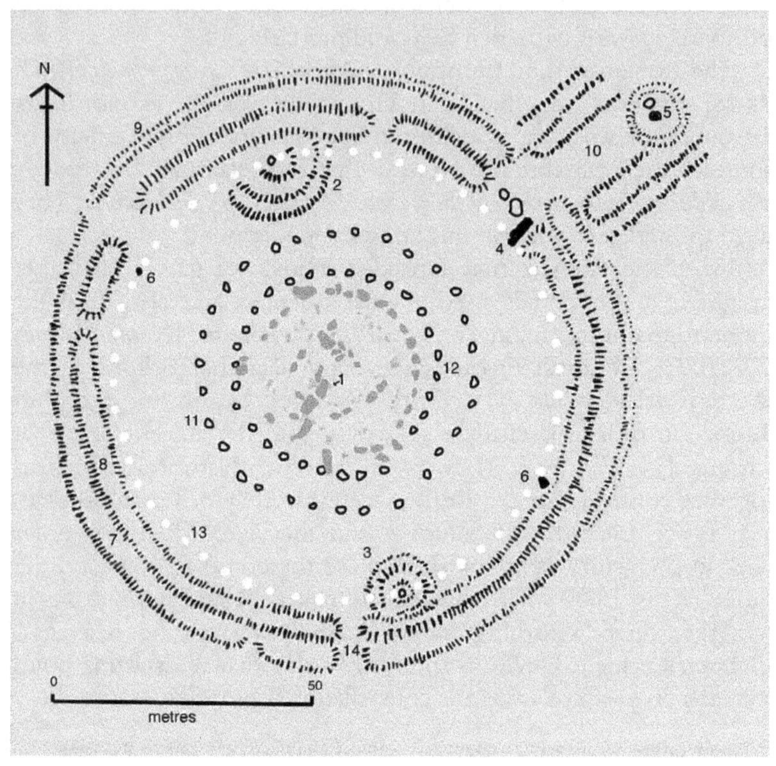

Stonehenge in its Landscape

Drawn by Adamsan - Cleal, Walker, & Montague, (London, English Heritage 1995) Pitts, M, Hengeworld (London, Arrow 2001) *Click on the diagram for a link and the full key.*

11 = 30 Y-holes
12 = 29 Z-holes
13 = 56 Aubrey holes

Although it is the standing stones that attract the eye, it is the rings of chalk-filled holes that reveal the link between Saturn and the Moon

We may not know the original application of the 56 Aubrey Holes, but this numerical correspondence cannot be mere coincidence. We may deduce that Stonehenge was originally built as a temple to the god Cronus, visible in the sky as the planet Saturn.

Returning to the significance of the 29 Z-holes and the 30 Y-holes. We may see that these could mark the 29 orbits of Saturn in 30 years rather than (or in addition to) signifying the days of lunar months. *No horizon alignment of sarsens is required.* The Saturn correspondences may be deduced from the calendar alone without the need to build stone circles. The solar alignments may be seen as mere architectural design features incorporated into the structure by clever architects applying knowledge that was already ancient. The argument that the Aubrey Holes and the Y/Z holes date from non-contemporaneous elements of the monument is also no obstacle as it only requires the continuous application of a very ancient lunisolar calendar. The significance of the concordance between Saturn and the moon every 56 orbits could only have been appreciated by a society that employed an accurate lunar calendar and who religiously observed Saturn over more than a human lifetime.

Following modern DNA science, we no longer have any impediment to recognising that druidic astronomy, as it was recorded by the Roman writers, was inherited from the practical astronomy of the stone circle builders. It doesn't matter whether you want to call these Neolithic astronomer-priests 'proto-druids' or by some other name.

The Calendar of Coligny

We also have evidence of the accurate luni-solar calendar against which the Druids could schedule the appearances of Saturn. In 1897 fragments of a Gaulish calendar plaque were unearthed at Coligny in the Auvergne-Rhône-Alpes region of France. Specialists have reconstructed the Coligny Calendar as a five-year cycle of lunar months. In addition to a year of twelve alternating 29- and 30-day months we see two intercalary months inserted at the start and in the middle of the third year; and evidence of a variable month (equivalent to our modern February) which must be present if the days are to be held to the solar year. However, a 5-year cycle alone simply does not work as a lunisolar calendar; it does not repeat and an error soon accumulates.

As I have shown in various books and articles, when combined with a hypothetical 6-year cycle then the 5-year Coligny cycle becomes a repeating 11-year lunisolar cycle with 4 intercalary months. [16 & 17] This was the neolithic calendar that the Druids inherited and against which they could schedule the orbit of Saturn over its longer 30-year 'ages'. [18] It doesn't really matter how you wish to arrange the days of the months: whether to hold them to the solar year, or to the moon, or to Saturn's rhythm. For example, every fourth year we *could* insert a 32nd of March instead of a 29th of February and our modern Gregorian calendar would still function. However, we may see from analysis of the Coligny fragments combined with the information supplied by Pliny that in its later form it was intended as a lunisolar calendar. [19]

This 11-year calendar cycle is ancient. It is not 'Celtic'. **Plato** also mentions alternating 5- and 6-year ceremonial periods associated with an ancient civilisation of the Atlantic coast. [*Critias 119*] Consider this for a moment: *this cannot just be a numerical coincidence*. If you follow the logic then the 5+6 calendar must be at least as old as the mid-Neolithic; if you want to take Plato more literally then it would be even older. However, even to mention Plato will have the establishment archaeologists running for somewhere to hide.

You don't have to accept everything that Plato offers in order to believe that knowledge of an ancient European calendar could have been preserved in the Egyptian Temple of Neit dating back to the fourth millennium BC. The reference to an alternating cycle of 5 and 6 years seems to have languished in the ancient Egyptian source, without either Plato, Solon, or the Egyptian priests of Neit recognizing it as a working calendar. Again, it fails on the dismissive mindset of university scholarship towards legends and ancient history. We see clear indication here of an archaic astronomy, overlooked by archaeologists for so long because it did not fit with the picture of the past that they had been taught. This is why we must always build from the most ancient sources rather than following the trail of modern excavations and papers.

It is also pertinent to ask *why* the astronomer-priests of the Neolithic found it so vital to set astronomical alignments in stone to establish the vagaries of the calendar. The earliest aligned monuments were clearly *practical* observatories rather than community religious sites. After all, not many of the congregation could fit inside the Newgrange passage for a religious ceremony! I have offered elsewhere the most likely reasons why such precocious astronomy arose in the years around 3000 BC. [20]

Is it the function of modern archaeologists to take forward our knowledge of prehistory or is their role to hold us back? The perception remains that only artefacts dug from the ground may constitute evidence of the past and that archaeologists are entitled to *own* prehistory. It was an infuriating attitude fifty years ago and it is just as annoying today. It is certainly not the intention here to be critical of those field archaeologists who produce the primary excavation evidence for others to use. However, it would be progress if they would show equal respect for the historians, astronomers and mythographers who also seek to discover what our ancestors were doing. It would be so much better if they had not squandered half a century to acknowledge that ancient Europeans were capable of basic naked-eye astronomy.

Conclusions

The complex stone circles and passage graves were not necessary to devise a practical calendar. We may see that the earliest aligned monuments dating from the late fourth millennium BC (the Stonehenge 1 era) had a practical purpose for observing both the seasonal variations and the thirty-year cycle of Saturn/Cronus; but by the later Iron Age these astronomical alignments had become ritualised in religious observances. Later generations forgot their original purpose.

With the arrival of the immigrants from the Steppes in the early third millennium BC, commonly known as the Beaker People, the older British population were absorbed and chased out to the western fringes – but the astronomical wisdom of the Druids was respected and adopted. Many of the ancient ritual sites were rebuilt to serve the religious rites of the newcomers. We see this in the remodelling that accompanied Stonehenge phases 2 and 3. The older religion of the god Cronus seems to have persisted alongside a newer 'Solar' religion based on Apollo and the other Titans, with the older beliefs surviving most strongly in the Scottish Isles right up to Roman times.

We may view the evolution of a temple associated with the visible gods in the sky as analogous to the addition of minarets to a former church by the Muslims, or the building of a Christian cathedral in the middle of a converted mosque, as in Seville. Whenever early Christian missionaries wished to convert pagans, they would usurp and rededicate their temples; and thus redirect the congregation to the new beliefs. The remodelling of Stonehenge in the Late Neolithic to its extant form (Stonehenge 2 and 3 eras) is just another example of religious conversion. The incoming 'beaker people' from the east wished to convert the temple from the older beliefs based on Saturn/Cronus, to their own religion based on Apollo. The 'new testament' was metaphorically added to the old!

Perhaps now we may progress to consider *why* Neolithic people developed such a precocious interest in astronomy in the early third millennium BC, which drove them to build so many aligned stone circles and passage graves; and why this excellence seems to have been lost again by historical times.

***Note 1**

Reverend Gidley, citing Welsh sources, remarked on p 69 of the links between the Druids and the Phoenicians, saying "*Saturn therefore appears to have been the planet which Phoenicians and Druids most highly revered*". Gerald Hawkins investigated Gidley's suggestion but thought only in terms of horizon alignments to Saturn, declaring that he found none.

***Note 2**

I recall these dates exactly because it was the NASA Mercury and Gemini missions that stimulated my own schoolboy interest in in astronomy. My copy of *Stonehenge Decoded* is of a similar vintage. I have been studying these matters, on and off, for quite a long time!

Relevant Hyperlinks

https://www.academia.edu/38485311/Review_of_Dublin_conference_Pathways_to_the_cosmos

https://www.cambridge.org/core/journals/antiquity/article/keeping-time-at-stonehenge/792A5E8E091C8B7CB9C26B4A35A6B399

http://www.sci-news.com/archaeology/stonehenge-solar-calendar-10598.html

https://www.megalithia.com/stonehenge/history.html

https://www.english-heritage.org.uk/visit/places/stonehenge/history-and-stories/archaeologists-of-stonehenge/

https://www.english-heritage.org.uk/visit/places/stonehenge/history-and-stories/history/research/

https://books.google.com.gi/books?id=pmYWAAAAYAAJ&printsec=frontcover#v=onepage&q=Saturn&f=false

https://archaeologydataservice.ac.uk/archives/view/eh_monographs_2014/contents.cfm?mono=1089007

https://www.worldhistory.org/Hyperborea/#:~:text=In%20Greek%20mythology%2C%20Hyperborea%20was,worshipped%20the%20sun%20god%20Apollo.

https://www.third-millennium.co.uk/cronusplutarchandamysteriousstranger

https://www.ancient-origins.net/artifacts-other-artifacts/coligny-calendar-1800-year-old-lunisolar-calendar-banned-romans-002429

https://www.third-millennium.co.uk/under-ancient-skies

https://www.third-millennium.co.uk/_files/ugd/e5604c_d9093eb264fd4bf9944df17d1abef5a6.pdf

https://www.third-millennium.co.uk/_files/ugd/e5604c_44a4db7e37e24a2a8ea6b820e4870914.pdf?index=true

https://www.third-millennium.co.uk/spirals-on-long-meg

References

1 Henty, L. (2019). "Pathways to the Cosmos – The Alignment of Megalithic Tombs in Ireland and Atlantic Europe". Dublin Castle, Ireland, 15th September 2018. *Journal of Skyscape Archaeology*, *4*(2), 246–251. https://doi.org/10.1558/jsa.37392

2 Darvill, T. (2022). Keeping time at Stonehenge. *Antiquity, 96*(386), 319-335. https://doi:10.15184/aqy.2022.5

3 Aubrey, J. (1666) *Brief Lives*, edited by Oliver L. Dick, Secker & Warburg, London, 1949

4 Gidley, L. (1873) *Stonehenge: Viewed by the Light of Ancient History and Modern Observation*, Brown & Co, London.

5 Piggott, S. (1968) *The Druids*, Thames and Hudson Ltd, London, ISBN 0-500-27363-4

6 Hawkins, G.S. (1965) *Stonehenge Decoded*, Souvenir Press, London

7 Thom, A. (1967) *Megalithic Sites in Britain*, Oxford University Press,

8 Thom, A. (1964) Megalithic Astronomy in Standing Stones, *New Scientist*, 12 March

9 Newham, C. A. (1972) The Astronomical Significance of Stonehenge, Moon Publications, Gwent

10 Hoyle, F. (1977) *On Stonehenge,* Heineman Educational Books Ltd, London

11 Newall, R.S. (1959) *Stonehenge*, Her Majesty's Stationery Office, London

12 Patterson, N., Isakov, M., Booth, T. et al. (2021) Large-scale migration into Britain during the Middle to Late Bronze Age. *Nature* 601, 588–594. https://doi.org/10.1038/s41586-021-04287-4

13 MacKie, E. (2006). "New Evidence for a Professional Priesthood in the European Early Bronze Age", in Todd W. Bostwick and Bryan Bates: *Viewing the Sky Through Past and Present Cultures: Selected Papers from the Oxford VII International Conference on Archaeoastronomy*, Pueblo Grande Museum Anthropological Papers No 15. City of Phoenix Parks and Recreation Department, 343–362. ISBN 1-882572-38-6

14 MacKie, E. (1977) *Science and Society in Prehistoric Britain*, Paul Elek, London

15 Oppenheimer, S. (2012) *The Origins of the British: The New Prehistory of Britain*, Constable and Robinson, London. ISBN: 978-84529-482-3

16 Dunbavin, P. (2005) *Under Ancient Skies: Ancient Astronomy and Terrestrial Catastrophism*, Third Millennium Publishing, Nottingham, ISBN 0-9525029-2-5

17 Dunbavin, Paul (2020) On the Coligny Calendar and the Calendar in Plato's Critias, in *Prehistory Papers,* pp 23-30 Third Millennium Publishing, Beverley, ISBN: 978-0-9525029-4-4; *or* Dunbavin, Paul (2018) in *Chronology & Catastrophism REVIEW*, 2018:2 pp 50-53.

18 Dunbavin, Paul (2020) The Neolithic Calendar, in *Prehistory Papers,* pp 13-22, Third Millennium Publishing, Beverley, ISBN: 978-0-9525029-4-4 (a previously unpublished 2006 paper)

19 Olmsted, G (1992) *The Gaulish Calendar*, Dr Rudolph Habelt GMBH, Bonn

20 Dunbavin, P. (1995) *The Atlantis Researches: the Earth's Rotation in Mythology and Prehistory*, Third Millennium Publishing, Nottingham, ISBN:0-9525029-0-9

3

Joseph's Famine - a Catastrophe Forewarned!

Summary:
The Joseph Story as found in the Bible and Koran is not the only version of a seven-year famine in antiquity. The others may be less well known but offer additional detail for us to examine. Do all these stories have a common source? Or do they each independently record a real ancient climate phenomenon? Here is a brief review of some of the sources and the related science that may explain how a seven-year climate rhythm could be created.

Firstly, to establish that the enquiry herein is historical and scientific in nature and expresses no opinion as to religious beliefs. We find versions of the famine of Joseph in all the main religions of the middle east; Christian, Jewish and Islam. We need not doubt that the faithful of all religions accept the truth of the events described – it is only rational modern science that might seek to question it as a mythological tale. In doing so, they evade responsibility to explain *how* a seven-year cyclical famine could occur and *when* it might have happened.

The version that we find in *Genesis 39-42* within modern versions of the Bible need only be summarised as everyone surely knows the details from childhood. We hear of how Joseph is sold into slavery by his brothers and is later imprisoned. He correctly interprets the dreams of his fellow captives, Pharoah's butler and baker, who had displeased him somehow. When, two years later, the king is troubled by bad dreams that his advisors cannot interpret, the butler remembers Joseph and recommends his skill to the (unnamed) Pharoah.

Pharoah perceives seven fatted cows in a lush meadow, but then seven thin and malnourished cattle appear and eat-up the fattened beasts. Next, he dreams of seven ears of ripe corn; but these are followed by seven more withered stalks *blasted by a strong east wind.*

Joseph interprets the two dreams by the same prediction. He tells Pharoah that the dream warns of seven years of abundance and excess produce of the Nile that will be followed by seven years of famine, more severe than has ever been known. Again, we are told of the *east wind.* He advises Pharoah to store the excess grain of the good years to prepare for the famine.

Pharoah appoints Joseph to oversee the storage of the grain harvest; and the seven good years and the seven bad years evolve as predicted. We are told that famine affected the entire world (or at least the region around the eastern Mediterranean) and that people came from every land to buy Egypt's corn. It also brings Joseph's family to Egypt and so the story continues.

Variant forms survive in other religions, but we need only focus here on the climate details and the description of the famine.

According to Biblical scholars the era of the Patriarchs was the third millennium BC and that of Joseph in Egypt should be placed around 2000 BC. This date would correspond to the 11th Dynasty of the early Middle Kingdom as the Egyptologists would have it. However, Egyptian chronology can be considered as exact. We also find evidence of Asiatic traders known as *Aamu* visiting Egypt during the reign of Senusret II (c.1897-1878 BC). [1]

The kings of the twelfth dynasty (Middle Kingdom) widened the flow of a natural waterway that runs parallel to the Nile, into a canal known as the *Bahr Yussef* (Arabic: "the waterway of Joseph"). The canal would channel the excess flood waters from the upper Nile into the Fayum basin thus creating a reservoir that Herodotus called Lake Moeris According to his description and others, this was much more extensive than the modern Birket Qarun. [*Herodotus II,147-50*] The creation of a reservoir is the very opposite of a famine and so would not corroborate a belief that the climate crisis associated with Joseph occurred during this dynasty. However, it does tell us that the need to provide for years of scarcity had become an acute problem compared to the wealth of the Old Kingdom. Rulers of the Middle Kingdom may have been fully aware of the warnings embodied in the Joseph story.

The East Wind

The present author's method is to look for 'mythological fossils' in an ancient historical narrative or legend. These would be precise numbers, names, or additional details that are not strictly needed to support the story. When an author devises a fictional plot then every detail serves a purpose to the main story or sub-plot; however, a true history may also contain extra elements and digressions that have no obvious relevance. We find few of these in the story of Joseph; it resembles a structured fictional plot. The only precise numbers offered are the seven years. The king is not named nor any details that would help us establish his dynasty. We know not where his palace lies; is it in the delta or the upper valley? However, we *are* told about a persistent east wind. Why is this detail present?

In Pharoah's dream it is the east wind that destroys the crops during the seven bad years. Is this the cause of the famine or is it merely one of the symptoms? We may see that we could remove this reference and the storyline would proceed just as well. Later, within the Exodus story we hear that an east wind brings the plague of locusts [*Exodus 10.13*] and later it accompanies the parting of the Red Sea. [*Exodus 14.21*] Perhaps a meteorologist could confirm exactly the conditions needed to produce such abnormal weather in the eastern Mediterranean.

Strong folklore has evolved around winds from the east that bring ill fortune: "*when ere the wind be in the east, it brings no good to man nor beast*"! For Britain and Ireland, it is the east wind that brings heavy winter snow as occurred in 1987. Between 24 February and 4 March 2018 western Europe experienced the *Beast from the East*, a week of incessant east wind (not gusts) that blew down fences and any poorly built structures. Dubbed Anticyclone Hartmut by the European meteorologists, it seems to have been triggered by ice melt in the abnormally warm Barents Sea. In the northern hemisphere, the winds circulate in a clockwise direction around an anticyclone and when coupled with a normal cyclone to the south it can channel continental cold air all the way from Siberia.

The prevailing climate of Egypt, for at least the past five-thousand years, is hot and dry, dominated by the influence of the desert. Mild rain falls only on the coast in winter and winds are light, usually from the northwest. An east wind is a rare phenomenon in Egypt and is normally considered mild and refreshing. However, in the Levant and further east, as in Europe, the east wind has accumulated a negative folklore since ancient times. The Biblical famine story should therefore be regarded as an Israelite or Babylonian view of the climate rather than Egyptian. [2]

Intermediate Periods in Egypt

There is every reason to believe that the during the Old Kingdom Pyramid Age the full desert conditions had not yet set-in and the immediate proximity of the Nile remained more like the savannah that had prevailed throughout the Sahara during earlier millennia. In the collapse that followed the long reign of Pepi II we find conditions of severe famine recorded in the *Admonitions of an Egyptian Sage* as found in the Ipuwer papyrus. This most likely corresponds to events of the 7th to 10th dynasties of Manetho that have long been known as the First Intermediate Period. Other sources would confirm that central authority broke down for nearly two centuries and power lay in the hands of warring regional nomarchs. The composition of the text is thought to date from the early part of the Twelfth Dynasty and so was written after conditions had improved. It is important to note that the source papyri are later copies. [3] We see no evidence within the extant versions of any respite or warning of what was to come. However, this long period of recurrent scarcities would have been comparatively recent history to the kings of the Twelfth Dynasty.

Many commentators would prefer to link the events in the Ipuwer Papyrus to the Biblical Exodus, upon which I shall add no further comment here. We may perhaps see the unusual climate conditions of the Joseph story better recorded in the *Prophecies of Neferti* where we hear of foreigners from Asia and Libya raiding the fields and the ploughmen are prevented from doing their work. Neferti complains that no-one can determine the time of day because the sun is veiled by so much cloud. The river is reduced to a trickle and people can wade across. Curiously, we also hear that the course of the river has changed and ships cannot navigate:

...for their course has become the riverbank and...the place of water has become a riverbank...

...the south wind will oppose the north wind, and the sky will not be with one single wind. *

These valuable climate indicators have long been neglected. [4] Although we need not doubt the deprivations at this period, there is no direct confirmation to equate the First Intermediate Period to the seven good years and seven bad years of Joseph. The Biblical account evokes a unified administration under a strong king, not the chaos that we hear of in the sage's warnings.

The Famine Stela

There are reasons to suggest that the memory of seven good years and seven bad years is centuries older than the First Intermediate Period. There is another account of a seven-year famine in the Famine Stela on Sehel Island (first cataract) near Aswan. Although believed to be an artefact of Ptolemaic age the inscription records a seven-year famine during the reign of King Djoser, builder of the Step Pyramid, right at the start of the Old Kingdom (c.2750 BC).

The inscription contains elements that are analogous to the Biblical Joseph and when first discovered in the nineteenth century, scholars were quick to view it as confirmation of the Bible. Conservative modern Egyptologists would now be more cautious; however, there is no reason to regard the inscription as a later forgery – any more than a historical papyrus would be so considered. We may consider it as another variant of an ancient warning that, when famines occur, they will usually last for seven years.

To summarise the inscription, the king Neterkhet (Djoser) was troubled that the Nile flood had failed for *seven years*, and the grain stores were near empty. The people were dying and there were foreigners everywhere. He sends Imhotep south to discover the source of the Nile and assess why the flood does not come. However, Imhotep reaches only as far south as Elephantine Island, just before the cataract, and here it is Imhotep rather than Pharoah himself who receives the revelation from the god Khnum in a dream; he returns to inform the king that it is Khnum who controls the waters. Djoser restores the temple of Khnum at Elephantine and soon the Nile flood returns to normal.

We may perhaps view the Sehel engraving as a replacement for a lost earlier inscription, to remind later generations of the importance of maintaining the temple on Elephantine.

Ishtar and Gilgamesh

We find a parallel reference to a seven-year famine preceded by a period of plenty within the Babylonian *Epic of Gilgamesh* as discovered on cuneiform tablets from the ruins of Nineveh (seventh century BC). Anu, the father of the gods, reluctantly grants the request of Ishtar, goddess of fertility, to unleash the Bull of Heaven, saying:

If I do what you desire there will be seven years of drought throughout Uruk when corn will be seedless husks. Have you saved grain enough for the people and grass for the cattle?

Ishtar replies:

I have saved grain for the people, grass for the cattle, for seven years of seedless husks there is grain and there is grass enough. [5]

Ishtar unleashes the 'Bull of Heaven' which causes great destruction on the Earth, until the hero Gilgamesh slays the Bull. Scholars are unsure what this heavenly bull represents, but one may venture that it recalls an astronomical phenomenon, perhaps in some way associated with the constellation of Taurus.

Although seven good years before the famine are not specifically mentioned in the Gilgamesh epic, the reference is so similar to the Joseph story that we may be sure it comes from the same root Babylonian tradition as would later find its way into the Hebrew Bible. The historical Gilgamesh was a king of the Sumerian city-state of Uruk at the beginning of the Sumerian Early Dynastic Period (c. 2900 – 2350 BC). *We would therefore have to regard the famine warning as at least this old.* However, the composition of the epic in its extant form is usually placed later, around 2100 BC, contemporary with the First Intermediate Period in Egypt.

A Famine in Ancient Lydia

Herodotus also tell us of an eighteen-year famine in Lydia (Turkish Aegean coast) that took place some unspecified number of centuries before the Trojan War. [*Herodotus I, 94-96*] The famine was so severe that half the population were forced to emigrate. This could record the same period of scarcity as in the Joseph Story; but other dating indicators would suggest that it better belongs to the later second or third intermediate period, during the second millennium BC. However, even if it is not the same climate episode the underlying cause could be the same. A famine enduring for (at least) 18 years at the Aegean coast would not rule out that the respite of seven years of milder conditions caused quite different problems in Anatolia; or perhaps the bad years came before the good years, leaving no opportunity to prepare. It may be that the famine records the beginning of a permanent climate adjustment. Unlike Joseph's famine, Herodotus does not mention an east wind.

Irish Legends and Newgrange

We also find a seven-year weather phenomenon recorded within Irish sources, as in the legend called The Wooing of Etain. Scholars have tended to treat Irish legends as less authentic and reliable than stories of eastern Origin as they were preserved orally by bards and only written down in early Christian times. The precise meaning of details within oral history may fade and wander over time or their meaning may be 'lost in translation'. Long-standing academic prejudices also disparage any attempt to analyse myths and legends as anything other than imaginative fantasy. Many Irish (and Welsh) mythological stories must be regarded as oral fiction designed to preserve the important details of history rather than as precise chronological history. The bards knew that if history were not made interesting to their audience then it would be forgotten.

The story of Etain takes place a generation after the construction of Newgrange and the other passage graves at the Bend in the Boyne. Place name legends record that Newgrange was built by the Dagda, a god-king of ancient Ireland who is associated with some strange astronomical events. However, the Newgrange mound has been archaeologically dated to 3150±100 BC. [6] Recent DNA evidence has confirmed that Ireland was rapidly repopulated by new immigrants around this time. [7] This confers a degree of authenticity to the story of Etain, which may hold a garbled record of events taking place in the years around 3100 BC.

The important elements of the story again concern the details of climate. We hear of the beautiful princess *Etain* who incurs the enmity of the powerful druidess Fúamnach when she steals the love of her husband *Mider.* She turns the princess into a scarlet fly (*see note 2*) and then summons-up *seven years* of lashing winds to blow away the fly. When the winds cease the fly returns, so she lets loose seven more years of strong winds, and this time the poor princess is forever lost.

We may ponder what the original symbolism of this scarlet fly may have been, but the important details here are the two periods of seven years and the memory of incessant winds occurring shortly after the building of Newgrange. One may wonder why the Irish should consider the wind to be so important to record. Anyone who knows Ireland, or the Atlantic coast of Scotland, will appreciate that wind and rain from the west is the norm and it is the warm sunny days that are remarkable. Although the legend does not specifically describe an east wind, it is clear that the story was structured to preserve the memory of the seven-years of wind; it does not refer to the typical Atlantic storms, rather to an incessant period of abnormal wind. **

The significance of this story is that it again gives us a memory of two consecutive seven-year periods plus high winds, as is found in the Joseph story. The added value comes with its link to an archaeologically dated monument with astronomical alignments; associated with legends of astronomical anomalies that took place around the time of its construction.

Conclusions

The famine story of Joseph was a warning to future generations that if a period of abnormal plenty arises then the people should prepare for it to be followed by the opposite. The Pharoah and some events in the story may be fictional but they embody the recollection of a real climate event. This need not require that Joseph or the patriarchs should be fictitious characters, merely that the warning was deliberately inserted there by the Biblical chroniclers so that it would be remembered for as long as the history survived. The coincidences are compelling:

- The story most likely recalls an astronomical event that occurred during the Egyptian predynastic (late fourth millennium BC) or at the very beginning of the dynastic era.

- The synchronism with the Irish legends of Newgrange would set this event around 3100 BC. It would seem to be *stretching probability* too far if the memory of a seven-year climate rhythm associated with severe winds, coming from two independent and geographically distant sources, were not to recall the same real climate phenomenon.

- The climate fluctuation was a *worldwide event* rather than a local weather feature. The third indicator: that the memory of a seven-year famine *predates* both the Babylonian Epic of Gilgamesh and the Egyptian pyramids, would further reinforce the independent Irish dating marker.

There are a number of ways to look at these indicators. If Biblical scholars have the correct era for the Patriarchs, then *either* we must view the Joseph Story as a fictional addition, or as a real event misplaced at this era by later chroniclers. The second alternative is that the true era from Abraham to Joseph should be set *earlier*, concurrent with the Egyptian predynastic and First Dynasty, when there is some evidence of an earlier period of Egyptian hegemony over the Levant. [8] A hybrid of this scenario would be that the true date of the Patriarchs was earlier, but the famine story built into the Joseph narrative recalls a later event.

The most realistic physical explanation for these events would be a wobble of the Earth's rotation, an instance of the Chandler wobble as known to geophysicists, but of a greater amplitude to the insignificant polar motion that is observed today. A significant wobble should be accompanied by other unusual phenomena such as pole tides which would manifest as changes to the coastline and the flow of rivers. [9] I leave open here the cause of such an event, which I have discussed many times elsewhere. [10]

The seven good years would accompany a mild period of *reduced* seasonality (i.e., the obliquity was temporarily reduced by the wobble) whereas the severe famine and east wind was caused by *increased* seasonality, which triggered arctic melting, thus producing the abnormal conditions needed for a persistent east wind. However, in Egypt and the near-east its effects were *relatively* mild; people survived the catastrophe and recorded it. Other parts of the world were less fortunate; nobody survived to remember it other than as confused myths. The memory of an east wind preserved within the stories of Joseph's famine and the Exodus leaves open the possibility that less severe episodes of the Chandler wobble recurred at later periods of prehistory. ***

**** Note 1***

The Egyptian prophecies of Neferti are reminiscent of those found in the so-called 'Prophecies of Merlin' in the British pseudo-history of Geoffrey of Monmouth and supposedly drawn from an ancient Celtic source. These similarly warn of climate disasters and that 'the arena of the winds will be opened once more'.

***** Note 2***

The most likely explanation would be that this scarlet fly recalls the Monarch butterfly, known in Britain and Ireland as the Milkweed, a rare migrant that is sometimes carried across the Atlantic by the prevailing westerly winds. An easterly wind would blow the butterfly back to America. At some point in the retelling of the Irish tale the symbolic link between the red butterfly and the east wind has been lost.

****** Note 3***

In 2022 researchers announced the discovery of a seven-year rhythm in the magnetic field emanating from the Earth's core. The researchers remained unable to explain the cause of the waves.

Relevant Hyperlinks

https://www.academia.edu/4536995/Chronology_of_Biblical_Patriarchs
https://www.academia.edu/1824221/The_Aamu_of_Shu_in_the_Tomb_of_Khnumhotep_II_at_Beni_Hassan
https://www.academia.edu/9849857/The_Fayum_in_Egypt_and_the_Lake_of_Moeris_in_Herodotus_
https://www.theweatheroutlook.com/twoother/twocontent.aspx?type=libgen&id=1503
https://worddisk.com/wiki/2018_British_Isles_cold_wave/
https://rmets.onlinelibrary.wiley.com/doi/10.1002/wea.3467
https://www.researchgate.net/figure/The-interaction-of-Cyclone-Emma-nearing-from-the-SW-and-Anticyclone-Hartmut-covering_fig4_350673667
https://rsc.byu.edu/abinadi/east-wind-old-new-world-perspectives
https://www.worldhistory.org/article/981/the-admonitions-of-ipuwer/
https://www.academia.edu/5301324/Prophecies_of_the_Prophet_Neferti_of_Ancient_Egypt_transcribed_from_a_grave_find_ancient_papyrus
http://www.attalus.org/egypt/famine_stele.html
https://www.gotquestions.org/Joseph-Imhotep.html
https://study.com/academy/lesson/ancient-egyptian-god-khnum-temple-symbol-facts.html
https://wiki.harvard.edu/confluence/display/k104639/The+Epic+of+G

ilgamesh+-+Pulkit+Agrawal
https://bardmythologies.com/midir-and-etain/
https://www.third-millennium.co.uk/irishgodkings
https://www.sciencedirect.com/science/article/pii/S1674984716300349
https://trs.jpl.nasa.gov/bitstream/handle/2014/46897/CL%2316-3115.pdf?sequence=1
https://www.pnas.org/doi/10.1073/pnas.2115258119

References

1 Kamrin, Janice (2009) The Aamu of Shu in the Tomb of Khnumhotep II at Beni Hassan, *Journal of Ancient Egyptian Interconnections*, Vol. 1:3, 2009, 22–36 http://jaei.library.arizona.edu

2 Hull, Kerry (2018) "An "East Wind": Old and New World Perspectives," in *Abinadi: He Came Among Them in Disguise*, ed. Shon D. Hopkin (Provo, UT: Religious Studies Center; Salt Lake City: Deseret Book, 2018), 167–208.

3 Faulkner, R.O. (1972) Admonitions of an Egyptian Sage, in William Kelly Simpson (ed) *The Literature of Ancient Egypt*, Yale Univ. Press. (see pp 210-229)

4 Faulkner, R.O. (1972) Prophecies of Neferti, in William Kelly Simpson (ed) *The Literature of Ancient Egypt*, Yale Univ. Press. (see pp 234-40)

5 N.K. Sanders (1972) The Epic of Gilgamesh, Penguin, Harmondsworth (translation on pp 87-88)

6 Ray, T. P. (1989) The winter solstice phenomenon at Newgrange, Ireland, accident or design? Nature, 337, 343-5

7 Cassidy, L.M., Maoldúin, R.Ó., Kador, T. *et al.* A dynastic elite in monumental Neolithic society. *Nature* **582,** 384–388 (2020). https://doi.org/10.1038/s41586-020-2378-6

8 Andelkovic, Branislav (2012) Hegemony for Beginners: Egyptian Activity in the Southern Levant during the Second Half of the Fourth Millennium B.C, *Issues in Ethnology and Anthropology*, n. s. Vol. 7. Is. 3 (2012) https://www.academia.edu/6409058

9 Gross, Richard (2016) *The Ocean Pole Tide: A Review*, Jet Propulsion Laboratory, Pasadena; a presentation at the Asia Oceania Geosciences Society, 13th Annual Meeting, July 31 to Aug. 5, 2016, in Beijing, China

10 Dunbavin, Paul (2003) *Atlantis of the West*, Constable & Robinson, London, ISBN: 1-84119-716-5; https://www.third-millennium.co.uk/atlantis-of-the-west

4

When The Sky Leaned Over (In Ancient China)

Summary: *Chinese mythology offers us a myth of the earliest times that is quite different from that found in western mythologies. Rather than a memory of a great flood at the dawn of time, we find instead a memory of a time when the sky leaned over, and rivers changed their courses. Typically, this is treated as a creation myth, or as primitive cosmology, rather than as recording a real event. This article will investigate the astronomy associated with the ancient event as it is described; how it may be co-ordinated with western myths; and suggest an approximate calendar date for the cosmic event based upon modern evidence of archaeology, climate and sea-level changes.*

For those of us who are unable to study the Chinese sources directly then we must rely upon the various translations by western Scholars. Among these are Joseph Needham's monumental work *Science and Civilisation in China* [1] and the abridged version by Colin Ronan [2]. The nineteenth century translations of the mythology by James Legge and those by Edward Werner in the 1920s remain as useful as ever [3]. The mythology given in these sources will suffice for a cross-disciplinary investigation.

The myths and legends recall an early rebel named *Kung Kung* (sometimes transliterated as Gong Gong) who fought with a legendary emperor *Chuan Hsiu* (Zhuan Xu) for the control of the empire. In the violence of the ensuing warfare Kung Kung struck his head against the pillar that supposedly supported the sky. Consequently, the balance of the entire world was disturbed causing the sky to lean-over towards the north-west; all the stars moved from east to north-west and the rivers began to flow towards the south-east. This episode would apparently explain the floods of the great rivers as they determined their new courses across the flat plain of northern China. Another version of the story would describe the goddess *Nü Wa* (sometimes Nüwa or Nü-kua); she along with her brother (and husband) *Fu-hsi* is credited with repairing the hole in the sky and restoring order to the world after the period of chaos. For most scholars, both Chinese and western, it is deemed adequate to dismiss all this as just a form of primitive creation myth.

In these memories of Kung Kung and Nü Wa we may see the attribution of natural catastrophes to real kings and queens reigning at the time (or perhaps they claimed to control them). This is much as we find in other societies, such as ancient Egypt or Ireland, with the rulers purporting to act as intermediaries with the all-powerful deities. Inevitably, with the passage of time, these powerful personalities merged as demi-gods with the true deities. Some myths would make Nü Wa the creator-mother of mankind supposedly 18,000 years after the creation of the world by P'an-ku. In this we may again see similarities with the long mythical chronologies found in Egypt, Mesopotamia and India. These cosmogony myths disguise for us the era when real history should begin.

The Chinese historical period only really begins at 1675 BC with the Shang Dynasty, before which everything must be considered legendary. There are no king lists equivalent to the Egyptian or Mesopotamian chronology; and so, confirmation of the legendary dynasties and rulers remains open to debate. Prior to the Shang was the Hsia Dynasty, loosely to be dated between 2100 BC and 1600 BC. Although long considered legendary, archaeology now suggests the existence of a recognisable civilisation in the low-lying plains. We hear of a ruler named Yu in whose time severe river flooding occurred. He is said to have controlled the overflows by dredging the rivers and channelling streams. Counting back the reigns of these early rulers in the legends gives an approximate date no later than 2850 BC for the supposed era of Fu-Hsi and Nü Wa. Further discussion of the legendary chronology and related archaeology may be pursued in the links below:

The worldview of the later Confucian historians demanded that China should always have been subject to the central authority of an all-powerful emperor. In the earliest times however, the extent of the Chinese 'empire' must be limited to the northern plain around the mouth of the Hwang-Ho, known as the Yellow River due to the colour of the loess deposits through which it flows. The accounts of the founding of the Shang Dynasty (c.1600 BC) and the semi-legendary Hsia Dynasty (c.2100 BC) both commence with rulers whose primary concern was the control of devastating river floods at the mouth of the Hwang Ho. For earlier periods we have only the shadowy accounts of rulers like Fu-Hsi and Yao who seem almost like demi-gods, comparable to Heracles or Osiris in the western myths.

In wedding her brother Fu-hsi, empress Nü Wa is credited with the invention of the institution of marriage in what had previously been a matriarchal society. Fu-hsi is also credited with many innovations, among them the breeding of silkworms and the introduction of the first calendar. The supposed era of Kung Kung and the cataclysmic events must therefore be placed sometime earlier than these legendary rulers.

The myths go on to say that Nü Wa stabilised the cosmos by cutting-off the feet of the great tortoise upon whose back the world rested. Later Chinese cosmology would envisage the world as an inverted, square-cornered bowl, with the four cardinal points situated at each corner, which was either likened to the back of a great turtle, or simply floating upon the ocean. The sky above was viewed as an inverted circular dome, which rested upon and rotated about a great mountain, the Un-rotating Mountain; also known as the Imperfect Mountain: Mount Buzhou. The mountain was deemed 'imperfect' because the repair made by Nü Wa had left the sky leaning over.

When investigating the astronomical consequences underlying such myths it may be simpler to cut through the confusion of later interpretations, by both ancient and modern commentators, and to trust the wording of the original legendary source, as here translated:

> *Heaven's pillars broke; the bonds with earth were ruptured,*
> *Heaven leaned over to the north-west,*
> *Hence the sun, moon, stars and planets were shifted,*
> *And earth became empty in the south-east.* [4]

We may test these legends alongside the latest archaeology. Chinese archaeologists recognise an early Neolithic civilisation known as the Yangshao culture in the Loess plateau of the upper Hwang Ho; recognisable by its distinctive red pottery and artefacts with intricate coloured designs; later sites would show evidence of millet farming. The original Yangshao discovery in Henan Province during the 1920s is now viewed as an outlier of the principal site at Banpo near Xi'an, dated 4500 – 3750 BC. Archaeologists also consider that the Yangshao were a matriarchal culture, which we may equate with the memories of Nü Wa as an early empress or goddess.

After about 3200 BC the Yangshao sites abruptly declined, to be supplanted by a new culture centred in the lower reaches of the Hwang Ho and Yangtze rivers. This new culture is termed the Longshan after the principal site on the Shandong peninsula. All the known early sites are situated on low hills above the flood plain and the transformation of customs is identifiable by its distinctive pottery style; black and undecorated. Yangshao pottery has been found at some Longshan sites, but not the other way around; thus, archaeologists suggest that this new culture spread from Shandong into western China.

Within this overview, which developed from the early discoveries of pottery, a more complex picture emerges. Archaeologists now recognise a number of local cultures in northern China, trading and influencing each-other over a long period before a truly unified 'empire' came into existence. Also dating to the third millennium BC is the solar-aligned platform at Taosi. Alignments to the summer and winter solstices would indicate the early origins of a formal calendar echoing the references found in the legendary sources.

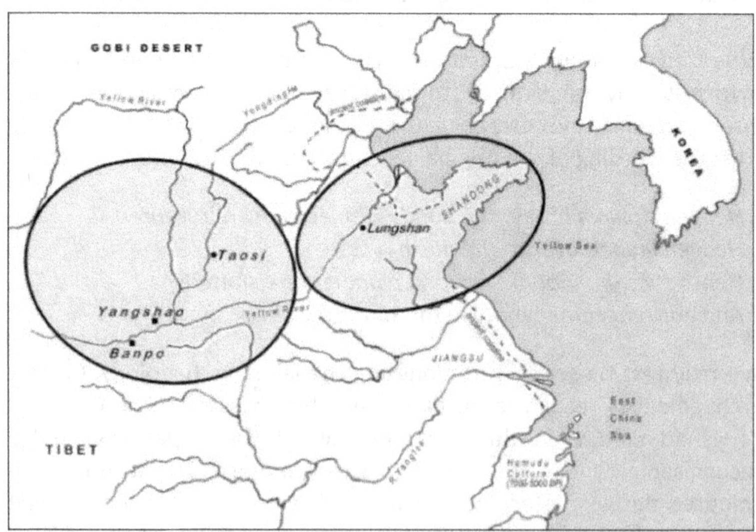

Figure 1 A summary map showing the principal sites and regions mentioned in the text.

Of significance is the abrupt decline of the Yangshao in the higher valleys and the beginnings of an agricultural civilization in the lower plains where none had been before. It has always been something of an enigma to explain why the earliest Chinese civilisation developed higher up the river valleys rather than in the fertile plains. Back into Ice Age times the Shandong peninsula was certainly an island surrounded by a shallow sea (analogous to the shallow European continental shelf) but precisely where the coastline lay in the later Holocene has been a matter for debate, since it is now disguised by so many years of intensive agriculture. Radiocarbon dates from coastal studies may help to place a more precise date on this transition.

A comprehensive study by Wang & Zhao [5] cited 'hundreds' of radiocarbon dates from Holocene sediments, between the Yellow Sea and Hainan island as evidence for Holocene sea level variations. Their data suggests a maximum transgression of the sea all along the coast between 7000 and 3000 BP with most dates falling between 6000 and 5000 BP, varying in different regions. They further suggest that since that time, the sea has retreated 'step by step' to present shores. Each 'step', of course, could represent a rapid change – but field researchers have to word their studies with a uniformitarian caution and respect for long established theories. In a paper covering similar bounds, Xiong et al are brave enough to suggest:

"*there are significant misfit between sea-level data and glacial isostatic adjustment models, and a revision to the existing ice melting history for the early Holocene is possibly needed*". [6]

A study of Holocene sea level changes in the Fuzhou basin (opposite Taiwan) revealed hill-top settlements dated to 5500-5000 BP that are now 80 km inland from the modern coast. These were formerly islands within an estuary that occupied the entire basin. Since that era, the coastline has retreated. [7] They find that the plain was rapidly occupied by rice farmers as the sea withdrew – as close a reference to a sudden and unexplained change of sea level as we might expect to a find within an academic study.

Recent investigations in Jiangsu province (just south of Shandong) reveal that the coastal plain was beneath seawater or low-lying wetland throughout the early Holocene. Much of the Lixiahe Plain remained a coastal lagoon until 6000–5500 cal. BP. [8] Other studies suggest that the rice-growing Hemudu culture that occupied the coastal region of the Lower Yangtze river was interrupted when the region alternated between intertidal mudflats and freshwater wetlands during the mid-late Holocene. [9] These conservatively worded specialist studies do not of course suggest a catastrophic or sudden change of sea level, but they would confirm the legendary accounts of great river floods.

Climate researchers also detect a transition at this same era. Between 6000–5000 BP, the climate of eastern China remained relatively warm and wet, and forest cover was extensive. However, the subsequent retreat of the forests and increased grassland is attributed to a decline in temperature and precipitation during the 5000–4000 BP period. [10] The cool humid period (4800-3400 BP) was followed by milder arid conditions. [11] This would be in line with comparable evidence of a mid-Holocene warm period that is evident from other parts of the world.

So, what might be intended by that enigmatic report in the Kung Kung myth: *...earth became empty in the south-east?* Translation ambiguities apart, this is a strange form of words. Does it mean that the land became uninhabited? Or does it imply a complete desolation of all vegetation and life? It would be a fair description of mudflats emerging from the sea after a rapid sea-level change. This is an example of something that I have referred-to elsewhere as a 'fossil' within a myth, which can be checked against the best science available. If you prefer to view the Chinese myths and legends as just primitive beliefs to be dismissed then I cannot help you; however, should you seek to validate them then this enigmatic phrase could only be remembering the period around five-thousand years ago when researchers find clear evidence of new and uncultivated land emergent from the sea, along with the cultural break that is recognised by the archaeologists.

The myths recall the sky tilting over and the courses of sun, moon and stars being disturbed. It may not be immediately apparent to the non-astronomer that this implies many of the effects that are described in myths from other parts of the world. If the obliquity changed then it must affect the calendar: the solstice sunrise, the seasons, and the latitude of the tropics and Arctic Circle. When we hear myths from other nations, of the sun going away or periods when its motion was irregular, then it is important to appreciate that these may be describing the same event as is recalled in China.

In the equivalent cosmogony myths from Japan, we hear of the sun goddess *Amaterasu* who hides herself away in a cave and has to be lured-out with trickery by the other gods. Again, the era of sea level change and emergence around Japanese coasts can be dated by archaeological finds to the Jomon period around 5,000 years ago. Although the Japanese myths may be more naïve and offer less detail than the Chinese stories, they again remember an abnormal solar event.

Archaeologists now recognise southern China and Indochina as the point of origin for the Lapita pottery culture found in Melanesia and the Bismarck Islands. [12] This culture was the forerunner of the Polynesian migrations, now confirmed by DNA evidence. [13] It was around 5,000 years ago that they began their island-hopping voyages into the Pacific in a sequence that can be traced via Taiwan, Philippines and on to Melanesia and Polynesia by 1500 BC. Once again, the ancestral sites are found on former small islets on the coastal plain of south-east China; another coincidence to add to the cultural break further north at this same era.

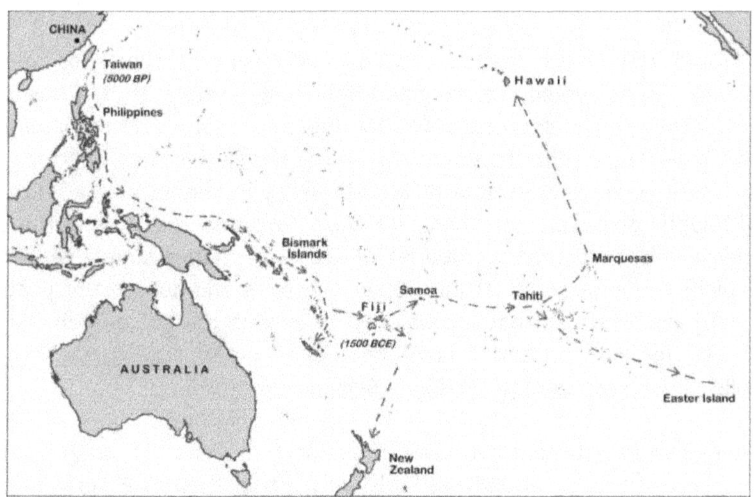

Figure 2: The Polynesian Migrations. DNA analysis now confirms the theory that the dispersal of the Lapita-Polynesians began from Taiwan and southern China c.5000 BP.

Although Polynesian myths vary from one island chain to another, they have a common root in their beliefs about the demi-god Maui, who is variously credited with fishing the Pacific islands out of the ocean and also with lengthening the hours of daylight to give the people more time to go about their daily tasks! In Hawaiian myths the movements of the sun are said to have been irregular and unpredictable before Maui snared the sun and made it behave. Underlying these naïve myths must be some real astronomy that predates the Polynesian dispersal. The typical modern researcher who might take an interest in mythology is unlikely to be an astronomer and so may miss the significance; conversely scientifically minded astronomers are unlikely to take much notice of myths. Hence, the coincidences within the myths and legends remain neglected as a potential source of evidence about real ancient events.

The emergence of islands from the Pacific is essentially the same phenomenon as barren coastal land rising from the ocean. The attempts by Maui to lengthen the hours of daylight may be a naïve experience, by a tropical people confined on oceanic islands, of the seasonal variations of daylight that are normal in the temperate zones; they may be rationalised by a transient nutation of the axis that would bring temperate seasonal variations to an isolated tropical community that had never experienced them before.

A rapid change of sea-level, producing emergent coastlines and islands, is as would be expected following a pole shift. Coastal emergence of the scale recorded by the specialists would demand a permanent pole shift of amplitude no more than a third or a quarter of a degree of latitude – modest, but still large by modern experience. Although pole-shift theories are not favoured by the various specialists, the prevailing theories of sea-level change simply cannot explain the *emergence* of east-Asian coasts in addition to the post-glacial sea-level rise that is employed to explain the *submergence* of coasts in Europe and North America (see: https://www.third-millennium.co.uk/raised-beaches-and-submerged-forests).

There can only be one worldwide 'eustatic' sea-level. Emergence at the east-Asian coasts and Pacific islands would therefore demand a mechanism to raise the land by some 20-30 m on top of that required to annul the sea level rise of some 120m attributed to polar melt since the Ice Age. Only a theory based on pole shifts can resolve such anomalies; it would leave a world-wide pattern of emergence and submergence in alternate quarter-spheres.

It is important to appreciate that tiny shifts of the poles are triggered every time that a crustal earthquake occurs. The phenomenon is well understood by geophysicists and must trigger a transitional episode of axis-wobble before it can settle to a new position. A larger excursion of the axis of rotation, as recorded by the Chinese, merely demands a 'quake' of greater amplitude and an explanation as to what might trigger it. Visualize that a quake deep down in the mantle or the core causes a change to the geoid (the flattened shape of the rotating earth); the centre of gravity jumps to a new position; the figure axis must shift to pass through the new centre of gravity, hence the rotational poles on the surface migrate and a wobble commences as the axis of rotation seeks the new axis of figure. At the surface this would manifest as temporary variations in sea-level called pole tides, until the ellipsoid of the planet permanently settled to its new axis; the coastline is left in some places above and in others below the former shoreline. Along the Chinese coast, the sea-level apparently fell, whereas in other parts of the world there was submergence at the same era.

A geographical pole shift must be distinguished from a change to the obliquity. In popular literature these concepts are often muddled. A motion of the geographical poles (a wobble) is measured relative to axes that rotate with the Earth – a rotating frame of reference. A change of obliquity, or an 'axis tilt' in common parlance, is measured relative to a frame that is fixed in space. This may be compared to the forced nutation that occurs due to the gravitational pull of the sun, moon and planets on the equatorial bulge. The solid earth and oceans move together and therefore do not cause pole tides. The Chinese myths that would portray the sky leaning-over are describing an apparent change of obliquity rather than a pole shift. So, what might be the connection between this, the river floods and the coastal emergence?

A change of obliquity requires an external force from space, but a geographical pole shift could be triggered by movements of mass internal to the Earth. However, this could imply some earlier external event that had left an imbalance waiting to be triggered. We may compare this to the tension on a fault that builds prior to a crustal earthquake but on a larger scale. It is disturbing to think that there might be such an imbalance of mass beneath our feet right now, in the mantle or the core, just waiting to be triggered! However, the Kung Kung myth, *as described*, would seem to be describing a force from space that was the immediate cause of both the axis-tilt *and* the creation of empty land, with many subsequent episodes of river flooding recurring in later dynasties.

While it may be the norm for single-subject specialists to dismiss myths as just the naïve tales of our ancestors, this is less tolerable when so many parallels can be seen between the myths of unrelated cultures in other parts of the world. To give just a few other contemporary examples: If we look to the western myths such as the Mesopotamian flood of c.3100 BC, as derived from the Babylonian king lists, then we see another event that requires a change of geodesy to properly explain it. In Irish myth we find memories of the sun standing-still, which are associated with the building of Newgrange (c.3150 BC); and in Manetho's chronicle of the Egyptian Third Dynasty we are told of an abnormal waxing and waning of the Moon, which so terrified the Libyan people.

From a cross-disciplinary analysis of such myths we may discern the degraded memory of a worldwide cataclysmic event and we are given an approximate era to look for more concrete evidence. Pole-shifts are the missing link that could turn the myths into history. Rather than dismissing ancient stories like that of Kung Kung, perhaps we should instead be asking what was the nature of the cosmic force that could so drastically disturb the earth's axis in the way that our ancestors have recorded.

Relevant Hyperlinks:

https://www.writtenchinese.com/neolithic-china-beginnings-chinese-civilization/

https://www.ancient.eu/Longshan_Culture/

http://factsanddetails.com/china/cat2/sub1/item32.html

http://www.chinaknowledge.de/History/Myth/personsgonggong.html

https://www.britannica.com/topic/Lapita-culture

https://anthrogenica.com/showthread.php?7766-Oceanian-Genetics-Beginners-Guide-and-FAQ

https://www.third-millennium.co.uk/raised-beaches-and-submerged-forests

Notes and References

1) Needham, R. *Science and Civilization in China* (vols 2 & 3) Cambridge Univ. Press (1959)

2) Ronan, C. (1984) *The Shorter Science and Civilisation in China*, vols, 1 & II & III, Cambridge University Press.

3) Werner, Edward, T.C. (1922) Myths and Legends of China, George G. Harrap & Co. Ltd. London Bombay Sydney.

4) See Ronan, vol 1, p 84, quoting the translation of the book: Huainanzi by James Legge.

5) Wang, S and Zhao, X. (1992) Sea-level changes in China-past and future: their impact and countermeasures, In McCall G J.H. et al. (eds.), *Geohazards* pp.161-169.

6) Haixian Xiong, Yongqiang Zong, Peng Qian, Guangqing Huang, Shuqing Fu, Holocene sea-level history of the northern coast of South China Sea, *Quaternary Science Reviews*, Volume 194,2018, Pages 12-26, ISSN 0277-3791, https://doi.org/10.1016/j.quascirev.2018.06.022. (https://www.sciencedirect.com/science/article/pii/S0277379117305218)

7) Rolett, BV, Zheng, Z, Yue,Y (2011) Holocene sea-level change and the emergence of Neolithic seafaring in the Fuzhou Basin (Fujian, China), *Quaternary Science Reviews* 30 (7-8), 788-797

8) Lan Li et al, (2017) Relative sea level rise, site distributions, and Neolithic settlement in the early to middle Holocene, Jiangsu Province, China, *The Holocene*, Volume: 28 issue: 3, page(s): 354-362 https://doi.org/10.1177/0959683617729442

9) Keyang he, -et-al, Middle-Holocene sea-level fluctuations interrupted the developing Hemudu culture in the lower Yangtze River, China, *Quaternary Science Reviews,* May 2018

10) Du Linyao, Ma Minmin, Lu Yiwen, Dong Jiajia, Dong Guanghui, How Did Human Activity and Climate Change Influence Animal Exploitation During 7500–2000 BP in the Yellow River Valley, China?, *Frontiers in Ecology and Evolution*, Vol 8, 2020
https://www.frontiersin.org/article/10.3389/fevo.2020.00161
DOI 10.3389/fevo.2020.00161, ISSN 2296-701X

11) Weiskopf A. R. *Vegetation, Agriculture and Social Change in Late Neolithic China: a phytolith study*; University College London Thesis (2010).

12) Diamond, J.M. Express Train to Polynesia, *Nature*, 336, p. 307-8. (1988)

Other References:

Rawson, J. *Ancient China - Art & Archaeology*, British Museum Publications, London (1980)

Waltham, Clae, *Shu Ching, Book of History, A modernised edition of the translations of James Legge*, George Allen & Unwin Ltd, London (1971)

Birrell, A. (1999). James Legge and the Chinese Mythological Tradition. *History of Religions, 38*(4), 331-353. http://www.jstor.org/stable/3176322

Yang Lihui & al. (2005), *Handbook of Chinese Mythology,* Oxford: Oxford University Press, ISBN 978-0-19-533263-6

****

5

The Phaistos Disc: Minoans, Trojans and Etruscans

Summary

A cross-disciplinary discussion centred around the Minoan Phaistos Disc; pursuing the theory that it was a simple 30- and 31-day solar calendar; its possible connection to the Etruscans; or perhaps to the Trojans and the legendary Trojan origins of the Romans. Many timeless legends offer us overlapping versions of the migration of tribes from the Aegean Sea region to Italy and even beyond, to Britain and Ireland. If we could untangle some of these legends then it might be possible to compare the events to hard evidence of climate change, famines and archaeology; and to suggest a chronology for some of the migrations. The enigmatic Phaistos Disc and its possible use as a calendar may offer clues to supplement the other evidence.

Discovered in 1908 at the palace site of Phaistos in southern Crete the Phaistos Disc has proven to be something of an enigma. On a fired-clay disc 15 cm in diameter and 2 cm thickness are some 242 'words' composed of 45 recurring glyphs, arranged in clockwise spirals on each side. No irrefutable theory has yet emerged as to what the symbols may signify or the true purpose of the disc. One thing that archaeologists seem to agree upon however, is that the artefact is not a modern forgery. Similar symbols occur on another Minoan object – the bronze axe head from the Arkalochori cave [1] Other glyphs show a resemblance to the undeciphered Linear-A script.

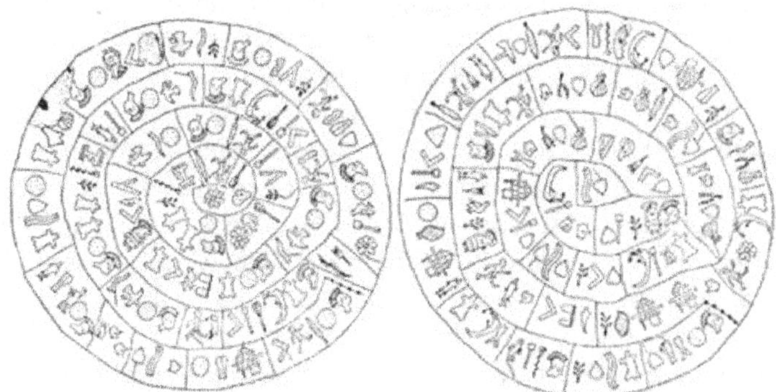

The Phaistos Disc (www.tokenrock.com – click the picture for access)

There is no agreement among specialists as to whether the script should be read from the outside in, or from the centre out. However, linguists consider that there are too many symbols to comprise an alphabet, yet too few to be hieroglyphs each signifying a word (like Egyptian). The consensus is therefore that each symbol represents a syllable (like Japanese). We should also ask: *what was the significance of the spiral arrangement?*

The simple detail that the disc was of fired clay (the only such example found on Crete) would suggest that it was intended for long-term use and so needed to be robust. Just as we might retain interesting objects as souvenirs, perhaps they did so too. Another possibility to consider is that it could be one surviving example of a 'mass produced' object cast from a mould, or 'printed' on to wet clay; there may be other discs just like it waiting to be found. This would at least prove that it was truly a Minoan artefact rather than an import from somewhere else in the Aegean region. Archaeologists date the disc loosely to the mid-second millennium BC. During the second and third millennia BC Minoan influence extended throughout the islands of the Aegean Sea and to the mainland coasts around it.

My personal interest in the Phaistos Disc goes back to my book *Atlantis of the West* in 2002. [2] For some reason, the publisher: *Constable*, chose a colourful image of the Phaistos Disc for the cover! "It's visually stunning", I was told. "Well, if you say so", was my response at the time – but it was far from what the book was about!

The spiral format of the disc, showing three-and-a half turns on each side making seven turns in total, suggested that it might be a seven-year 'spiral calendar'; I had made the case at the time that a spiral wobble of the Earth's axis caused seven-year climate rhythms during the early third millennium BC, consequent upon an astronomical event.* On this theory, each boxed 'word' would represent a season and so forecast when to expect abnormal seasonal weather, i.e.: *mild winter, hot summer, cool summer*, etc. There are numerous examples of spiral carvings on seasonally aligned Neolithic monuments dating from the third millennium BC. Although the Phaistos Disc cannot be dated as early as the third millennium BC, calendars are conservative and would preserve an older structure. If you don't like this theory, then you would need to propose some other reason why the spiral format was chosen.

Coiled-snake spirals with seven turns are also known from Egypt and are usually considered to be a board game called Mehen. Perhaps the Phaistos Disc was also a mass-produced gaming board (see also: game-board | British Museum). When eventually the script is deciphered, the disc may turn-out to be quite mundane after all. Perhaps it just made a nice table mat!

Another possibility to float is that the disc was a simple *monthly calendar* to remind the owner of the named days of the month. We see 31 'words' on side A and 30 on side B – suggestive of the twelve idealised 30- and 31-day solar 'months' as are later found in the Roman calendar. Each word or token could therefore be a day of the month, named after a Minoan god or goddess.

This format would be a precocious invention of the Julian Calendar that Caesar would acquire from Cleopatra's court astronomer; rather like biologists would term a 'parallel evolution' – a similar adaptation to the same real-world problem. ** Speculative? All one can reply is that: *the disk would work as a calendar* if you moved a counter around the spiral each day; no different than ticking-off the days of the month on your desk calendar with a pen!

The structure of the modern Julio-Gregorian calendar preserves the 28-day variable month of February (*Februarius*) from the old Roman calendar – but it isn't really needed. If the arrangement were a simpler (7 x 30) + (5 x 31) = 365 then an extra day could just be added to one of the 30-day months each fourth year (or just turn the disc over). Perhaps as in the Egyptian civil calendar they let the seasons wander. The 30-31 day 'coincidence', which just happens to create an artefact that can be employed as a calendar, is one of those unlikely circumstances that suggest design rather than chance. The significance of this coincidence will be further discussed below in relation to the Etruscan and Roman calendars.

The author's desktop Phaistos calendar – it works just fine!

Since 2002 the possible links between the Etruscans of central Italy and the Aegean region have been reconsidered and this has invited comparison between the Cretan disc and an Etruscan spiral artefact: the *Magliano Disc*. This connection is reinforced by modern DNA research, which has tested so many older assumptions that have lain unchallenged in the textbooks. Archaeologists would prefer to view the Etruscans as a progression from a native Italian culture that had been in that region since the Neolithic, evolving via the Iron Age Villanovan culture (c. 900–700 BC); The earliest recognisably 'Etruscan' artefacts date only from the 7th century BC when the culture also began to display influence from the new Greek colonies in the south of Italy and Sicily. Classical Greek authors referred to the Etruscans by the name: *Tyrrhenians*.

The purpose of the Magliano disc can scarcely be determined any better than for the Phaistos disc, but specialists think that they recognise the names of some Etruscan gods within the spiral inscription. [3] This has prompted suggestions that both artefacts might have had a religious motive, perhaps a prayer. But look at the practical calendar on your own wall and you will see days and months named for ancient Roman and Germanic gods (i.e.: Monday = 'moon day', Friday = 'Freya day', etc). Other calendrical interpretations would compare Etruscan divination to their astrological beliefs and those of the Minoans. [4]

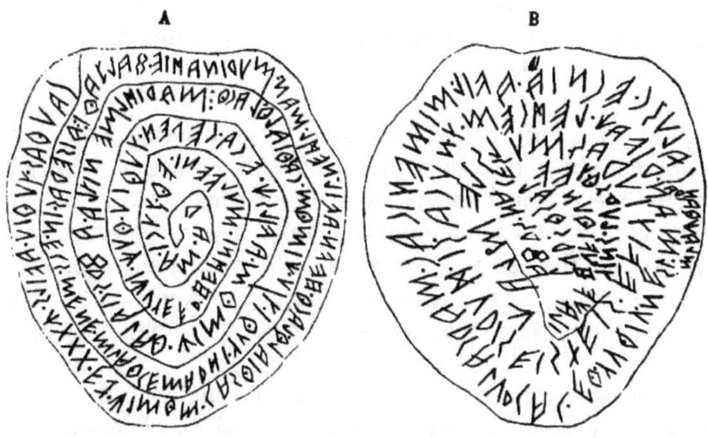

The Etruscan Magliano Disc (Source: www.ancient-origins.net)
The Magliano Disc is dated to the Fifth Century BC. Stamped onto an 8 cm diameter lead disc are spiral inscriptions of five turns on each side; written in an Etruscan script that can still be only partially translated. However, Etruscan was written in an alphabet rather than a syllabary.

The belief that the Etruscans originally came from Anatolia is as old as the Romans and many more recent specialists have also proposed connections with Asia Minor, especially with the Lydians and their neighbours, the Lycians. In the 1950s Michael Ventris (who deciphered the Cretan Linear B script) made a case that Linear B was Etruscan, before it became clear that it was an archaic form of Greek. More convincing is the relationship between the Etruscan and Greek alphabets; specialists can read how the words were pronounced by analogy with Greek, but their meaning cannot be understood save for a few proper names and numbers.

Links between the Etruscans and the islands off the Aegean coast of Anatolia were first suggested in a legend recorded by Herodotus who was a native of Halicarnassus on the coast of Asia Minor: the region of Lydia. [5] The story recalls *Tyrrhenus* the son of King Atys of Lydia. In the reign of Atys there occurred a prolonged famine; and so, after eighteen years of starvation the king decreed that half the population must emigrate in search of better prospects. This reference to a precise *eighteen-years* is a typical example of a 'mythological fossil' that betrays a real event; a fictional storyteller has no need to state a precise period. It is the present author's method to seek-out these 'fossils' together with coincidences between unrelated historical and mythological sources.

Herodotus says that the Lydians drew lots to decide who should remain and who should emigrate along with Tyrrhenus; ships were built, and the colonists set sail. After passing many other countries, they eventually settled in the region of Umbria, in central Italy, where they changed their name to *Tyrrhenians* after their eponymous leader. We cannot know precisely when these supposed events occurred, but a loose date in the late second millennium BC is generally assumed.

This story raises the possibility that other wandering Bronze Age colonists may have settled elsewhere in the Mediterranean and beyond. Perhaps other sea-faring Greek and Aegean nations embarked on similar migrations in their desperation, just as we see economic migrants in modern times. We may note other timeless famine stories such as the Biblical Joseph and the Egyptian Ipuwer Papyrus (first intermediate period c.2100 BC) as examples of ancient famine catastrophes; with other possible climatic fluctuations at the second and third intermediate periods; and even as far back as the mid-Neolithic. There may have been numerous ancient famines, triggering migrations, which the repetition of similar-sounding elements has merged into a single narrative; such is the nature of oral myths and legends.

Herodotus did not assert that all the Etruscans of his own era were descended from the colony of Tyrrhenus, merely that their heirs still lived there. Recent DNA studies would suggest that only some isolated communities in modern Umbria could claim descent from the Etruscans. Specialists would prefer that the migration, if true, occurred during the Neolithic around 5,000 years ago, or earlier, when other migrations from Anatolia to the west occurred. [6] Could Herodotus be recalling a legend quite as old as that? If so, then it overlaps the period of High Minoan maritime culture that dominated the Aegean islands and coasts, before it was devastated by the Thera eruption around 1645 BC. Perhaps the wandering Tyrrhenians took the idea of the spiral disc with them to their new homeland?

We must also rely upon Herodotus with regard to other timeless migration legends; he tells us of a colony of Cretans at Miletus on the Anatolian coast that dates from the era when King Minos expelled his brother Sarpedon from Crete (a legend of uncertain date but loosely sometime in the late third Millennium BC). Again, this would suggest a close relationship between the Lydians and the Minoans. The language of their Anatolian neighbours the Lycians is also believed to have belonged to the Luwian Group and only distantly related to Hittite. Herodotus also confirms that the Minoans were not Greeks:

The Lycians came originally from Crete, which in ancient times was occupied entirely by non-Greek peoples. [7]

We are also told that the Lycians took their mother's name and operated an apparently matrilinear, or even matriarchal system of inheritance. Herodotus says that in some customs they resembled the Cretans, in other ways they were more like the Carians.

Of other west-Anatolian nations, the Carians and the Caunians, Herodotus cites their own beliefs that they too came from Crete. The language of the Carians was also related to the extinct Luwian group. Therefore, any of these lost Anatolian languages might be the non-Greek script that is represented as a unique 'printed font' on the indecipherable Phaistos disc. The linguistic evidence remains inadequate so we still cannot rule-out a native non-Indo-European origin for the Cretans.

The customs of the Lydians, as Herodotus describes them, do indeed stand comparison with those of the Etruscans, most notably the free social conduct of the women. Herodotus describes the liberty enjoyed by Lydian women, who were free to associate and choose their husbands. Etruscan women retained a similar independence, in contrast to later Roman marriage customs. Unlike Roman women they could attend public functions as the equals of their husbands; they could own property and were educated. This equality of status between the sexes seems to have been a characteristic of many indigenous Mediterranean cultures, including the Minoans. Indeed, we may note a parity of roles, even outright matriarchy, among descriptions of ancient Libyan and Egyptian women; and of course, on the island of Malta. This contrasts with the warlike male-dominated cultures of the Latins, Greeks, Celts and other nations further north, whom we may consider as Indo-European intruders from the Steppes.

In 2007 two DNA studies revealed that some people living in the Umbrian region of Italy do indeed show evidence of an Aegean origin: specifically, from the island of Lemnos. The correspondence was most prominent in the mitochondrial DNA of the female line. [8] [9] If this may be considered as evidence in support of the migration of Tyrrhenus then we should have to view the ancient kingdom of Atys and his 'Lydians' (or 'Meiones' as they were formerly called) as extending further north along the coast of Anatolia - perhaps even as far as the traditional site of Troy at the entrance to the Dardanelles. During the Hittite era the kingdom was known as Arzawa and may have held political authority over nearby islands such as Lemnos.

The influence of later Greek and Carthaginian colonies in the south of Italy is well known from the historical settlements that began in the Etruscan era and survived until the Roman expansion. It may be that this has disguised earlier immigration by closely related Aegean peoples. The DNA relationship would suggest a link with the older inhabitants of Greece and the Aegean: the Minoans, Trojans, Pelasgians and the Anatolian groups, rather than the Indo-European Dorians and Achaeans who arrived later to the mainland. The Etruscans and the Minoans even look remarkably alike in their facial features and hairstyle, as we may see in their colourful frescos.

The Etruscan myths of origin remain obscure because their scripts cannot be deciphered – but those of their Roman neighbours are well known. A new theory gaining acceptance is that the Latins were related to the Trojans. [10] The Latin tribes seem to have been already established in Italy contemporary with the Etruscans and this is certainly what the familiar traditions suggest. In brief, these relate that Aeneas the Trojan fled to Italy after the Trojan War where he married the daughter of the local king *Latinus.* How many Trojans accompanied Aeneas is unclear; his son Ascanius went on to establish the city of Alba Longa where, several generations later were born Romulus and Remus: the legendary founders of Rome. The traditional date for the foundation of Rome is placed at 753 BC – and almost immediately they found themselves at war with the Etruscan cities. For a long period up to 510 BC Rome was ruled by Etruscan kings.

We may consider the migration of the Tyrrhenian colony to Umbria as an example of an *invasion*, since they established a flourishing kingdom of city-states in central Italy, retaining their culture and displacing or absorbing the local inhabitants. Although archaeologists might prefer that the Etruscans were a native non-Indo-European nation, the legend implies a substantial population influx added to the mix.

By contrast, the legends of Roman origin are best viewed as an *immigration* by a small Trojan elite who merged with the Latins, influencing their culture and language but leaving little trace in the DNA. At this distance in time, it is difficult to distinguish what was native Latin and what might have been Trojan. The later fusion with the Etruscans has blurred this relationship still further and we cannot now be sure how much of Roman culture and religion was borrowed from the Etruscans; certainly, they influenced the alphabet and numerals that we use today. Ultimately, both cultures are *Aegean* in inspiration, from their art through to their mythology.

Little is known about the workings of the Etruscan calendar save for its use in divination, but we do know that it influenced the development of the Roman calendar. It was an Etruscan king of Rome: *Tarquinius Priscus* who established the so-called 'Republican Calendar'; another Etruscan king had wanted to move the start of the year to midwinter but after he was overthrown the idea was forgotten – until Caesar's reform. The first Roman calendar supposedly introduced by Romulus himself had consisted of 10 months plus a vague midwinter hiatus; the two winter months being later additions. There were six months of 30 days plus four of 31 days (sometimes referred-to as the 'pre-Julian' calendar) making a total of 304 days, plus the winter gap. The individual days were not named, save for the markers (kalends, ides and nones). These too were Etruscan ('ides' meaning a division); originally they marked the lunar phases, but the calendar had ceased to be strictly lunar by some point in the fifth century BC.

We see here too-many coincidences. In addition to the similarities of *art* and *social customs*, we find the coincidence of comparable *spiral artefacts* and possibly the precocious development of a *solar calendar* with 30- and 31-day months at both ends of a migration legend. Could it be that the origins of the Roman and Gregorian calendar that we still use today go all the way back to Minoan civilisation or to one of their Aegean neighbours in ancient Anatolia?

A further development within recent decades has offered some clues about the Minoan calendar of the Bronze Age. In 2011, Henrikksson and Blomberg showed evidence of an alignment to the autumn equinox at the palace of Knossos. They propose that in addition to a lunar calendar, the Minoans understood the solar year with twelve solar months and a leap-year. [11] They would also suggest a knowledge of the stars adequate for navigation. Another theory is that the Minoan 'double-axe' symbol, found at various sites on the island, represented the constellation of Orion and its annual rising.

A related theory by Greek author and researcher Alexios Pliakos is that the small stone trays known as <u>*kernoi*</u> that are found at many Minoan sites (167 at latest count) were also a form of ritual divination calendar. [12] Archaeologists had considered the *kernos* to be a form of libation table with holes or cups to hold offerings or incense. The discs show much variation in the arrangement of the holes, which Pliakos suggests would remind the holder of the proper usage for a particular feast-day. Some kernoi have only 10 holes and a circular layout, while others have a quite different layout. The hypothesis of Pliakos is that the solar year was divided into 10 months plus a period of 5 days for festivals. He would suggest that each 'Minoan solar month' was therefore 36 days long, a figure arrived-at simply by dividing 360 by 10; however, this number has no astronomical significance. It may be that a lunar cycle was retained for religious observances (as with Easter in the Gregorian calendar) used alongside a solar calendar for more practical day-to-day matters. [13]

However, the kernos-theory would neglect that 'coincidence' of the spirals of 30 and 31 'words' as found on the Cretan Phaistos disc. If the calendar instead comprised 10 solar months of 30 or 31 days plus a hiatus over autumn or winter, then it becomes almost identical to the first Roman calendar. Similar problems find similar solutions – or perhaps the Minoan solar calendar was the prototype for them all. The sky above is the same for everyone. A common misconception among non-astronomers is that astronomy is difficult, and that some ancestral genius is required to devise a calendar. The reality is that naked-eye astronomy is easy; calendars evolve over generations from simple forms, refined by experience and necessity.

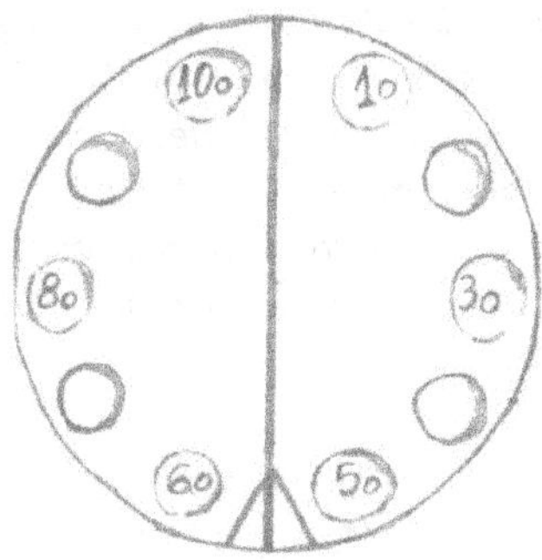

An example of a kernos with 10 holes excavated during the building of the Stratigraphical Museum at Knossos.
(Source: Figure 4 from the paper by Alexios Pliakos).

According to the theory, the solar year was divided into two halves, or 'seasons', with five solar months each, plus the period of five days for festivals indicated by the chevron. Other kernoi also show smaller holes that are interpreted as the special feast-days.

These parallels of the solar calendar, when placed alongside the DNA and the cultural similarities, may expose a Bronze Age connection between Italy and the Aegean-Anatolian region. It may offer confirmation that the Lydian migration described by Herodotus was real and that it occurred sometime between 1600 BC (the presumed date of the Phaistos Disc) and c.900 BC when the Villanovan Culture first appeared in Italy. Neither should we rule-out that migration from the Aegean islands to Italy and beyond was almost continuous throughout the earlier period of Bronze Age seaborne trade. The later Roman Empire too, was a melting-pot of cultures; an earlier influx of genetically related Trojan or Minoan colonists, from the same regions of the Aegean, would be difficult for specialists to distinguish in the modern DNA.

We must await decipherment of the Minoan and Etruscan languages to provide hard evidence of the parallels in their calendrical astronomy and the enigmatic spiral discs. In the meantime, Perhaps this cross-disciplinary enquiry has offered a few helpful insights that specialists would otherwise miss, without stretching the evidence too far.

****

* **Note 1:** *The spiralling motion that I proposed in 1995 and 2002 was merely the Earth's Chandler wobble and the Core wobble, as known to modern geophysicists, but increased to a more significant amplitude.*

** **Note 2:** *A theory that the Phaistos disc was a calendar of 30- and 31-day months was proposed in a 1999 book called: "The Bronze Age Computer Disc".* [14] *The author took his concept a little too far, spoiling a good case with too many astronomical theories (perhaps due to pressure from the publisher to create a more marketable book). These are issues that a fellow author can understand; to paraphrase the Monty Python sketch: "who among us can say we have not made that error from time to time – I know I have!"*

Relevant Hyperlinks

https://the-phaistos-disk.webnode.com/arkalochori-axe/
https://www.tokenrock.com/explain-phaistos-discs-93.html
https://www.ancient-origins.net/unexplained-phenomena/curious-phaistos-disc-ancient-mystery-or-clever-hoax-002089
https://www.people.ku.edu/~jyounger/PHDisc/
https://www.thoughtco.com/who-were-the-etruscans-118262
https://www.livius.org/sources/content/plutarch/plutarchs-caesar/caesars-calendar-reform/
http://www.perseus.tufts.edu/hopper/text?doc=Hdt.%201.93&lang=original
https://www.britannica.com/science/calendar/The-early-Roman-calendar
https://omniglot.com/writing/lydian.php
https://omniglot.com/writing/lycian.php
https://omniglot.com/writing/carian.php
https://linguistics.osu.edu/herodotos/ethnonym/asian/caunians
https://upload.wikimedia.org/wikipedia/commons/b/b2/Anatolian_03.png

References

1) Timm, Torsten (2004). "Der Diskos von Phaistos - Anmerkungen zur Deutung und Textstruktur". *Indogermanische Forschungen* (109): 204–231. doi:10.1515/16130405.204. S2CID 170325659

2) Dunbavin, Paul (2003) *Atlantis of the West*, Constable & Robinson, London, ISBN: 1-84119-716-5; https://www.third-millennium.co.uk/atlantis-of-the-west

3) Copeland, Mel (1981) Etruscan Phrases: Translation of the Magliano Lead Disk "M" http://www.maravot.com/Translation_Magliano.html

4) Carter, Lance (2017) Celestial Magliano Disc Deciphered https://www.academia.edu/31038379/Celestial_Magliano_Disc_Deciphered

5) Herodotus, I, 93-94

6) Dunbavin, Paul, (2020) The Stonehenge Builders came from Turkey: so what's new? in *Prehistory Papers*, pp 164-169, Third Millennium, ISBN: 978-0-9525029-4-4 https://www.third-millennium.co.uk/stonehenge-builders-dna

7) Herodotus, 1, 174

8) Ghirotto, Silvia et al, Origins and Evolution of the Etruscans' mtDNA in *PLoS One*. 2013; 8(2): e55519. Published online 2013 Feb 6. doi: 10.1371/journal.pone.0055519 PMCID: PMC3566088 PMID: 23405165

9) Tassi F, Ghirotto S, Caramelli D, Barbujani G., Genetic evidence does not support an Etruscan origin in Anatolia, *Am J Phys Anthropol.* 2013 Sep;152(1):11-8. doi: 10.1002/ajpa.22319. Epub 2013 Jul 30.

10) Dillon, Kenneth J. The Phaistos Disk Seems to Be Trojan: https://www.scientiapress.com/phaistos-disk-trojan

11) Henriksson, G. & Blomberg, M. (2015) Minoan Astronomy in: *Handbook of Archaeoastronomy and Ethnoastronomy* (pp.1431-1441) DOI:10.1007/978-1-4614-6141-8_141

12) Pliakos, A (2015) Minoan Solar Calendars Carved in Stones and the Riddle of Kernoi https://www.academia.edu/41121968/MINOAN_SOLAR_CALENDARS

13) Ridderstad, Marianna (2009) Evidence of Minoan Astronomy and Calendrical Practices

https://www.researchgate.net/publication/45880446_Evidence_of_Minoan_astronomy_and_calendrical_practices

14) Butler, Alan (1999) *The Bronze Age Computer Disc*, London & New York, ISBN:9780572022174

6

Callanish, Cronus and a Mysterious 'Stranger'

Summary:

Two essays from Plutarch's Moralia describe voyages made by the North Britons to an Atlantic island, which Plutarch equates with the Ogygia of Homer. Plutarch gives two related references to the voyages, the first in 'Obsolescence of Oracles' is brief; and the second in 'The Face in the Moon' offers more detailed geography. Conventional scholarship would view these references as little more than an attempt by Plutarch to equate some Celtic myths with those of Greece. However, an examination of the underlying astronomy and the aligned Neolithic monuments of Britain would suggest that there is much more to it than that; and that they offer us clues to the true antiquity of the Druids and their calendar.

In Plutarch's moral essay, *Obsolescence of Oracles* (*De Defectu Oraculorum*) one of the speakers is a certain Demetrius, who in an aside remarks upon the eternal imprisonment of Cronus. [1] He relates that Cronus was confined in a cave on an island close to Britain, guarded as he slept by the ancient Briareüs and various other daimones (demi-gods). In the recognised Greek mythology Cronus was ruler of the Titans and the father of Zeus; the Romans would equate him with their own god *Saturn*.

In *The Face on the Moon* *(De Facie Quae in Orbe Lunae Apparet)* Plutarch goes further and gives us a better opportunity to identify the geography; moreover, he identifies one of the islands with the Ogygia of Homer's Odyssey. [2] This island, supposedly lay some five-days sailing west of Britain in the direction of summer sunset; three other islands lay in-between, equidistant from the mainland and from each other. On this distant isle was an oracle where the faithful could receive the prophecies of Cronus in his dreams. He also refers to this part of the North Atlantic as the Cronian Sea and says that sometimes it could become 'congealed' (frozen?) but the geography is rather blurred and we cannot be sure quite what is intended, or indeed on which island we should seek the sleeping Cronus. It may be that Plutarch himself was confused by the geography in his sources and merely passes it on to his own readers. *

The Loeb translations of these essays are now freely available in the open-sources (linked above) and so need not be quoted here in full. However, it is important to note that the source text for *The Face in the Moon* is incomplete; the beginning of the essay is missing.

Beyond the Cronian Sea was the 'great mainland'; evidently a continent that lay a further 5,000 stades beyond Ogygia, across the Cronian Sea. On a gulf of its coast, resided a colony of Greeks who had migrated there from Britain via Ogygia. They believed they were the descendants of Greeks who, in ancient times, came west in the train of Heracles and over a long period of years had merged with the people of Cronus. Thus, they still revered Cronus, second only to Heracles.

Plutarch reveals that regular expeditions to this distant island continued right up to his own day; the voyages commenced from an island off the coast of Britain, which there are good reasons to suggest was the Isle of Lewis. Every thirty years when the Star of Cronus (the planet Saturn) returned to the constellation of Taurus, the crossing would begin. The faithful would set-off in a number of rowing boats, putting-in at outlying islands on the way (also occupied by Greeks) before the long haul to Ogygia began.

Demetrius is introduced as a grammarian who discussed philosophy with Plutarch and Cleombrotus of Sparta during a meeting at Delphi, on his way home to Tarsus; the date is identified as 83-84 AD by reference to the Olympiad. [3] Demetrius says that he was instructed by the emperor to survey the islands beyond Britain, but we cannot be sure which emperor sent him: Vespasian or Titus. He mentions many isolated islands and he had himself visited one of the nearer isles, inhabited only by a few holy men from whom he had learned the story of Cronus. The particulars are repeated in *The Face in the Moon,* by the Carthaginian, Sextius Sulla; he argued that many of the Greek myths were wrong and adds the important detail that the story came directly from the native Britons – he is not citing an earlier Mediterranean author. This dialogue took place later than AD 84 and so Plutarch could already have been influenced by Demetrius. A solar eclipse, probably that of 5 January AD 75, is mentioned as 'recent', but the best opinion of the translators will only put the date of the dialogue as sometime later than this. [4] Plutarch died in AD 120.

Confirmation that the starting point for the Atlantic voyages was the west coast of Scotland comes from the astronomy. It is perhaps best here to simply quote the words of Sulla. Firstly, he cites Homer:

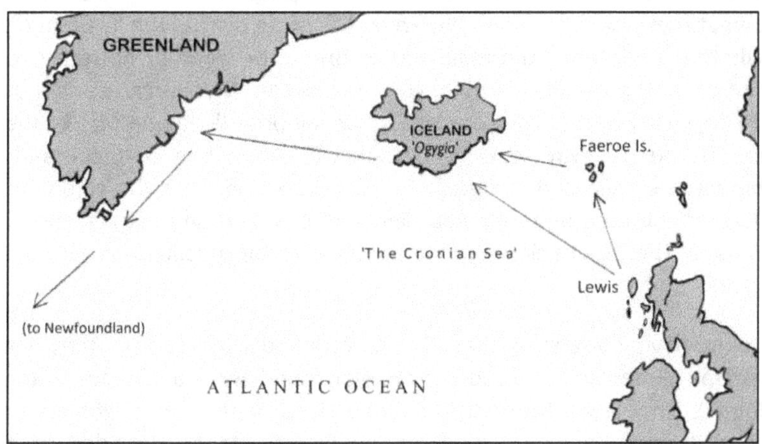

An isle, Ogygia, lies far out at sea,

a run of five days off from Britain as you sail westward; and three other islands equally distant from it and from one another lie out from it in the general direction of the summer sunset. In one of these, according to the tale told by the natives, Cronus is confined by Zeus, and the antique Briareüs... [5]

Later he comments:

The great mainland, by which the great ocean is encircled, while not so far from the other islands, is about five thousand stades from Ogygia, the voyage being made by oar... [6]

Ancient Voyages?

The statement that the direction of the voyages was towards the summer sunset tells us that the location of Ogygia lay to the northwest. Iceland lies some 670 miles (1085 km) northwest from Lewis, but whether this could be sailed or rowed in just five days seems improbable; and the distance of a further 5,000 stades to the distant mainland beyond the Cronian Sea, suggests a voyage of about 575 miles (925 km).

We are also offered a latitude for the final destination: a gulf lying upon a similar parallel to the Caspian Sea. This extra detail would equate it with Newfoundland or perhaps Nova Scotia rather than Greenland. It is here that the muddled geography defeats us. It is sometimes not clear, when Plutarch goes on to discuss the 'mainland', whether he intends the mainland of Britain or whether he refers to the distant 'great mainland' beyond the ocean. Moreover, we cannot distinguish whether the cave of Cronus supposedly lay on one of the islands on the way to Ogygia (Iceland?) *or* on one of the islands between Ogygia and the great mainland beyond. Was the colony of 'Greeks' situated on the 'great mainland' or was it on the mainland of Britain? This lack of clarity has led to a variety of speculations over the years.

Some have suggested that the narrative describes a journey via Iceland, Greenland and Labrador to Newfoundland – analogous to the later Viking sagas. More conservative classical scholars might prefer that it describes a shorter journey via the Inner Hebrides from mainland Britain to the Outer Hebrides. Others more conservative still cannot conceive that Homer's Ogygia lay beyond the fictional Mediterranean theatre. However, although the Isle of Lewis may sometimes seem remote to outsiders there is certainly no need to wait thirty years to go there; and the voyage was surely not so daunting even in ancient times! None of the explanations quite fits Plutarch's geography.

The narrative then moves on to discuss the 'stranger' who returned from the distant island. He is not named and it may be that he was introduced in the lost beginning of the essay.

> *Here then the stranger was conveyed, as he said, and while he served the god became at his leisure acquainted with astronomy, in which he made as much progress as one can by practicing geometry, and with the rest of philosophy by dealing with so much of it as is possible for the natural philosopher. Since he had a strange desire and longing to observe the Great Island (for so, it seems, they call our part of the world), when the thirty years had elapsed, the relief-party having arrived from home, he saluted his friends and sailed away...* [7]

We cannot be sure whether the stranger passed all of his religious servitude in Ogygia, or on the distant mainland, or on some intermediate isle where Cronus was believed to sleep; such is the uncertainty. All that really matters is that after thirty years he returned. We may wonder what was so 'strange' about him? Perhaps he was a native, born on the distant isle? Plutarch tells us that eventually he made his way to Carthage where Cronus was still a much-revered god. [8] There he met with Sulla, who later narrates the details to Plutarch.

The astronomical circumstances as they are given allow us to retro calculate the date of the events. We already know from the narrative that Demetrius was in Britain before AD 84, which was the era when Agricola took Roman forces into Caledonia. There is little reason to doubt that Demetrius of Tarsus was a real historical person. Any visitor to the Yorkshire Museum may see two votive offerings in Greek, left by a visitor named Demetrius at the site of the Roman legionary fort (RIB662 & RIB663). The first fortress at Eboracum is believed to have been built in AD 71 as the base for operations further north. We can be sure that Demetrius made his explorations to the west coast earlier than AD 84, probably in AD 82 protected by Agricola's army. [9]

The thirty-year return of Saturn to the constellation Taurus gives three possible dates for the 'stranger': AD 57, AD 87 and AD 117. No precise observational astronomy is needed; both the local observers and those in the distant colony would know that when Saturn returned to the proximity of the Hyades or the Pleiades then the relieving voyage should begin in the following summer. It is most likely that he made his pilgrimage west in AD 57 and returned in AD 87, allowing time for his later experiences in Carthage to have taken place during Plutarch's lifetime. We cannot rule out that his voyage occurred in an earlier thirty-year cycle but we can rule out AD 117. Nothing in the narratives requires that Sulla and Demetrius ever met each-other. However, Sulla is directly quoting his conversations with the 'stranger' when he says that some Greek myths were incorrect; and that 'stranger' had learned these specifics directly from the chamberlains at the oracle of Cronus.

Next Page: *three views thirty years apart showing Saturn in Taurus as it sets in the west, with the moon near conjunction. Taurus is a sprawling constellation and so its centre was probably taken as either the Hyades or the Pleiades.*
[retro calculations via Skymap Pro]

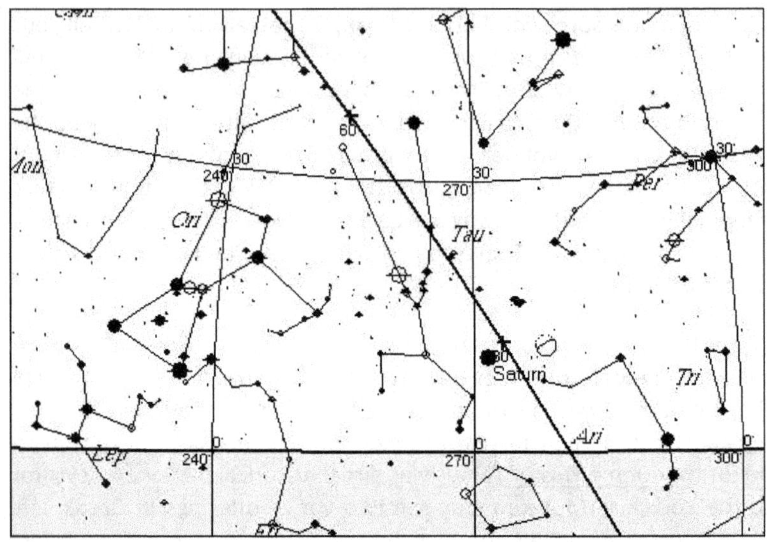

3 January 57 AD

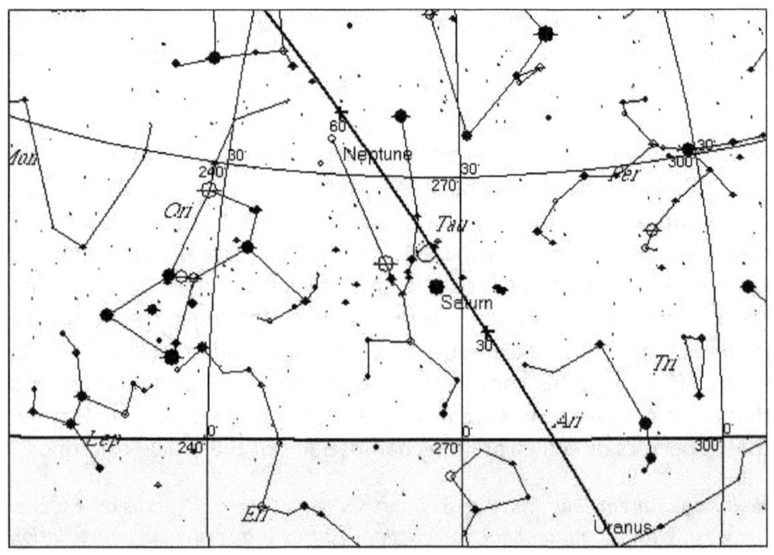

3 January 87 AD

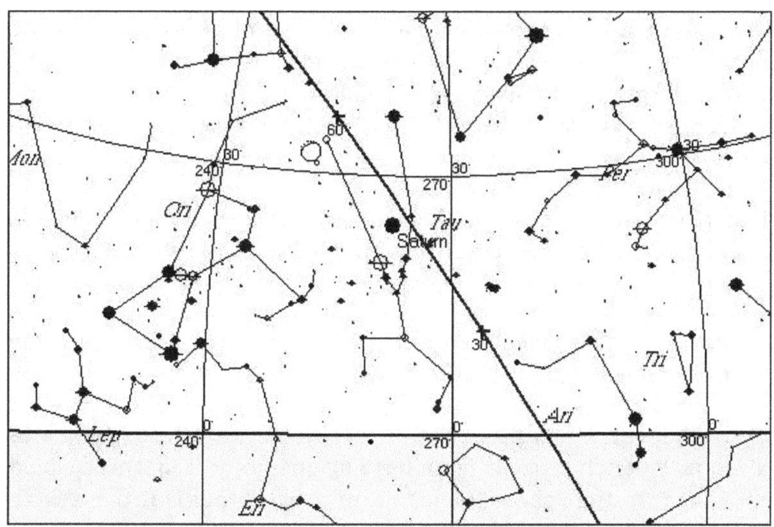

3 January 117 AD

Pliny, in his *Natural History* also offers much that is revealing. In discussing the calendar of the Druids, he too mentions the thirty-year 'ages' – but he does not make the link with Saturn. [10]

> *...above all on the sixth day of the moon (it is the moon that marks out for them the beginnings of months and years and cycles of thirty years) ...*

At this festival, a bull sacrifice was performed, showing us that this long cycle had both a religious and a practical significance; and we may presume there were other seasonal festivals. Pliny's geography of the Western Isles and the polar seasons is also informative. After detailing the islands around Britain, he goes on to describe the distant northern island of *Thule*:

> *The most remote of all those recorded is Thule, in which...there are no nights at midsummer... and on the other hand no days at midwinter....*
>
> *Some writers speak of other islands as well, the Scandiae, Dumna, Bergos, and Berrice the largest of them all, from which the crossing to Thule starts, called by some the Cronian Sea.* [11]

The largest island: *Berrice*, is plainly the Isle of Lewis – for he has previously counted all the Orkneys, Shetlands and Hebrides. The voyage across the Cronian Sea to Thule must surely recall the same sea-crossing as does Plutarch, only the name of the destination changes.

Plutarch prefers the name *Ogygia*. The name *Thule* has come via earlier geographers and ultimately from the fourth century BC voyage of Pytheas, of which Pliny observes:

> *Pytheas of Marseilles writes that this* [the polar seasons] *occurs in the island of Thule, 6 days north from Britain.* [12]

This comment would fit well with the five-day voyage to Ogygia as given by Plutarch, except that a heading due north from Lewis would take them to the Faeroe Islands not to Iceland; perhaps these were one of the intermediate islands as described. Again, the vague geography defeats conclusive identification; today we know the true geography, but it is understandable that the ancient geographers assumed different names for the same island to be different locations. Strabo, who treated the voyage of Pytheas as a fiction, gives an account of the climate and inhabitants of Thule that would fit better as a description of the Outer Hebrides. [13]

In the Loeb translation (p 181-183) Cherniss and Helmbold comment that Plutarch's account of the 'great mainland' beyond the ocean was likely inspired by Plato's Atlantis; and his remark about the congealed sea to be a reference to the debris of the sunken island. Such a comment is typical of conservative classical scholarship, which would treat Greek and Roman writers as the only legitimate source of ancient wisdom; all ancient texts are to be viewed merely as classical authors citing each other and ultimately as fictional recreations of myths. To discuss Plato's narrative as a degraded memory of something real would be to enter the realm of the lunatic.

In *Timaeus*, Plato describes the Atlantic voyages as taking place before the sinking of the lost island (and thereby implies that the knowledge was ancient). Via the island it was formerly possible to sail to the continent on the far side of the ocean before the way was blocked and forgotten. [14] if we accept the internal content of the underlying sources then we have one story of a continent beyond the ocean that ultimately came from the temple of Neit in Egypt; the other came via native British tradition; both remembering similar historical geography. However, we wander off-subject to pursue these topics further.

Why should modern historians find the notion of ancient transatlantic voyages so implausible? At this same era and for thousands of years the Polynesian explorers were rowing across the vast Pacific, navigating by the stars. Why then deny this same capability to European mariners? However, such exploration requires acceptance of a higher standard of navigational astronomy than is usually ascribed to northern 'barbarians' at this era. This is another text-book preconception of classical scholarship that has to be challenged. Naked-eye astronomy is *not* difficult; it merely requires diligence and a reliable calendar against which to record and predict the movements of the celestial bodies. We should never lose sight that ancient astronomy was actually just *precise astrology*, to interpret the signs of the 'visible gods' in the sky.

We should also consider that the inhabitants of the Western Isles and Ireland may observe the echelons of migratory geese and swans flying off to the northwest and returning again each year. They could reasonably assume that land existed in that direction, just as Polynesian navigators would look for these indicators to find islands in the vast Pacific. Long before any Greek or Carthaginian navigators reached Britain, we may presume that local fishermen were venturing out into the Atlantic and using the sky above for navigation.

Callanish and the Stone Circles

On the Atlantic coast of Lewis, on the inlet of Loch Roag lies the Callanish stone circle. Although the oldest stones date from as early as 2900 BC, the unique cross-shaped monument that we see today is a relatively late construction, dating from after 2000 BC. The cruciform arrangement disguises the fact that at its heart is a stone circle with a central monolith and a (later) chambered cairn built within. Beaker pottery has also been found at the site. The monument fell into disuse around 800 BC and in the damp climate it began to be enveloped in a layer of peat.

The original stone circle presumably had the same calendrical and religious purpose as all the other circles. So, what was its original purpose? The latitude of Callanish is such that the lunar standstills, when at their most southerly extreme every 18.6 years, rise and set behind the hills on the southern horizon. However long rows of stones are not essential to mark an alignment and so it is more likely that these possessed some processional significance for religious ceremonies. The inlet of Loch Roag is a prime candidate as the port of embarkation for ancient voyages into the western ocean and so Callanish may have retained a ritual significance as a place of pilgrimage for the later Druids long after its original astronomical usage was forgotten.

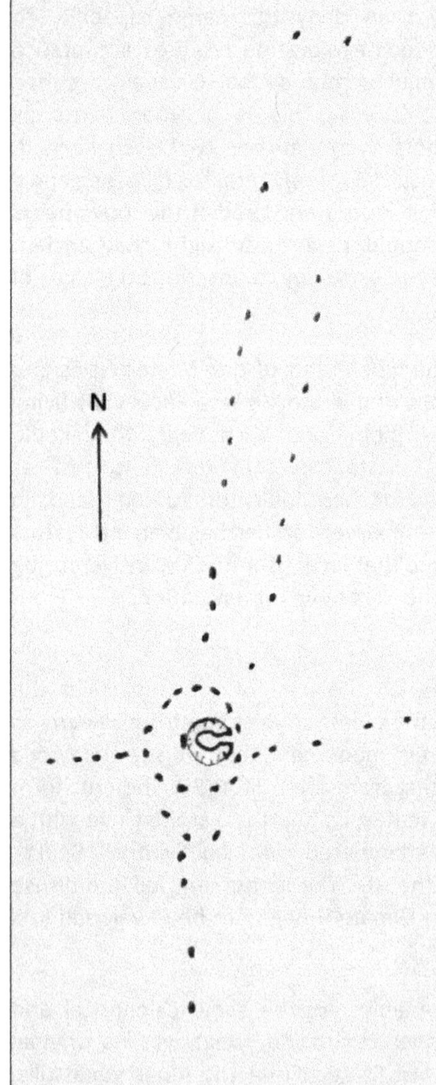

Left: the Layout of the circle and avenue at Callanish (click on the diagram to access Google Maps).

Again, we would go off-subject to pursue a discussion of the Callanish alignments here. The astronomical alignments have been well studied, one of the earliest being Captain Boyle Somerville in a 1912 article in *Nature*. [15] He thought he could see some navigational purpose to the alignments, suggesting orientations to Capella and other prominent stars – but his work predated any accurate means of archaeological dating. Later investigators such as Hawkins and Thom proposed the lunar horizon alignments in the 1960s,

A recent study by Dr Gail Higginbottom would claim to have statistically proved the alignments for the first time. [16] The paper provoked popular responses that Callanish and other similar monuments must have been laid-out by ancient astronomers. This would be rather like saying that the people playing football in the stadium must be footballers. Why should it be required for an academic to state the obvious in an appropriate journal in order for it to be accepted as fact? The ancient builders did not have the luxury of precise modern computations and surveying equipment. An approximate alignment to a seasonal marker was good enough for purpose and the best way to attain accuracy was to align to the celestial body as it rose or set at the furthest point on the horizon. They simply made use of whatever horizon feature was available at each site.

Rather we should perhaps be asking, what compulsion drove the Neolithic people to build these outdoor stone alignments all over Britain and beyond. Initially there must have been a practical imperative to understand the seasons, but later this lapsed into religious ritual.

Some commentators on Callanish, going back to John Toland in the eighteenth century, have thought that the 'temple of the spheres' in the land of the Hyperboreans beyond the Celts, as described by Hecataeus (quoted by Diodorus Siculus) is more likely to have been Callanish than Stonehenge; it was more accessible by sea and would better comply with the statement of Hecataeus that at this temple the moon came very close to the earth. [17] This could describe the coincidence that when at its most southerly extreme the moon just skirts the horizon at this latitude; however, against this it must be said that the same seasonal lunar indicators would be needed at every stone circle, regardless of latitude. **

If one may digress at this point to consider *Stonehenge*, as being illustrative of the function of other circles, then we have another aligned 'temple', dating from the same era; like Callanish it also passed through later stages of renewal. If we look beyond the giant stones that dominate the site then we also have the ring of 56 chalk-filled holes, known as Aubrey holes after their seventeenth-century discoverer. These are thought to date from the first phase of the monument around 3000 BC and may once have held wooden posts, or perhaps the bluestones before the monument was reorganised. Around the main sarsen ring are the Y and Z holes. However, these have been dated to the later phase of the monument when the giant sarsen stones were erected.

Since there are 29 of the Z-holes and 30 Y-holes these have long been assumed to represent the days of lunar months. Therefore, it is reasonable to suggest that the 56 Aubrey holes also served a practical calendrical purpose for the original builders.

Theories that Stonehenge was an observatory to predict eclipses were proposed by Gerald Hawkins in 1963. [18] This was followed by the more general theories of Alexander Thom of solar and lunar alignments at many other stone circles. 19] Following Hawkins and Thom, in 1977 the renowned cosmologist Sir Fred Hoyle took up the subject of the Aubrey holes. His scheme built upon Hawkins's theory that Stonehenge, at least its earliest phase, was as an elaborate observatory to predict eclipses. However, he would dismiss any connection between the megalith builders and the later Druids. [20] His introductory words on page one are important to note for the historiography of this subject:

> *The Druids had nothing to do with the construction of Stonehenge, which was completed a thousand years before the Celtic peoples invaded the British isles.*

Alas, again, this kind of statement is a delusion of modern scholarship: the assumption that ancient wisdom is only as old as its earliest mention in a classical source. It is rather like saying that the medieval cathedrals could have had nothing to do with Jesus because they were built more than a thousand years later. Of course, ancient knowledge and religion could have survived to form part of druid teaching. In saying this, Hoyle, who was performing a cross-disciplinary study outside his expertise, was merely citing the accepted textbook wisdom of the day. This preconception persisted well into the twenty-first century until DNA science showed that the so-called Celtic invasion of the Iron Age never happened. Once this preconception is removed then we may readily accept the statements by contemporary historians that Druidism originated in Britain. [21] We may also see that Anglesey was the 'Jerusalem' of their cult, which might explain why the Romans went to such lengths to eliminate it as a centre of resistance. [22] Druid astronomy and wisdom was ancient; Celts in Gaul were converted to it, rather than the other way about.

Hoyle would build upon the 18.6-year period of the lunar standstill and conclude that the 56 Aubrey holes were a device for predicting the eclipse cycle, based on three such cycles or 55.8 years. Because of the prejudice that there was no link with the Druids, he did not consider either Saturn or the thirty-year druid cycle. The same may be said of the other modern investigators who were similarly constrained to consider the megalith builders as stone-age 'pre-Celts'.

In fact, as I showed in Under Ancient Skies in 2005 and in two later articles the Druids maintained a highly accurate lunisolar calendar based on an 11-year cycle. The number 56 provides the link between Saturn and the Moon. [23] There is an equivalence between the Moon and the synodic period of Saturn (the period between each opposition) that would be noticed by any society that sought to schedule its motion against an accurate lunar calendar: [24] [25]

717 lunar months	= 717 x 29.530598	= 21173.43days	= 57.97 solar yrs
56 synodic periods	= 56 x 378.09292	= 21173.2 days	(approx. 58 years)

The discrepancy is only about five hours and ancient people may well have considered the correspondence to be exact. It would seem much more likely that this equivalence between Saturn and the Moon was the significance of the 56 Aubrey holes rather than for predicting eclipses. There is only one chance in fifty-six that the choice of this number was a random coincidence.

A similar solar correspondence occurs after 59 years:

59 solar years	= 59 x 365.2422	= 21549.29 days
57 synodic periods	= 57 x 378.09292	= 21551.29 days

Therefore, after 59 years the configurations of Saturn in the sky are repeated exactly two days later in the solar year. Either or both correspondences could then be used to check the accuracy of a lunisolar calendar and allow corrections to be made after 60 years, analogous to the Gregorian century rule.

We should also note the astronomy of the 30-year cycle and Saturn.

29 synodic periods	= 29 x 378.09292	= 10964.694 days	= 30.02 solar yrs.

The discrepancy is only about a week or one quarter-moon; and 30 plus 29 also gives the 59-year checkpoint. Too many coincidences here.

Therefore, we may see that the rings of 29 and 30 postholes at Stonehenge need not represent the months at all, but rather they may be related to Saturn rituals. The occultations of Saturn by the Moon may also have been significant astrological events for divination and ceremony. Once we remove the artificial constraint that druid science was 'Celtic' and accept that their astronomy was older, then it becomes apparent what they were doing. They meshed their lunisolar calendar with Saturn in the same way that the Mayans and the Babylonians meshed theirs with cycles of Venus; and they used it to validate the day count and maintain its accuracy.

Plutarch's essays supply the missing link; they show the relationship between the thirty-year druid cycles, the ancient cult of Cronus, and his visible star: the planet Saturn.

There are no references in classical sources to suggest that the Britons took any interest in eclipses, whereas we do find clear references to Cronus and the thirty-year druid cycle. The complex eclipse theories proposed by the modern specialists, to explain the function of the stone circles, have been another diversion that has led us in the wrong direction.

Neither is Plutarch the only classical author to offer parallels between Greek and 'Celtic' mythology. Also neglected have been the various fragments of lost knowledge that would equate Celtic gods and myths with those of the Mediterranean. In Caesar's commentaries, probably summarising Poseidonius and earlier historians, we are told that the doctrine of the Druids was imported into Gaul from Britain where it was found already existing. The Celts of Gaul, he says, recognised all the same gods as the Romans, but curiously he fails to mention Cronus! It may be that the cult of Cronus/Saturn was best remembered only in Britain and the North. [26] The 'stranger' told Sulla that one should especially honour the moon (the goddess Cora) demonstrating once again the importance of the Saturn-Moon relationship.

Hecataeus and Herodotus, writing hundreds of years earlier, said that the northern Hyperboreans had maintained a friendship with Athenian and Delian Greeks since the most ancient times, exchanging both gifts and visitors with each other. [27] Raffael Joorde has recently suggested that the 'travel guide' by Hecataeus of Abdera drew on the lost book 'On the Ocean' by Pytheas. [28] ***

Also significant must be the conviction of Plutarch that some Greeks had migrated to the west of Scotland in the era of Heracles. Perhaps DNA science can one-day offer some insight on this. In the Irish Book of Invasions (*Lebor Gabála Érenn*) we are told of successive waves of invaders from 'Greece' via Spain: Nemedians, Firbolgs and Danaans. After the Firbolgs were defeated by the Danaans some of these earlier 'Greeks' were driven from Ireland to take refuge in the Scottish islands, among a shadowy indigenous people called Fomorians. Does this not echo the same story that Plutarch gives us? And where should Heracles fit into all this?

So far as we know, there is no archaeological evidence of Neolithic occupation on Iceland or the Faeroes. The lost cave and oracle of Cronus remains for archaeologists one day to find!

Conclusions

The coincidence that Saturn made one of its 30-year returns to the constellation Taurus, around the same date that the explorer Demetrius was in Britain confers an authenticity on the story of the stranger's voyage as also contemporary with Agricola. There would be only one chance in thirty that this was coincidence. The 'stranger' therefore most likely made his pilgrimage to Ogygia and to the oracle of Cronus thirty years earlier in AD 57, returning in AD 87. This would have given ample time for his subsequent visit to Carthage to be recorded and conveyed to Plutarch during his later life, but probably after he had already been influenced by Demetrius.

Plutarch's use of the name *Ogygia*, rather than *Thule,* for the distant island tells us that his inspiration has come via a Greek source, probably Demetrius, rather than from older sources such as Pytheas and those geographers who cited his book. Plutarch, or his source has therefore equated the two locations and preferred the Greek name.

The Ogygia of Plutarch and the Thule of Strabo and other geographers are the same place – *Iceland*. Whether this was the same place as Homer's Ogygia is a complication we need not pursue here.

The voyage to Thule/Ogygia most likely began from various points on the British mainland and called at the inner and Outer Hebrides, where the pilgrims assembled their fleet of rowing boats before embarking on the long journey to Thule. The convoy most likely set out from the east coast of Lewis as may be inferred from Pliny. Therefore, Plutarch's description of the journey may be an amalgam of two similar-sounding voyages; firstly, a regular religious pilgrimage via the Hebrides to Ogygia, combined with a recollection of less frequent expeditions to Greenland or America beyond. These Atlantic crossings may have been as distant in time to Plutarch as the Vinland sagas are to us.

Such knowledge as we can assemble from the various sources would suggest that the religion of Cronus was truly ancient and must go back at least to the building of Callanish, Stonehenge and the other stone circles. The ancient calendar as preserved among the Druids was concerned not only with the short-term lunisolar cycle, but also with long-term observation of Saturn – the star of Cronus – and its geocentric orbit. The coincidence of the 56 correspondence between Saturn and the Moon is too precise to be dismissed as coincidence. *Astronomy doesn't lie!* These longer cycles would give an opportunity for the calendar to be adjusted, equivalent to the century rule of the Gregorian calendar. To accomplish this, they would almost certainly have needed an era and a system of calendar dates like those we find in the Mayan calendar. Unfortunately, this ancient knowledge is lost because the British Druids refused to commit their secrets to writing.

The antiquity of the religion of Cronus and thereby of the calendrical astronomy is given by the age of the aligned monuments – Callanish, Stenness, Stonehenge, Newgrange and others dating from the late fourth millennium and early third millennium BC; and also, by Plato's *Timaeus*, which *if taken at its word*, describes an account preserved in Egypt of similar ancient voyages into the Atlantic. The temple of Neit dates from as early as the First Dynasty of Egypt (c.3100 BC). Therefore, we may posit that the myths surrounding Heracles, Cronus and the other Titans take us back to even earlier times: to the earlier Neolithic and Mesolithic of the North.

As to when the regular 30-year voyages finally ceased, this depends upon how long you believe the ancient religion and the culture that supported it could have endured in the Hebridean Isles of Scotland. It may have persisted until the Romans under Constantine raided and subdued the northwest tribes sometime around 313 AD. [29] In their enfeebled state the tribes were then absorbed among the Picts from the North and the Scots from Ireland and their ancient ways were forgotten. Certainly, after Saint Columba and others introduced Celtic Christianity to the Western Isles then the old religion would have been suppressed. We may wonder if some vestigial memory of the Atlantic voyages were recorded by later Christian monks; and whether the ancient knowledge encouraged Viking expeditions to Iceland and Vinland beyond.

* **Note 1:** *A further possibility here is volcanic ash accumulating on the sea from one the many Icelandic volcanoes after an unusually strong eruption; an event that could perhaps be dated by specialists.*

** **Note 2:** *On a related subject, it will be instructive to read a recent paper by Rick Doble for an example of how preconceptions about the capabilities of Greek astronomers held-back an understanding of the Antikythera mechanism by at least 50 years.*

https://www.academia.edu/28931421/How_Preconceptions_Interfered_With_Discovery_Understanding_the_First_Computer_the_Antikythera_Mechanism_of_Ancient_Greece?email_work_card=title

*** **Note 3:** *The thorough analysis by Raffael Joorde of the surviving fragments of Hecataeus of Abdera concludes that the Hyperboreans on an island beyond the Celts were a description of the inhabitants of southern Britain; and that their culture survived in a recognisable form, distinct from the continental Celts, up to his own era: c.300 BC.* https://independent.academia.edu/RaffaelJoorde

https://www.academia.edu/27786980/Hecataeus_of_Abdera_and_his_work_On_the_Hyperboreans_about_300_BC_The_fragments_with_a_historical_commentary_2016_?email_work_card=view-paper

Relevant Hyperlinks

https://penelope.uchicago.edu/Thayer/E/Roman/Texts/Plutarch/Moralia/De_defectu_oraculorum*.html

https://penelope.uchicago.edu/Thayer/E/Roman/Texts/Plutarch/Moralia/The_Face_in_the_Moon*/D.html
https://oxfordre.com/classics/view/10.1093/acrefore/9780199381135.001.0001/acrefore-9780199381135-e-2105
https://www.greekmythology.com/Titans/Cronus/cronus.html
https://www.perseus.tufts.edu/hopper/text?doc=Perseus%3Atext%3A1999.01.0136%3Abook%3D7%3Acard%3D240
http://edithorial.blogspot.com/2014/04/from-tarsus-to-wales-earliest-greek-in.html
https://romaninscriptionsofbritain.org/inscriptions/662
https://romaninscriptionsofbritain.org/inscriptions/663
https://www.worldhistory.org/article/1078/on-the-ocean-the-famous-voyage-of-pytheas/?visitCount=2&lastVisitDate=2021-4-3&pageViewCount=3
https://astronomynow.com/2016/08/19/britains-pre-stonehenge-megaliths-were-aligned-by-astronomers/
https://www.sciencedirect.com/science/article/abs/pii/S2352409X16301808?via%3Dihub
https://mythology.net/greek/mortals/hyperborea/
https://www.academia.edu/27786980/Hecataeus_of_Abdera_and_his_work_On_the_Hyperboreans_about_300_BC_The_fragments_with_a_historical_commentary_2016_
https://f7e94415-3a55-48d9-ba14-ed235f05a65f.filesusr.com/ugd/e5604c_203d00faad9d40beac90ad2144700a8b.pdf
https://historicengland.org.uk/images-books/photos/item/P50825
https://www.third-millennium.co.uk/under-ancient-skies
https://www.abc.net.au/science/articles/2014/02/19/3947224.htm

References

1. Plutarch, Obsolescence of Oracles, 419, 18
2. Plutarch, The Face on the Moon, 941-942
3. Plutarch, Obsolescence of Oracles, 410,1-2
4. See the Loeb translation by Harold Cherniss and William Helmbold, page 11 commentary on the narrative at para 931,19.
5. Plutarch, The Face on the Moon, 941,26
6. Ibid
7. ibid, 942, B
8. Diodorus Siculus, V, 66, 5
9. Agricola, 24
10. Pliny, Natural History, XVI,250
11. Pliny, Natural History, IV, xvi, 102-104
12. Pliny, Natural History, II, lxxv, 187
13. Strabo, Geography, I, 4, 3
14. Plato, Timaeus, 25

15. Somerville, B. (1912) Astronomical Indications in the Megalithic Monument at Callanish, *J. Brit. Astron. Assoc.* Nov 1912, pp 83-96
16. Gail Higginbottom, Roger Clay, (2016) Origins of Standing Stone Astronomy in Britain: New quantitative techniques for the study of archaeoastronomy, *Journal of Archaeological Science: Reports*, Volume 9, 2016, Pages 249-258, ISSN 2352-409X
17. Hecataeus of Abdera, as quoted in: Diodorus Siculus, Book II. 47, 1-7
18. Hawkins, Gerald. F. (1966) *Stonehenge Decoded*, Souvenir Press, London
19. Thom, A. (1967) *Megalithic Sites in Britain*, Oxford University Press, Oxford
20. Hoyle, F (1977) *On Stonehenge*, Heineman Educational, London
21. Caesar, The Gallic War, VI, 13
22. Tacitus, Agricola, 18
23. Dunbavin, P (2005) *Under Ancient Skies*, Third Millennium Publishing, Nottingham, ISBN:0-9525092-2-5
24. Dunbavin, P (2018) On the Coligny Calendar and the Neolithic Calendar in Plato's Critias, in *Chronology & Catastrophism Review*, 2018:2 pp 50-53
25. Dunbavin, P (2020) The Neolithic Calendar, in *Prehistory Papers*, pp 13-22, Third Millennium Publishing, Beverley, ISBN: 978-0-9525029-4-4 (a previously unpublished 2006 paper)
26. Caesar, The Gallic War, VI, 13
27. Hecataeus cited in Diodorus Siculus. II. 47, 1-7
28. Joorde, Raffael; Dortmund; Hecataeus of Abdera and his work 'On the Hyperboreans' (about 300 BC): The fragments with a historical commentary
29. Eusebius, The Life of Constantine, IV, c, 50

7

British DNA: History and Legends of Origin Compared

Summary: *In December 2021, a DNA study of British population origins entitled "Large-scale migration into Britain during the Middle to Late Bronze Age" was published in the journal Nature.* [1] *This would attempt to fill the gaps left by earlier genetic studies, which could not resolve ancient DNA origins within the well-mixed modern population of central and southern England. The new study focused rather on older DNA from archaeological sites. The earlier studies also lacked the resolution to distinguish between Iron Age immigration and later Anglo-Saxon arrivals from the same regions. This article considers how the findings from this and other recent genetic studies may be reconciled with the traditions of origin and such contemporary historical sources of ethnography as are available. These may come via Greek and Roman authors, Welsh and Irish oral history, or the corpus of older ethnography that has grown-up prior to the new science of DNA. The picture that is now emerging from the genes is surprisingly congruent with the oldest historical sources.*

From turn of the millennium, genetic studies of ancestry begun to intrude into the comfortable picture of British prehistory as it has been built-up over the years by the archaeologists and linguists. [2] This had itself been forcibly revised in the second half of the twentieth century by the advent of radiocarbon and again by tree-ring calibration methods; however the older terminology and classifications for periods of prehistory, with some shuffling of dates continued in parlance. There was a presumption that ethnic origin could be related to the changes of artefacts, pottery and tomb styles, etc., as identified by archaeology, and that changes of culture implied population movements and migrations. The spread of languages then accompanied these assumed migrations of people. The attempts to date such cultures by cross-dating of pottery styles back to the chronology of Egypt, led to more general theories of 'diffusion' from the 1930s onwards, such that all cultural advance from Stone Age through Bronze Age to Iron Age came to be thought-of as emanating from Egypt and the near east; the use of bronze therefore must also have been brought west by continental invaders: the so-called 'beaker people'. The dawn of the British Iron Age was ascribed to a later invasion by continental Celts who brought their language with them and replaced the 'pre-Celts'. Although the revolution in archaeological dating modified these broad assumptions, it failed to fully penetrate studies of ethnography and linguistics. The new science of genetics finally threw this older picture up in the air and demanded a reassessment of prehistory.

To summarise: in 2015 a report on British DNA ancestry had revealed the regional ancestry within Britain and Northern Ireland [3] This was followed by further surveys and regional DNA maps, culminating in the comprehensive studies of modern regional DNA for Britain and Ireland (2016-19). [4] These studies had indicated that the indigenous *Western Hunter Gatherers* declined or were almost completely replaced by new people, the *Early European Farmers* originating from Anatolia perhaps as early as 4000 BC. The conclusion of the geneticists is that the hunter-gatherers therefore contribute negligibly to the make-up of the later population. From the DNA of *Cheddar Man* (c.7150 BC) we have a view of these earliest inhabitants after the ice age as dark skinned with blue eyes, although his closest surviving descendant – a teacher from Somerset – did not possess those attributes. However, some geneticists would argue that it is still not possible to identify physical traits: eyes, hair, skin-colour, etc from the genes. (*MailOnline 2 March 2018*).

From around 2450 BC (or perhaps earlier) the DNA now reveals another population transformation; the earlier Neolithic farmers were almost completely replaced by people of '*Steppe ancestry*' who would go on to comprise 90% of the later population.[5] The geneticists associate this with the arrival in western Europe of the Bell Beaker Culture as recognised by archaeologists, expanding from the east after 3000 BC; and by linguists as speakers of the various Indo-European languages. Within this overview it was possible to identify many regional DNA differences in Britain, which loosely correspond to the pre-Roman tribal boundaries. However, within the well-mixed modern population of central and southeast England the earlier genetic studies could not distinguish finer variations nor any major immigrations after about 1300 BC – the late Bronze Age and early Iron Age. [6]

The long-accepted view of British prehistory from archaeology and linguistics, before the revelations of the genes, had placed the first appearance of farming in Britain and Ireland from around 4000 BC. The arrival of people who planted wheat and barley is contemporary with the building of the earliest dolmens, long barrows and field walls. A decline in agriculture and regrowth of woodland is noted by some archaeologists in the years before 3000 BC, followed by a gradual recovery. [7] Along with this recovery came a change in monument styles from the long barrows to round barrows, astronomically-aligned passage graves and stone circles. For archaeologists, pottery will always figure prominently and the finds of the bell beaker pottery, replacing earlier forms, is evident from around 2500-2200 BC – a seemingly gradual transition from Neolithic to the Bronze Age. However the change of monuments clearly precedes other cultural changes associated with the beakers. The transition to the use of iron tools and weapons, the 'Iron Age', is now placed around 800 BC. This is the era when we first find hill-forts throughout Britain, perhaps an indicator that in earlier times such fortifications were not needed. In older literature the Iron Age was associated with an assumed *invasion* of continental 'Celts' who brought with them their languages, ancestral to modern Welsh and Gaelic, replacing the 'pre-Celts'. This terminology remains in use by linguists although the idea of a Celtic 'race' has become moribund. It may be noted that the dates suggested for the DNA, archaeological and linguistic shifts do not conveniently coincide.

The 2021 report in Nature by Patterson and a team of geneticists makes heavy reading for the non-specialist, being replete with the jargon and the abbreviations used by geneticists, which of course it must in order to satisfy peer review. Gone are the familiar classifications of racial groups, such as Celts, Indo-Europeans and 'Aryans' that we have to recognize when comparing modern with older studies; to be replaced by new terms and abbreviations such as WHG for 'western hunter gathers', etc. (*see note below*). One has now also to cope with genetic terms such as 'alleles' (alternative forms of a gene at the same site on a chromosome) and 'haplotypes' (a group of alleles inherited from a parent) as well as 'mitochondrial DNA' (inherited only from the mother within the mitochondria of a cell). With archaeological findings we may at least visit an ancient site or view an artefact in a museum; with linguistics we may trace a source text; a physicist can repeat the maths. However, with genetics, we have to accept the conclusions of the teams of specialists and their referees. Future investigators are invited to "*develop theories integrating the genetic findings within archaeological frameworks*". It would seem that only archaeology matters and little or no value is to be placed upon the precious historical sources and the legends that have been preserved by the very people whose DNA they are investigating. The historian will always advise you to stay close to the oldest available sources.

An example of the difficulties that the blizzard of new terminology brings for non-specialists may be seen in the report on the BBC News website, which summarised the main conclusions, boldly stating: "*Scientists have uncovered evidence for a large-scale, prehistoric migration into Britain that may be linked to the spread of Celtic languages*". However, to quote from the report itself the conclusions are rather more guarded:

> *Population movements are often a significant driver of cultural change, including in the languages people speak. While periods of intense migration such as the one we infer here do not always result in language shifts...*

And later:

> *Our failure to find evidence of large-scale migration into Britain from continental Europe in the IA* [Iron Age] *suggests that, if Celtic language spread was driven by large-scale movement of people, it is unlikely to have occurred at this time.*

It would seem that one may take to such scientific studies those preconceptions with which you arrive; and go away with whatever you expect to find. The centuries of indoctrination about an Iron Age invasion of 'Celts' that we have so long been taught is difficult to rebut; its control is both overt and subliminal in every textbook that we read about British prehistory, whether it be archaeology, ethnography, linguistics or culture. The new DNA study would instead place the likely era of mass migration *earlier*, during the mid to late Bronze Age;

a period when we know of other population movements and dislocations within the historically better-documented Mediterranean cultures.

A special note in the 2021 report is meticulous to distinguish the meaning of the term 'migration', as employed by archaeologists, from its usage in genetics. The former would like to infer, from a change of artefacts, a rapid 'invasion' by a foreign culture bringing the objects along with new people; whereas the geneticist would prefer to see migration as "gene flow": the longer-term infiltration of genes into a population via generations of inter-marriage and individual or family relocations originating from the same source. Here I shall refer to the former as 'invasion' and the latter rather as 'immigration'. It is also best not to become entrapped by the long-standing archaeologists' classifications such as: Mesolithic, Neolithic, Bronze Age, Iron Age, as if bronze-users could never make stone tools or that Neolithic farmers could not go hunting in the forests. If a Mesolithic tribesman plants a garden then does he become a farmer? It is both absurd and uninteresting to talk about 'beaker people' or the distribution, for example, of Tievebulliagh axes as if artefact styles must have ethnographic significance. Such labels should be applied loosely lest they constrain our understanding of a complex past.

Climate and Sea Levels

Another view of the recent past is available from specialist studies of climate and sea-level variations over this same period. These should not be divorced from the proposed migrations of farmers that occurred while these environmental changes were ongoing. The current consensus view of when Britain physically separated from Europe, following the rise of sea level at the end of the Ice Age, is that the North Sea flooded, around 6500 BC. The separation of Britain from Ireland is usually considered an earlier event; however Mesolithic hunter gatherers, such as *Cheddar Man*, had been in the islands long before the final separation. The climate was at its warmest and most equable during the Atlantic pollen zone between c.5500-3000 BC. When the first farmers arrived, Britain was still heavily forested.

A sharp change from this climate regime to stronger seasonal rhythms then set in between about 3000 BC and 500 BC – the Neolithic and Bronze Age. The Atlantic-Sub-Boreal transition (loosely 3000 BC) corresponds quite well to the era when archaeologists detect a population decline and a hiatus in agriculture; [8] and *a few hundred years later* (c.2450 BC) the DNA evidence now suggests an almost complete replacement of the first farmers of Britain by the immigrants from the east. [9] All of the migrations and evolution of the population suggested by the DNA evidence were taking place during the period for which we have dynasties of kings and historical events from Egypt and the near-east, telling us of famines, wars and migrations. For Britain we have no such datable history before the arrival of the Romans, but they must have experienced the same climate influences as we find in the Mediterranean history. We see the well-attested famines during the First Intermediate Period of Egypt. We find mid Bronze Age displacements within the Mediterranean associated with the so-called Sea Peoples, perhaps triggered by famines in more than one region; and the eighteen-year famine described by Herodotus. [*Herodotus, I, 93-96*] However, the *causes* of these climate shifts is not the primary focus here, other than as the background within which the population changes were ongoing. It will not be possible to fully understand the trigger for the migrations until the various specialist views of the past can be reconciled.

Julius Caesar and the Roman Sources

Here however, I shall focus upon another parallel view of British prehistory that can be extracted from the traditions, legends and historical references. A sound place to begin would be to consult the best and oldest classical historical sources; but by common consent even the best is not as good as we might wish! As a subset we have: *Caesar, Tacitus, Strabo, Polybius, Diodorus Siculus, Ptolemy, Dio Cassius, Plutarch, Pliny, Bede and Nennius*. All of these authors offer us peeks into the people of pre-Roman Britain that fail us when we try to drill deeper into precise geography and dates. The tribal divisions that we find in Ptolemy's geography reflect the situation just prior to the Roman conquest of the first century AD rather than in earlier centuries – much can change in a millennium. We find also, more vague references to islands in the Atlantic within earlier Greek sources, where some interpretation is required. No extant classical author leaves us a history of pre-Roman Britain; rather we have to rely upon mere fragments of *Poseidonius* and *Pytheas* as cited by the later historians.

The sources cited by Caesar in his commentaries on the Gallic war are uncertain, although authorities believe that much of his background ethnography came from the lost histories of Poseidonius. We find overlap with the references by Strabo and Diodorus Siculus, but these too may have drawn on the same earlier writers. It can be difficult when considering Caesar's propaganda, to distinguish his first-hand observations and education, from those he has taken from the historians. He tells us about 'recent' Belgic immigrants who farmed around Kent and the southern coasts but offers no clarity as to how long they had been there.

The tribes further inland, he says, were different; he remarks on the social organisation of tribes "*in the interior*", who claimed "*on the strength of their own oral tradition*" to be aboriginal to the island. These same tribes shared wives (if this be the correct term to use) with fathers and brothers within extended families. [*Gallic Wars V.14*] Frustratingly, we cannot distinguish which tribes he is actually describing or how far north they were, but references by other Roman authors may help us to narrow this down.

Dio Cassius and Herodian

In the later Roman wars against the tribes in the north, before they were called Picts, the emperor Septimus Severus came to Britain and his campaign of AD 208-212 is described by Dio Cassius and Herodian. We are given a description of the social organisation of the *Caledonians* and *Maeatae* that is more informative than from the earlier writers. Dio tells us that they did not farm the land, but lived on their flocks, wild birds and fruit, but, for some reason, they declined to eat the fish. Both Dio and Herodian tell us that they lived naked and unshod, despite the cold, to exhibit their tattoos. Most importantly he says that they "*possess their women in common and in common rear all their offspring*". [*Roman History, LXXXVII, 12*] This may give us another version of the social organisation vaguely mentioned by Caesar.

Most revealing of all is a quote from a Caledonian woman, said to have been made to the Empress Julia Augusta: "*we fulfil the demands of nature in a much better way than do you Roman women, for we consort openly with the best men, whereas you let yourselves be debauched in secret by the vilest*". [*Roman History, LXXXVII, 16*] This little snippet is so valuable. It sweeps aside the male-centric viewpoint of 'wife-sharing' that we find in the other reports, revealing the women as empowered and equal. The absence of marriage customs explains why we find matrilinear royal inheritance among the later Picts, where succession went to a brother or to sister's son, in the female line (the father's royal heritage being unreliable). There were no patriarchal 'families' as we might understand them and children were brought up within a communal nursery. We may perchance that, as with modern 'liberated' women, they tended to have fewer children.

We also see this free social organisation in the writings of Solinus (around AD 250) who is describing the tribes of the west coast and islands. [*Polyhistor 22. 9-12*] Although the geography is confused, he describes the king of the Hebrides who has access to many women but may have no wife of his own. He echoes other writers, that no man has a wife and "use their women in common". [10] Of the mainland, he tells us that most of the barbarians tattooed their bodies with animal designs but it is unclear whether the islanders also did this. It would seem that any tribe that tattooed their skin might be considered Picts, but it is simplistic to assume that all Irish and British tribes who tattooed themselves were ethnically the same people.

We have another glimpse of these tribes during of the later campaign of Theodosius (AD 368-9) when Picts and Scots allied with *Attacotti* (or *Atecotti* in another source) were raiding the Roman province. We may see that these were neither Picts nor Scots from Ireland; the term is being used derogatively in the sense of: natives, savages, 'Indians'! The historian John Morris, a specialist in the post Roman Dark Ages, accepted the meaning of this name from the Celtic linguists to mean: 'very-old-ones', or aborigines. To cite the view of Morris, the Atecotti were aboriginal inhabitants who survived alongside the Picts and who wrote the enigmatic ogham inscriptions; in his view these were: "*the language of the aboriginal people who dwelt in Britain before the coming of the British and before the builders of Brochs and duns...who inscribed a little of their language centuries later, when they were familiar with Pictish memorials and the Irish alphabet.*". [11] Note that Morris, writing in the 1970s, was still in the pre-radiocarbon mould of an Iron Age invasion by continental Celts.

Some of the southern tribes may have followed their own variant of this communal social organisation. Unfortunately, there is no way to know how far south the customs extended and where the cultural and linguistic boundary should be drawn back into the Iron Age and earlier times. Perhaps one day the geneticists will find a way to determine this transition more precisely. We have a clue from later Scottish history as to how such a change of language and culture might come about. In 565 AD Kenneth Mac Alpin, king of the Scots of Dalriada, inherited the Pictish throne by rightful matrilinear succession from his Pictish mother, thus uniting the two kingdoms. Language change and suppression of the Pictish culture within Medieval Scotland then duly followed. We may envisage that in earlier millennia other invasive southern kings could have gained control of northern tribes in a similar manner via matrilinear succession, resulting in change to patrilinear succession and the retreat of the aboriginal language and culture ever-further northwards. However, pockets of the older culture could have persisted in isolated regions. [12]

The unique British social customs should be of importance for genetic studies but do not seem to have been considered. Scientists in general are unlikely to cite non-scientific historical sources, or to ascribe value to them. The ancestry within communal societies where women could choose their own partners, without the constraints of monogamous 'marriage', should show its effect in the genes over the generations. It selects different characteristics for survival and should reveal itself mainly in personality and behaviour. If a foreign conquering overlord and a small band of elite followers begat numerous offspring in preference to the local males, then it becomes another way that immigrant-genes could spread within a population without mass immigration. We should also consider who is doing the choosing? Is it the men or the women? Where women have choice it is likely that they would all prefer the same few alpha-males, leading to a concentration of those genes going forward. By contrast patrilinear marriage leads to larger families and population growth; it allows a wider selection of male genes to pass to the next generation.

Foreign ruling-elites may also impose their own language and customs with little effect on the genes; the Normans brought language change to southern Britain but the Romans did not! Slavery and vassalage was commonplace in the ancient world. The integration of slaves, perhaps through the female line *over many generations*, is another way that foreign genes could enter a population without political change (see 'Orkney' here below). We may also assume that both genocide and pandemic were common in the ancient world and could account for the complete replacement of a regional population. Again, this cannot be inferred solely from the chance preservation of DNA in a few archaeological finds.

Lactose Tolerance in the Iron Age

A curiosity arising from the new DNA evidence comes in the findings about the precocious evolution of lactose tolerance within the (southern) British population. The condition is more uncomfortable than fatal. It seems that the gene for assimilating cow's milk evolved a millennium earlier in Britain than in adjacent Europe from which they are considered to have migrated.

In Caesar's commentaries we are told that Britain was densely populated and that most tribes *in the interior* lived on milk and meat; cattle being very numerous. [*Gallic Wars 5, 12-14*] Compare this with his ethnographic comments about the continental Germans of the same era. He describes the tribes of the Hercynian Forest as shunning agriculture in preference for milk, cheese and meat, and supplementing their diet with hunting forays, where they would capture wild elk and auroch in pits. [*Gallic Wars, VI, 26-27*] A century later, Tacitus would still describe the Germans as indolent farmers, preferring to plant a field for corn one year, then clear a new plot the next, due to the abundance of spare land. [*Germania, 45*]

The explanation for the lactose mutation in Britain becomes apparent. Caesar is describing the tribes in the 'interior' of Britain, not those Gauls who had arrived recently from the continent. The transition from hunter-gatherers to farming is usually considered as progress to a higher culture: 'civilisation'; whereas it may better be seen as a *necessity* being the mother of invention. Hunting for meat and gathering fruits requires less labour than planting fields and tending flocks; it can be performed by tribes in balance with nature, whereas farming requires forest clearance, field walls and irrigation, which then need to be defended by kings and armies. Iron Age European tribes still had the option to venture into the virgin forests to take wild animals, whereas in offshore Britain, these natural resources had long been depleted; therefore animals had to be farmed for meat much earlier than on the continent. One cannot drink the milk of wild beasts, but for pastoral farmers it is an incidental source of sustenance. People who did not farm might starve; farmers who did not drink milk might starve, but those who drank it could be lactose intolerant; hence those who possessed the gene for tolerance were preferentially selected. No immigration or culture change needed, if anything it signifies a long period of stability.

Tacitus

A summary of early British ethnography is supplied by Tacitus. [*Agricola, 11*] Although he is primarily concerned with the Flavian conquest of the North, he comments on physical characteristics, noting that the red hair and broad limbs of the Caledonians were similar to the Germans, though he is vague as to which part of the continent he compares. He likens the tanned complexion and curly hair of the recently conquered *Silures* (South Wales) to some Iberians; and says that the inhabitants of the south coast most closely resembled the Gauls opposite. He finds little difference of language between Britons and Gauls – yet how far inland is he considering? In the *Germania* he states that the language of the Baltic *Aestii* (a tribe in Germanic Suebia who did not speak German) was more like that of the Britons – but again fails to be precise. [*Germania, 45*] He mentions the *Brigantes* (Yorkshire-Lancashire) and describes the most northerly inhabitants collectively as "Caledonian Britons"; so we cannot work out how far north this cultural divide was situated prior to Roman interference.

The brief overview left by Tacitus is of immense value as it preserves a snapshot of the population at a period when tribal divisions still constrained movement and inter-marriage. We may still observe these regional differences of physical attributes in the modern British population, if we take care to notice, despite two thousand years of further integration. These variations should be of interest to historical geneticists and cannot be gained solely from archaeology. It is regrettable that DNA analysis cannot yet conclusively identify the physical characteristics of these ancient nations.

Strabo and Diodorus Siculus

An important link between Britain and the near-continent was the ancient religion of the Druids. Caesar alone informs us that the order originated in Britain but from Diodorus Siculus we gain more detail about the Druids' activities in Gaul; they retained their influence there even a century later – until their shrines on Anglesey were burned by Agricola. We may therefore assume that there was a religious pilgrimage route in both directions: with Gaulish students visiting Britain and the Britons attending the annual assembly in the centre of Gaul. Just as Latin would later become the medium for Christian unity, there may have been a need for a common Celtic language through which the Druids could spread their oral wisdom and teachings; and this could explain the continuity of Celtic languages from Gaul to Anglesey and perhaps to Ireland also. The former assumption that Druidism was introduced to Britain (and to Ireland) along with an invasion of Iron Age Celts is no longer tenable; their religious culture was ancient and the newcomers from the east (whether invaders or migrants) became converts. Of particular interest is the Druids' calendar which there is every reason to believe was very ancient, dating back to the astronomically aligned monuments of the Neolithic.[13]

Diodorus Siculus repeats the claim of some British tribes to be aboriginal and says that they still used war chariots in the manner of the Greeks prior to the Trojan War. Strabo gives us fragments of the voyage of Pytheas (c.330 BC) derided by him and his contemporaries, but with geography that we may now endorse. Since his voyage was a circumnavigation of the island, it gives us a glimpse of the coasts but adds no extra detail about the people of the interior. Of Ireland he mentions some cannibal practices and comments on their marriage customs. Overall, other than on the ways of the Druids, these two authors add little to the available ethnic information about the common people or their rulers.

Nennius and Geoffrey of Monmouth

Following the Roman departure from Britain the written sources of pre-Roman history fail completely and our knowledge of post-Roman Britain is little better. Nennius (820 AD) apologetically tells us that he "made a heap" of such history as he could find. In the *Historia Brittonum* attributed to Nennius he tells us that the Britons had set down no written record and indeed we know from the Roman writers that druids and bards were forbidden to write down their knowledge. Such history as had been preserved orally was lost when the Druids were slaughtered and their teachings suppressed. From the Roman author *Pomponius Mela* we hear that the old religion was preserved via illicit meetings in secret forest glades. [*De Chorographia, III, 2, 18-19*] Among these teachings, perhaps a little of the pre-Roman history was orally preserved by the bards, to be written down for the first time in medieval Wales. We may assume that other Dark Age chroniclers made similar 'heaps' of history, all now lost, which were consulted by medieval historians; or that many lost traditions were only ever transmitted orally.

Nennius derived the Britons from the Roman 'Brutus' and the eponymous 'Britto', one of the Trojans who supposedly founded Rome after the Trojan War. Being driven out, he and his people migrated via Tours in Gaul, to a seemingly uninhabited Britain! We may discount this as Roman-era propaganda to offer Britons the same ancestry as their masters, but it would at least place a colonisation in the late Bronze Age timeframe suggested by the DNA evidence. We should perhaps not rule out that there were colonies of Mediterranean traders that have failed to leave a trace in either DNA or archaeology. This Roman propaganda-invasion also found its way into the more elaborate pseudo-histories of Geoffrey of Monmouth and the Welsh 'Bruts' that would attempt to fill the void of pre-Roman history. Another useful ethnic detail that we glean from Nennius is that the Picts too were considered as invaders, whom he says occupied Orkney and the North some 800 years later than the Britons (so say about 300 BC). Bede and others record that they were warriors from 'Scythia' (the vast region of modern Russia) and that they sought Irish wives; some Picts perhaps also settled in Ireland.

The Welsh Historical Triads

The historical validity of the Welsh Triads has been greatly disputed and have always had little influence upon the English academic view of British prehistory outside of Wales. This may be partly due to the deeply entrenched barriers of Celtic ethnicity that persist to this day. There are no ancient written sources because the triads were preserved orally; they seem to have been a method of teaching facts to bardic students in easily remembered clusters of three, with the full details and historical chronology preserved in other ways that have been lost. Some of the elements within the triads reappear in the prose *Mabinogi*. Welsh scholars would suggest that none of the triads are truly ancient; they were created during the void after Roman withdrawal, perhaps as late as the ninth century. Therefore, to imply that the later bardic historian Edward Williams (Iolo Morganwg) may have 'invented' the entire third series of triads is not quite the same thing as saying that he invented all the history that they contain; he merely followed what the earlier triad authors had done. [14] However, we may observe that the legends of origin within the triads are remarkably consistent with the picture that we are now given by the geneticists (or at least the genes do not disprove them). So if Iolo and the earlier triad-authors were guilty of inventing history then they did so with remarkable prescience.

In the triads from medieval manuscripts that are generally considered authentic, we find triad 36 which lists the three *gormes* or 'oppressive invaders' of Britain.

> *Three Oppressions That Came To This Island, And Not One Of Them Went Back: One of them the people of the Cor(y)aniaid, who came here in the time of Caswallawn (=Lludd?) son of Beli: and not one of them went back. And they came from Arabia.*
> *The second Oppression: the Gwyddyl Ffichti. And not one of them went back.*
> *The third Oppression: the Saxons, with Horsa and Hengist as their leaders.* [15]

This is the simplest form of the Welsh invasion legends. Although the triads are quite timeless, we may perhaps infer historical sequence in the order that the three facts are presented. The mention of the Saxons betrays the post Dark Age date of composition. The *Gwyddyl Ffichti* are the 'Irish Picts', sometimes considered to be among the Scotti who crossed to Britain only after the Romans left (the north British Picts being simply *Ffichti*). *Caswallawn* is the Cassivellaunus who opposed Caesar's raids, so this history does not take us back very far. Who the *Coraniaid* may have been is a subject of speculation; as they are listed first we may consider them as certainly earlier than the others? Rachel Bromwich suggested that Triad 51 was a later version that replaced the Coraniaid with the Romans. [16] How do you incorporate a fourth invader into a triad? Answer: drop the oldest one! In the *third series*, Williams elaborated by saying that they were a tribe who settled about the Humber estuary and later united with the Romans and Saxons – but this cannot be authenticated at all. Ptolemy's map shows the *Parisi* tribe east of the Wolds. Archaeologists have long investigated Iron Age fields and burials from East Yorkshire, known as the Arras Culture, dating to the mid-late first-millennium BC. [17]

Welsh scholars lament that Williams, in his supposed forgeries, would incorporate details from authentic manuscripts to make his fictions more believable; some would say that Geoffrey of Monmouth did the same, but it is not so simple. We just don't know how much lost oral history was circulating in early medieval Wales. It is useful to read the extended version (Triad IV) in the third series, which would bring the Coraniaid instead from Asia. Triad V lists tribes who were allowed to settle peacefully: the Caledonians, the Gwyddel (Scots) and Galedin (Gauls). Note that here the Caledonii are distinguished from the Picts and the Scots, but there is no other tradition that would bring them in as immigrants.

Triads I & II of the third series detail the *benevolent tribes* who arrived first and from whom the Welsh claimed descent. First came the *Cymry* themselves, after the Flood; then came the *Lloegrwys* (the Romano-Britons who became absorbed among the English) and thirdly the *Britons* from Llydaw (Brittany or maritime France). All these, the triads claim, were of the same ancient stock and similar language, having migrated from the regions around the Bosporus and Anatolia in some ancient era. This statement would have to imply that they spoke related forms of Celtic *from the earliest times,* which were mutually intelligible.

By analogy with the spread of the English language, we may see that even a mass invasion from the east coast did not penetrate beyond the highlands of Wales. The genetic study of 2015 determined that the populations of north and south Wales are only distantly related. [18] They were never a unity until the medieval necessity to resist the English. This would again suggest that if the British Celtic language came along with later invaders then they must have colonised Wales *from the west* – i.e. from the sea. Note that nothing in the Welsh tradition claims that the three benevolent tribes were aboriginal in the way that Caesar records, merely that they peacefully occupied an *uninhabited* island. Of course, it may only have been empty in the same sense that Australia and New Zealand were empty before the colonists arrived! The indigenous pastoralists were neither numerous nor strong enough to resist and, like the tribes of the Brazilian rain forests, they were displaced inland. We must look elsewhere to find the tribes who claimed to be the first inhabitants of Britain.

Irish Origins and Invaders

The 2021 genetic study did not encompass Ireland; however, one cannot discuss the early ethnography of Britain without considering the extensive legendary history of Ireland. Irish scholars tend to discuss their prehistory in isolation as if there were little influence from Britain. The Irish also had druids and bards and they too preserved history orally via poetry and prose; but crucially, although some stories have become muddled for the same reasons as the Welsh tales, crucially, it never suffered the four centuries of suppression by the Romans. The Irish view of their origins therefore remained relatively intact, until it too was deformed by Christian conversion and priestly attempts to squeeze the traditional narrative into Biblical doctrine. The summary here will focus principally on ethnic origins and any indicators of chronology contained within the stories.

The origins of the Irish are collected in the Book of Invasions (*Lebor Gabála Érenn*) recorded via various medieval versions from the eleventh century onward. Nennius also knew of some of the stories in the ninth century. The result is a collection of overlapping sources that lead to varying interpretations. Although scholars typically treat all the invasions as purely mythical, it does at least fill the gap in prehistory that has been totally lost from the equivalent Welsh sources. It allows us to compare that which may be historical and those parts that are even earlier 'mythology'.

The *Lebor Gabála* tells how Ireland was settled successively by six groups of people: the tribe of Cessair, Partholon, and Nemed; these were followed by the Fir Bolg, the Tuatha Dé Danann (Danaans), and lastly the Milesians. Most of the later pseudo-history concerns the Milesians, who are generally regarded as the Gaels; the modern people of Ireland. The first two legendary settlements died out, but from Nemed onward we have details that can perhaps be analysed as history. In the earliest period the land is described as in a formative state; the settlers cleared plains and endured floods. Ireland is described as lying empty and neglected for three hundred years, then again for 30 years until Nemed arrives. Of particular interest should be the struggles of the early settlers with an apparently indigenous enemy called the *Fomorians*. The name has various translations, among them a 'giant' or a pirate. We must consider whether this distorted image recalls a real indigenous population, as they recur repeatedly in later tales. The problem we have is that there is so much imagination in Irish fiction, which disguises where the true history may lie within it all – but this is a general problem when exploring the myths of all nations. We need not dwell here on the details of the various stories, fascinating though they are; we need not doubt that these too hide much valuable history.

The origin of the settlers is in essence as follows. Some sources would bring them vaguely from 'Greece', others from Iberia. The tribe of Nemed, were somehow related to the earlier Partholonians. The Nemedians were ultimately defeated by the Fomorians. Some of the surviving Nemedians from Greece later returned, now calling themselves the *Fir Bolg*. They, in turn, were conquered by the Danaans who drove the Fir Bolg into the west of Ireland and out to the islands; both had their own conflicts with the Fomorians until they were finally defeated by the Danaans in a great battle. The Danaans are also linked back to Greece and we find various interpretations of their origins and how they arrived in Ireland.

Sometime later, much later, there arrived a colony of the *Milesians*, supposedly from Spain (Galicia) and they conquered the Danaans, who, in the later stories would be elevated to the status of ancient gods and figures of myth, along with the Fomorians who become 'giants' and distorted fairy-tale caricatures. It is usual to identify the Milesians as the Gaels, who brought with them the Irish language. We have a similar story from Nennius, who records a warrior from Spain, who came with thirty ships, followed, he says, by many more who crossed over gradually. The Britons, he believed, had arrived earlier than these Irish invaders. [*Nennius 13-15*] However, the simple picture that the Milesians completely replaced the earlier inhabitants can be challenged on a number of grounds, not least the preservation of the older legends. Regional DNA variations in Ireland would now also suggest that the descendants of earlier settlers are still there. [19]

Of particular interest must be the Fomorians, who were clearly not considered as Irish, and who were present even when the first settlers arrived. We may view them as indigenous inhabitants who were trying to hold their lands against the intruders. We only have the Irish invaders disparaging view of them. In the *Historia Brittonum* attributed to Nennius, which was written earlier than the Book of Invasions, we are told: "*Bolg and his people held the Isle of Man* [Eubonia] *and other islands about*". Again in the Book of Invasions (Ballymote version) we are told that the Fomorians came from the western isles and from Scythia; [20] and that some of the displaced Fir Bolg went to live among them in Britain and in the islands, where they remained identifiable right up to the time of Christian conversion. [21]

As to when we could historically date the various invasions we are offered a clue from archaeology. Irish place name legends attribute the building of the passage graves at Newgrange and its neighbours to a king of the Danaans called *the Dagda*. [22] The construction of the passage graves can be dated via radiocarbon and recent DNA evidence to around 3150 BC and correlates to the period when modern science detects recovery after a real decline in agriculture (see ref 8). This would suggest that the invasion legends are as old as the Neolithic. As for which of the colonists brought the Gaelic language with them remains undetermined. We may also consider that these seaborne colonisations must have left their mark on the west coast of Britain, in Wales, Cornwall and Brittany – but as we have seen, for Britain, the traditions are more sparse. We may note again the remark by Tacitus as to the resemblance of the people of southwest Britain to those of Atlantic Iberia. It is worth consideration that the differences of language between Ireland and Wales may result from the different accents of the earlier people who were absorbed. Perhaps future DNA research will offer more conclusive evidence.

Plutarch and 'Greeks'

An interesting tale by the Greek author Plutarch offers us another view of the northern and western parts of Britain. In two of his *Moral Essays* he infers that a colony of Greeks had migrated to the Hebridean islands in ancient times. The modern Scot may wonder why Greeks would wish to emigrate from the sun-drenched Aegean to these windswept isles, as most would now prefer to go the other way each year. It seems to have been a religious colony seeking the perceived home of the Greek gods; therefore we may perhaps compare it to a Christian pilgrimage or the annual Muslim Haj.

Plutarch tells us about the explorer *Demetrius*, sent out from Rome during the reign of Emperor Titus to survey the islands west of Britain. [*Obsolescence of Oracles, 419, 18*] He relates that the oracle of Cronus was believed by the locals to lie on an island in that region. His true mission seems to have been to assess the tribal opposition and geography; to evaluate the feasibility of a military campaign on the west coast and a conquest of Ireland. In another essay Plutarch tells us that in ancient times a colony of 'Greeks' came west in the train of Heracles and settled in the islands and parts of the mainland. [*The Face on the Moon, 941-942*] It is worthwhile to quote the ethnic information that Plutarch offers:

> *On the coast of the mainland Greeks dwell... These people consider themselves continentals... and they believe that with the peoples of Cronus there mingled at a later time those who arrived in the train of Heracles and were left behind and that these latter...rekindled the Hellenic spark there which was already being quenched and overcome by the tongue, the laws, and the manners of the barbarians.* [Loeb translation]

Whence Plutarch obtained this opinion is uncertain but the narrative suggests that they reached him via Carthaginian sources; it has clear parallels with the Irish Book of Invasions. He says that the Greeks mingled with *'the peoples of Cronus*', who may be recognised as the earlier 'barbarian' inhabitants of that region. We are unable to place a date on any of these events, except that the 'Greeks' remained somehow recognizable until such date as Plutarch's source could record them. Any such colony, since it is linked with the legendary figure of Heracles, must recall an ancient time. The Aegean was always a complex ethnic region, with various pre-Greek island races and isolate languages related to those of Anatolia and Crete. It is likely that Mediterranean tin traders sustained a maritime trading contact with the Atlantic coasts throughout the Bronze Age; and that religious travellers seeking the god Baal-Cronus came along with them. [23]

If direct Greek colonisation does not reveal itself in the British DNA then it may be an indicator that it remembers a very old population movement, perhaps disguised in the Neolithic influx of people of similar 'steppe ancestry' or the even earlier arrival of the first farmers from Anatolia. We would therefore have to regard 'the peoples of Cronus' as a survival of the aboriginal inhabitants: the Mesolithic people, or the Western Hunter Gatherers if you prefer. Small colonies of later traders and pilgrims from the same region would therefore be difficult to distinguish from an older merged-population. There must be greater uncertainty the further back we attempt to unravel the contradictory strands of science versus history and legend.

Hyperboreans

The earliest mention of *Hyperboreans* 'the people from beyond the North Wind' comes from the poetry of Hesiod dating from 700 BC. By the earliest classical era, the Greeks had forgotten much of their own history from the Bronze Age. They preserved legends about people inhabiting the far north of Europe, beyond the mountains, where the cold wind and snow prevailed. The collective name may therefore encompass many nations at the northern limit of their known world. Due to the prevalence of Latin and Greek in classical education, the interpretation of the Hyperboreans as a purely mythical race dominates to this day, so it is perhaps asking too much of geneticists to find evidence of Hyperboreans in their DNA studies!

In Pinder's Odes, from 500 BC we have poetic references to the visits by Perseus and Heracles to the Hyperboreans, where they witnessed their games and the celebration of the god Apollo, whose religion was especially celebrated in Athens and on the island of Delos. According to Herodotus the Delians knew most about the Hyperboreans. He describes how, since ancient times, they had sent gifts each year to the temple on Delos along with two girls as messengers, escorted by a few men as their bodyguards; and he details their route from Hyperborea via the Adriatic Sea. [*Herodotus IV, 33-4*]

The ancient relationship between Greece and Hyperborea is further confirmed by *Hecataeus of Abdera* (c.320 BC). He offers the extra detail that the Hyperboreans (or at least some of them) lived on an island beyond the Celts. The passage as paraphrased by Diodorus Siculus describes a large island, which could only be either Britain or Ireland. [*Histories, II, 47*] The identification is further validated by the presence there of a 'temple of the spheres' in which the inhabitants would celebrate the sun god (Apollo) with music and hymns as they followed the nineteen-year cycle or 'year of Meton'. This temple has been suggested by various modern commentators to be one of the astronomically aligned stone circles, perhaps Stonehenge or Callanish. Therefore, we may perhaps date the era of this Hyperborean culture via archaeology, by reference to how late the stone circles continued in usage. Key data for ancestry and language study is the statement:

The Hyperboreans also have a language, we are informed, which is peculiar to them...

It is difficult to see this 'peculiar' (i.e. unique) language as British Celtic since the continental Celts were recognised as a cultural unit by even the oldest Historians. Hecataeus has already mentioned them and their language was not considered peculiar. It may record a non-Indo-European language or an isolate that was spoken prior to the Celtic languages. Again, we are not helped by the absence of any written inscriptions from early British archaeology; this conveys a false sense of backwardness when compared to Mediterranean cultures; whereas in fact, the undoubted wisdom of the Druids and Bards was maintained orally until it was eradicated by the Romans and later Christian conversion. We may see that the religion and wisdom of the Hyperboreans was greatly respected by the Mediterranean nations with whom they had contact.

In so far as we may equate Hecataeus with the older poetic references to Hyperboreans then he would seem to be describing the circumstances of Britain at a time *significantly earlier* than the other classical historians. We may also take from it a view of a peaceful political unity and high culture that had yet to fragment into the tribes of the late Iron Age. A recent comprehensive analysis of the fragments of Hecataeus would suggest that this Hyperborean culture *remained recognisable* at least until he could include the description in his fourth century BC travel guide. It is possible that the description was derived from the lost book '*On the Ocean*' written by Pytheas after his circumnavigation of Britain. [24]

Herodotus, writing earlier around 450 BC did not know of the existence of Britain, nor even of the western ocean, but he did know of the Hyperboreans from the poetry and he wanted to know where they were. This would seem to suggest that they had already disappeared as a unified nation before 450 BC. He knew only of a people called *Cynetae* (or Cynesians) beyond the Celts; so could these be the same people? They are more likely to have been the Belgae, whom Caesar tells us arrived at the Channel coast from across the Rhine around this time and may indeed have pushed the *Cantii* farmers into Kent. [*Gallic Wars II, 4*] We therefore see both historical and DNA testimony for the migration of Belgic tribes from across the Rhine into southern Britain in the centuries before the Romans. [25] We do not know for certain whether the original language of the Belgae was Celtic or Germanic (old English?); neither do we know how strongly, if at all, they had adopted Druidism. The lack of any similar DNA evidence for *invasion* from further north suggests that the culture of the tribes occupying the Midlands had changed little since the era of the Stonehenge builders – although this would not rule-out a trickle of immigration and coastal trading stretching back into the Bronze Age. So again we may ask: how long did their 'unique' language and communal culture persist in southern and central Britain?

Iron Age Tribes

The term 'Iron Age hill forts' has been in use since the earliest archaeology. There is little trace of fortifications in Britain before the late Bronze Age around 900 BC; certainly, they were fewer and less elaborate. The earlier 'henges' dating back to the Neolithic do not seem to have been defensive, rather they may have been community places to enclose animals. The evidence of a common style of monuments, as far north as Orkney, during the era when Stonehenge and the other stone circles were built, would suggest that the island of Britain formerly shared a unified governance and culture.

We may find something of this centralised authority lingering in the timeless legends of a 'King Arthur' as ruler of all the Britons, which we find in the later pseudo-histories. Perhaps there was a remembered age when the Britons believed, as in later eras, that the best place to defend the island from foreign invaders was in France! A millennium before the continental expansion of the Iron Age 'Celts' there may have been a cross-channel hegemony in which the doctrine of the Druids could spread. This would not be out of line with the new DNA evidence, which suggests that immigration to Britain peaked during the late Bronze Age. A trickle of continental immigrants over a long period is suggestive of that which could freely occur within an 'empire' under a stable ruling dynasty. As with the later Norman conquest, replacing the rule of a single king is far easier than the piecemeal Roman conquest of numerous unruly tribes. This could best explain gradual culture and language transformation without leaving a record in the DNA. We should always remember that for this same era Egyptologists can offer us pages of history about the dynasties of kings and their conquests, but for Britain and northern Europe we have only a void.

From the late Bronze Age onwards archaeologists detect evidence of fortified settlements ('hill-forts'), suggesting that the unity of earlier times may have broken down. [26]. However, the new genetics now tells us that there was little new immigration. Our knowledge of the ethnic divisions of pre-Roman Britain comes mainly via Ptolemy's geography, from coin hordes, and from the tribes mentioned in accounts of the Roman campaigns; but these only reflect the tribal divisions just prior to the Roman conquest. Other than for Caledonia, and the intrusive Belgic tribes, we have scant information to distinguish the various 'nations' either ethnically or linguistically, beyond the outline descriptions of Tacitus above. We may perhaps take this to infer that there was little distinctiveness for foreign observers to note, beyond the unique communal society and the survival of a peculiar language in the north.

The *Brigantes* ('hill-people') a confederation who occupied lands from the River Trent to Northumbria, were quick to ally with the invading Romans; their queen clearly seeing them as a less immediate threat than her tribal neighbours. Some early linguistic studies had suggested they were related to the Brigantes of Ireland, perhaps speaking the Insular Celtic of the Milesians. [27]. There is no certainty as to their language nor evidence that they ever tattooed their skin; however archaeologists determine that they were long established in the region. They must be a prime candidate as one of the tribes of the interior who preserved older customs. As with Wales, the 2015 DNA study found the Yorkshire Dales and Cumbria regions to be genetically distinct.

Picts and Scots

The geneticists may have put the final nail in the coffin of the 'Celtic Picts'. Celtic linguists continue to look (without success) for Celtic words within the later Pictish Ogham inscriptions; and the assumption of Celtic Picts remains embedded in the literature because of the supposed presence there of a p-Celtic 'Pictish' language. [28] This dogma stretches back to nineteenth century authorities; the archaeology has never really endorsed the idea and now the DNA evidence also reveals the uniqueness of the Scottish population. The new genetics suggests that an "ancestry convergence" took place across Europe during the Late Bronze Age (the proto-Celtic era 1300-800 BC) showing a homogenized proportion of heritage from the Early European Farmers. However this convergence did not extend to Scotland (or to Sardinia apparently) which continued to show a proportion of such ancestry unchanged since the early Bronze Age. The 2021 DNA study would emphasise that this argues against any substantial immigration to these regions from central Europe during this period. The report does not define precisely where we should draw the ancient cultural boundary or where pockets of older ancestry might have persisted further south.

All of the historical and legendary sources that we may consult are firm that the Picts came from 'Scythia', either directly by sea, or in Irish sources overland through Gaul. *Both may be true!* The relative clarity of the historical sources suggest that the Pictish invasion was a more recent 'Iron Age' event. The confidence that they were 'Celts' is purely a construct of the linguists. Rather we should expect (based on the legends of origin) that the Scottish population should reveal an ancestry closer to the pastoralists of Baltic Europe and Russia rather than from European farmers, well-mixed with Scots-Irish heritage.

Another DNA study, for the Orkney Islands, was published in early 2022 and offers us a curious story. [29] In a popular newspaper: "*Bronze Age immigration to Orkney 'mostly women'*" (*Daily Express*) which shows a misunderstanding by the journalists of the mitochondrial DNA ancestry. In summary, the research would indicate that Neolithic people persisted in Orkney longer than in the south, before being largely replaced by people of "steppe ancestry" during the mid-Bronze Age. However, the mitochondrial DNA would indicate that the female-lineage descends from the immigrants, with the older male-lineages persisting for longer – until they were ousted by another wave of incomers (the Picts?) during the Iron Age and later still by the Vikings. It would be interesting to see how the geneticists would view these findings in the light of the historical reports of communal social organisation, but there is no consideration of the historical sources within a study that is again dense with jargon. The 2015 study had previously shown the DNA ancestry of Orkney to be complex and varying from island to island. It may demonstrate, in microcosm, what was going on further south.

It would seem then, that Scots are not only distinct from the southern Britons but distinct from most of Europe; and also, it would seem, different from each other. We surely did not need geneticists to tell us that!

Conclusions

How should one sum-up the above comparison of DNA with the history and legends? We may see that the picture of British prehistory that emerges from the new science does not conflict with the one we have always had from the classical historians and the legendary sources. Should we even consider ancient history and legends to be sources of 'evidence'? Certainly, we see more congruence between the DNA and the history than by comparing it to the chronology that the archaeologists formerly proposed based on artefacts and excavations. However, we seem also to have more surviving historical references to the people of the northern and western coasts of Britain than we have for the east coast and interior of the island. This may reflect the fact that the west coast was accessible to Mediterranean voyagers, but also not to forget that this represents a minority of the mainland population, then, as it does today.

Most important to note is that none of the surviving traditions of British or Irish origin would describe the inhabitants as indigenous to the islands; they are all in one way or other *colonists* who remember a homeland in the east; migrating either via northern Europe or via Iberia and the Mediterranean. Therefore, we must conclude that the oral tradition believed by some aboriginal tribes in the interior of Britain, as mentioned by the various Roman authors, has not survived in any traditional source. We therefore have to infer who they were from those ancient tribal groups whose traditions we do *not* possess.

One may suggest a sequence as follows. The indigenous hunter-gatherers of the Mesolithic persisted in the forested interior as the first farmers colonised the best land of southern Britain and Ireland during the warm period of the mid-Holocene c.4000 BC. This is the era remembered in the oldest Welsh and Irish 'myths' rather than in their more concise 'legends'. This marks the era that archaeologists would term the early and middle Neolithic when the farmers were able to expand their range and forests were cut down; it corresponds to the 'elm decline' that climatologists have long discussed. Towards the end of the fourth millennium BC this population of early farmers was severely reduced by rapid climate change and perhaps also by natural catastrophe. There followed centuries of agricultural decline and regeneration of forests as peat bogs enveloped the neglected fields. This hiatus of around three-hundred years is now verified by the science. It should make scientists treat the legends that early British and Irish colonists inherited an 'empty' land with greater respect than hitherto.

A new period of climate stability allowed recovery and we see new monument styles: the era of the stone circles. A wave of immigrants or invaders from the Steppes eventually reached Britain and overwhelmed the recovering farmers during the Late Neolithic 'Stonehenge era' after 3000 BC. A long period of evolution followed during which Britain remained, for the most part, a unified culture into which generations of new settlers came over from the continent. We may equate this with the fabled 'Hyperborean' era. Further climate fluctuations during the mid-late Bronze Age (after about 1600 BC) and perhaps also new and hostile invaders, may then have led to a collapse of central authority, with fragmentation into the regional tribes and 'nations' during the Iron Age. The influx of new settlers declined. The DNA evidence allows us to put the vague history and legends into a loose chronological sequence that was not formerly attainable solely from archaeology.

The origin of the immigrants, *as it is suggested in the legendary sources*, does not conflict with those given by DNA, although geneticists may wish to 'fine-tune' the route to the west that the various genes took in their journey from Anatolia and the Steppes. The Irish invaders may have been a mix of the Aegean pre-Greek peoples similar to the first farmers, together with later Greeks who were part of the dispersal from the Steppes. The Welsh triads imply a similar origin from Anatolia and the Black Sea. The Picts and some of the earlier Irish invaders may have come instead via a northerly route through Germany and the Baltic coast. Colonists who came via the Iberian route included the people who spoke Celtic. We may suggest that the origin of seaborne migrants from Atlantic coasts reached Ireland and southwest Britain in more than one wave. We may then see other, probably late, arrivals from Gaul and the Rhine into the south and east. However, this is the region from which we have the poorest survival of history and legends to suggest origins, so we can only follow the Roman information. Overall, it would suggest that the oldest cultures survived longest in the north and west where they were protected behind the hills and other natural barriers.

The question of the arrival of the Celtic languages remains open and the DNA can neither confirm nor refute the traditional and historical sources. It would, however, overturn the long-standing belief that the Celtic languages arrived along with a single wave of Iron Age invaders; clearly they were present much earlier. If you wish to believe the Welsh traditions then the arrival of Celtic languages must be placed early, possibly at the same era as the legendary Irish invaders c.3000 BC. Alternatively, you may envisage a wave of Celtic-speaking settlers into Southwest England and South Wales, during the later Bronze Age, which left the older 'peculiar' language of the Hyperboreans steadily retreating to the North. However this older language was probably *not* Pictish. There is every reason to suggest that the Pictish language was a later arrival along with their historically remembered invasion from Scythia; and that the older language survived alongside it in western Caledonia right up to the historical Pictish period. It is the speakers of this older language whose myths and legends we have lost.

During the mid-late Bronze Age we may see a long period of some two thousand years of relatively stable and evolving cultural exchange with the continent, during which there may have been numerous incursions, both hostile and permitted, as we find in the Welsh triads; along with refugee migrants from the same regions as the earlier immigrants. We may compare with the European colonisation of the Americas, where immigrant farmers have overwhelmed the indigenous inhabitants within just five-hundred years. Here we consider a period of three-thousand years, during which patrilinear newcomers simply produced more children surviving to adulthood.

Numerous intrusions of tribes from the east into western Europe are recorded during historical times, from the Cimmerians and Scythians to the Cimbri and Teutons in the Roman annals; later the Huns, Goths and other barbarians massing on Roman borders, through to the later Mongol empire. There is every reason to believe that comparable intrusions from the Steppe region and beyond were ongoing throughout the thousands of years of the Neolithic and Bronze Age, driven by deteriorating climate. This population-pressure from the east pushed the established European tribes to migrate even further west and drove some across the sea. We need not always see conquests led by warlords, rather a steady trickle of 'refugees' who merged into their new homeland. Such trickle-migration does not show in the archaeology, but it is revealed in the genes.

As the new research would suggest, invasive tribes into southern Britain during the Iron Age were restricted to the south coast and East Yorkshire. It seems unlikely that these small groups alone could be responsible for the shift to Celtic language, as later history would suggest that whichever culture holds the English midlands will ultimately dominate the island. Furthermore, the fact that the archaeologically attested settlements were remembered by contemporary historians would suggest that there were no others worthy of note. The culture of Middle Britain thus remained little changed from earlier millennia, with the older language being gradually supplanted by the Continental Celtic of the Britons from the southwest at some time around 500 BC.

A note on terminology and abbreviations

The preceding should be viewed as a cross-disciplinary article for the interest of the general reader and historian, rather than as a genetic study. Specialist terminology ('jargon') has been held to the necessary minimum and explained where its usage cannot be avoided. You may find the following abbreviations in the 2021 report and elsewhere:

WHG	Western Hunter Gatherers	C/EBA	Chalcolithic/ Early Bronze Age
EHG	Eastern Hunter Gatherers	MBA	Middle Bronze Age
CHG	Caucasus Hunter Gatherers	M-LBA	Mid to Late Bronze Age
SHG	Scandinavian Hunter Gatherers	LBA	Late Bronze Age
WSH	Western Steppe Herders	IA	Iron Age
EEF	Early European Farmers		

Urnfield Culture – the 'proto-Celtic' nation, now often used by archaeologists in preference to the former ethnic term 'Celts'
'Steppe Ancestry' – now preferred to the former ethnic term 'Indo-European'
Yamnaya Culture – Neolithic steppe-pastoralists within the above grouping.
Corded Ware Culture – a Neolithic culture situated north of the steppe pastoralists.
Insular Celtic – now preferred to *q-Celtic* as the term for Irish Gaelic languages.
Continental Celtic – now preferred to *p-Celtic* as the term for British and Gaulish forms of Celtic.

Relevant Hyperlinks

These will provide additional research background, but hopefully the narrative will stand-alone should they become broken.

https://www.nature.com/articles/s41586-021-04287-4

https://www.bbc.co.uk/news/science-environment-59741723

https://www.independent.co.uk/news/the-family-link-that-reaches-back-300-generations-to-a-cheddar-cave-1271542.html

https://www.dailymail.co.uk/sciencetech/article-5453665/Was-Cheddar-man-white-all.html

https://www.newscientist.com/article/2161867-ancient-dark-skinned-briton-cheddar-man-find-may-not-be-true/

https://archaeologydataservice.ac.uk/archives/view/eh_monographs_2014/contents.cfm?mono=1089041

https://www.hud.ac.uk/news/2022/february/rewriting-genetic-history-of-prehistoric-orkney/

https://www.nbcnews.com/health/health-news/new-genetic-map-shows-ancient-british-divisions-linger-n326036

https://www.expressandstar.com/news/science-and-technology/2022/02/07/bronze-age-immigration-to-orkney-mostly-women-scientists-discover/

https://www.nature.com/news/uk-mapped-out-by-genetic-ancestry-1.17136

https://www.nature.com/articles/s41598-017-17124-4

https://en.wikipedia.org/wiki/Pollen_zone

https://www.academia.edu/10372980/Is_there_evidence_for_a_Neolithic_crisis_or_revolution_in_3000BC

https://www.abroadintheyard.com/maps-britain-ireland-ancient-tribes-kingdoms-dna/

http://www.attalus.org/translate/poseidonius.html

https://www.worldhistory.org/article/1078/on-the-ocean-the-famous-voyage-of-pytheas/

http://classics.mit.edu/Caesar/gallic.5.5.html

https://www.third-millennium.co.uk/_files/ugd/e5604c_465f3f96346041fb94f8e5f960804f1f.pdf

http://www.zendonaldson.com/twilight/camelot/triads/index.htm

https://www.maryjones.us/jce/LGEoverview.pdf

https://www.ancienttexts.org/library/celtic/ctexts/lebor3.html#39

https://www.nature.com/articles/s41586-020-2378-6

https://www.academia.edu/27786980/Hecataeus_of_Abdera_and_his_work_On_the_Hyperboreans_about_300_BC_The_fragments_with_a_historical_commentary_2016_

https://www.worldhistory.org/Hyperborea/

https://www.loebclassics.com/view/diodorus_siculus-

library_history/1933/pb_LCL303.39.xml?readMode=recto&result=1&rskey=HAqqHl
https://www.cell.com/action/showPdf?pii=S0002-9297%2807%2962721-9
https://www.academia.edu/71621445/Belgic_Atrebates_settlement_of_Britain_Draft_?auto=download
https://www.wales247.co.uk/ancestry-dna-shows-genetic-link-between-wales-and-spain
https://www.nbcnews.com/health/health-news/new-genetic-map-shows-ancient-british-divisions-linger-n326036
https://livrepository.liverpool.ac.uk/3135296/1/200781399_Feb2021.pdf
https://archaeology-world.com/scientists-find-that-tin-found-in-israel-from-3000-years-ago-comes-from-cornwall/
https://www.libraryireland.com/Pedigrees2/brigantes.php

Notes and References

Citations of ancient authors are given as square parentheses in the main text.

1) Patterson, N., Isakov, M., Booth, T. et al. (2021) Large-scale migration into Britain during the Middle to Late Bronze Age. *Nature* 601, 588–594. https://doi.org/10.1038/s41586-021-04287-4
2) Cristian Capelli et al. (2003) Y Chromosome Census of the British Isles, *Current Biology*, 13, 979–984, May 27, 2003, DOI 10.1016/S0960-9822(03)00373-7
3) Leslie, S., Winney, B., Hellenthal, G. *et al.* The fine-scale genetic structure of the British population. *Nature* **519,** 309–314 (2015). https://doi.org/10.1038/nature14230 https://www.nature.com/news/uk-mapped-out-by-genetic-ancestry-1.17136
4) Gilbert, E., O'Reilly, S., Merrigan, M. et al. The Irish DNA Atlas: Revealing Fine-Scale Population Structure and History within Ireland. *Sci Rep 7*, 17199 (2017). https://doi.org/10.1038/s41598-017-17124-4 https://www.nature.com/articles/s41598-017-17124-4
5) See page 1 of ref. 1 above
6) See detailed maps and summaries in refs 3 & 4 above.
7) Shennan, S. et al. (2013) Regional population collapse followed initial agriculture booms in mid-Holocene Europe. *Nat. Commun.* 4:2486 doi: 10.1038/ ncomms3486.
8) Bevan, Andrew, et al. (2017) "Holocene Fluctuations in Human Population Demonstrate Repeated Links to Food Production and Climate." *Proceedings of the National Academy of Sciences of the United States of America*, vol. 114, no. 49, National Academy of Sciences, 2017, pp. E10524–31, https://www.jstor.org/stable/26486018

9) See page 1 of ref. 1 above

10 Golding A.. 1587. *Solinus - Collectanea Rerum Memorabilium*, (reprinted in facsimile by Scholars Facsimiles and reprints, Gainsville, Florida, 1955).

11) Morris, John (1973) *The Age of Arthur: A History of the British Isles from 350 to 650*, Weidenfeld & Nicolson, London see pp 190-191

12) see ref 3 above

13) Dunbavin, Paul (2020) On the Coligny Calendar and the Calendar in Plato's Critias, in *Prehistory Papers*, pp 23-30 Third Millennium Publishing, Beverley, ISBN: 978-0-9525029-4-4

14) Bromwich R:"Trioedd Ynys Prydain: The Myvyrian 'Third Series" *Transactions of the Honourable Society of Cymmrodion* 1968 Part II pp 299-338 for Iolo Williams' Triads 1-50 plus Notes, and 1969 Part I pp 127-155 for Triads 50-126 plus Notes., *see p 301*

15) Bromwich, Rachel (1978) *Trioedd Ynys Prydein – The Welsh Triads*, University of Wales Press, Cardiff; see p 90

16) ibid p 92

17) Halkon, Peter & Starley, David. (2011). Iron, Landscape and Power in Iron Age East Yorkshire. *Archaeological Journal*. 168. 133-165. 10.1080/00665983.2011.11020831.

18) Sykes, Bryan, (2007) *Blood of the Isles: exploring the genetic roots of our tribal history*, Bryan Sykes, Bantam Press, ISBN 0593056523

19) See ref 4 above

20) Watson, W.J. (1926) *The Celtic Place Names of Scotland,* Edinburgh, (1986 edition ISBN 1-874744-06-8, pp 40-41

21) ibid, p 64

22) Cassidy, L.M., Maoldúin, R.Ó., Kador, T. et al. (2020) A dynastic elite in monumental Neolithic society. *Nature* 582, 384–388 (2020). https://doi.org/10.1038/s41586-020-2378-6

23) APA citation: The enigma of bronze age tin (2019, September 13) retrieved 28 February 2022 from: https://phys.org/news/2019-09-enigma-bronze-age-tin.html

24) Joorde, R (2015) Hecataeus of Abdera and his work "On the Hyperboreans" (about 300 BC): The fragments with a historical commentary, Raffael Joorde - Academia.edu

25) Pullen, William (2022) Belgic Atrebates settlement of Britain (Draft) | William pullen - Academia.edu

26) Campbell, Lorraea, (2021 Thesis) https://livrepository.liverpool.ac.uk/3135296/1/200781399_Feb2021.pdf

27) Counihan, Martin (2019) Ptolemy's Tribes of Ireland (revised) mjc@gmx.ie Second revised version, 1 March 2019 https://www.academia.edu/38482760/Ptolemys_Tribes_of_Ireland_revised_version_

28) Rodway, S. (2020). The Ogham Inscriptions of Scotland and Brittonic Pictish. *Journal of Celtic Linguistics*, 21(1),173-234. https://doi.org/10.16922/jcl.21.6
29) Dulias, K et al (2022) "Ancient DNA at the edge of the world: Continental immigration and the persistence of Neolithic male lineages in Bronze Age Orkney" by Katharina Dulias, George Foody, Pierre Justeau et al., 7 February 2022, *Proceedings of the National Academy of Sciences*.

Other References

- Language origin debate rekindled, *Nature*, 518, 19 February 2015, (Corrected 23 February 2015) pp 284-5 https://www.nature.com/news/polopoly_fs/1.16935!/menu/main/topColumns/topLeftColumn/pdf/518284a.pdf
- Hoag, H. Y chromosomes rewrite British history. *Nature* (2003). https://doi.org/10.1038/news030616-15 https://www.nature.com/articles/news030616-15
- Capelli, C. et al. A Y chromosome census of the British Isles. *Current Biology*, **13,** 979 - 984, (2003).
- Sykes, Bryan, (2007) *Blood of the Isles: exploring the genetic roots of our tribal history*, Bantam Press, London, ISBN 0593056523
- McEvoy, B et al (2004) The Longue Durée of Genetic Ancestry: Multiple Genetic Marker Systems and Celtic Origins on the Atlantic Facade of Europe, AJHG, Vol 75, Issue 4, P693-702, October 01, 2004, :https://doi.org/10.1086/424697

8

Narmer, Meri-nar and Queen Myrina

In the histories of Diodorus Siculus, we find an account of a warlike queen named Myrina and the campaign of her Libyan Amazons into Egypt; and her further conquests around the Levant and Asia minor. Egyptologists usually sweep this under the carpet as a myth, as it does not correspond with any other known history from dynastic Egypt. Similarly scholars of Greek will dismiss the attempts of Diodorus to rationalise, or 'euhemerise' the ancient myths – for some of which he is the only source. However, Egyptologists do recognise a predynastic or First Dynasty king called Narmer, who is often considered to be the same person as Horus-Aha or Menes, the founder-king of the First Dynasty and traditional unifier of the two lands of Upper and Lower Egypt. Here, focusing primarily upon history and mythology, this article will offer a cross-disciplinary view of the mid-Holocene era beyond Egypt; it will investigate the parallels between Myrina and Narmer and compare these with the current consensus about the unification of Egypt – a view from outside the box!

At the very beginnings of Egyptian dynastic history, we are presented with a profusion of royal names derived from archaeological finds and inscriptions. Nothing is yet certain. The various interpretations must be treated as cumulative informed speculation by generations of Egyptologists (who are of course qualified to speculate) and it is more important than ever not to regard early Egyptian 'history' as proven fact. Here, with apologies for brevity and summary, I shall attempt to focus and simplify rather than to follow every modern speculative thread.

Deep in the Egyptology textbooks we find the discoveries of late nineteenth and early twentieth century excavators. Prime among them is the Narmer Palette from the First Dynasty temple of Nekhen at Hierakonpolis, discovered by James Quibell in 1898. [1] One side holds a scene of a king wearing the red crown and apparel of Lower Egypt, leading a procession, amid a show of defeated enemies; below it are animal scenes and a central depression, used for the practical purpose of the palette – the mixing of make-up or face paint. On the other side we see the king (or perhaps a different king) wearing the white crown and beard of upper Egypt, in the triumphal 'smiting' pose while striking a defeated enemy with a mace. The scene has long been interpreted as commemorating the unification of Egypt at the commencement of the first dynasty; in later dynasties the pharaohs would wear the dual crown of the unified kingdom. However, we should not rule out that two different kings (or queens) are depicted in each scene with the crowns intended to distinguish them. We may ask: who defeated whom? And is there any significance that the vanquished foes are so clearly depicted as male?

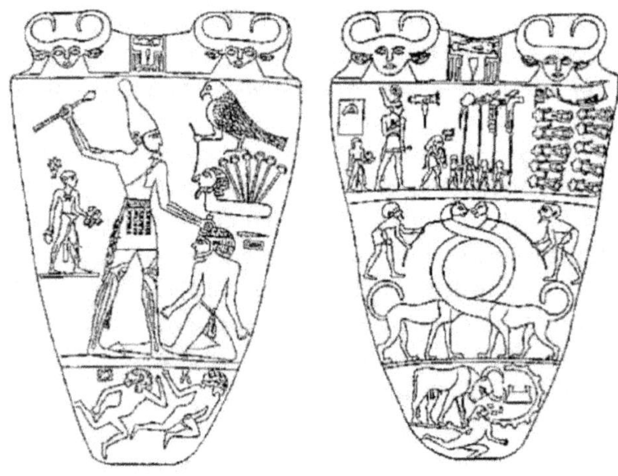

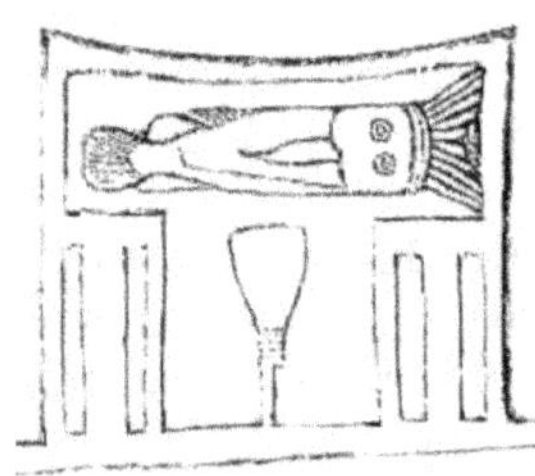

On the Narmer palette the catfish + chisel serekh of the royal name is shown at the heading on each side, but the same name (without an enclosure) appears to identify the king by this name, only on the 'red' side; seemingly associating that name with the ruler of Lower Egypt (the delta region). On the other side, the smiting-king instead has the hawk of Horus above papyrus in the same relationship at top right. So why must we assume that the figure wearing the white crown is also Narmer?

The serekh of Narmer is the most common among the royal serekh found in Egypt and the Levant from early dynastic times. At this early period the royal name was not yet placed in a cartouche, rather the Horus-name of the king was placed in an enclosure, perhaps denoting a royal palace or a temple. In later dynasties the Horus name declined in prominence and the birth-name or nebty-name was preferred, encased in a cartouche. [2] This change of priority adds further uncertainty about the identification of Narmer and the other early rulers.

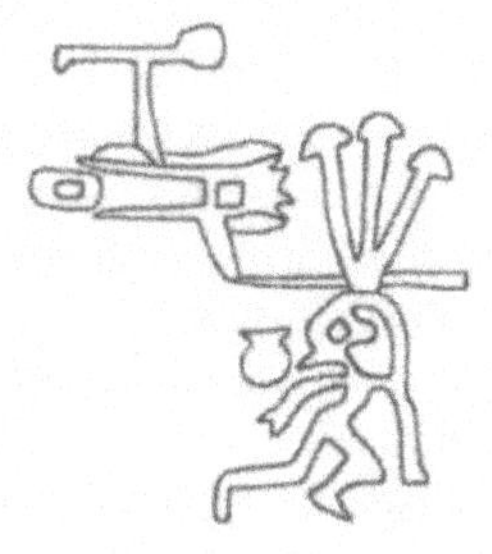

The apparently same 'smiting' that is portrayed on the Narmer Palette, is depicted on a broken label with the Narmer Serekh, from Abydos, found by the German archaeologist Günter Dreyer in 1993. In later Egypt, every year of a king's reign would have such a year-label marking a significant occurrence, i.e. 'the year when x occurred'. This label is taken to confirm that the scene on the Narmer palette was a historical event rather than mere symbolism. The king, here identified by the stylised 'catfish' and mace symbol, is shown beating a captive from the papyrus country: the Delta or perhaps, the Fayum. [3]

From the same deposit at Hierakonpolis is the Narmer 'wedding' mace head now in the Ashmolean Museum, Oxford. This too depicts a procession but is more celebratory in nature. It was interpreted by Petrie as a sed-heb wedding, to reaffirm the succession of the king. [4] The procession is led by a figure, who has the Narmer serekh displayed above, progressing towards (behind) another figure wearing the red crown, seated in an enclosure atop an elevated stepped-podium. In front, on a litter, sits the 'bride'. It is easy to see the scene as the wedding of a southern King Narmer to a northern princess once that idea has become firmly embedded in the literature. [5]

In the chronicle of Manetho and in later king lists we find the name *Menes*, the King *Min* of Herodotus, as founder of the First Dynasty and traditional unifier of the northern and southern crowns. Menes is described in one epitome as the first king 'after the flood', reigning for 60 or 62 years. The version of Eusebius says he reigned for only 30 years and achieved great fame by a war beyond Egypt's frontiers, but does not say where, nor list any great victories. Manetho's chronicle is the only 'historical' account we have that is free from modern interpretations. The remark that Menes was carried-off by a Hippopotamus (or a crocodile according to Diodorus) is often used to dismiss Manetho's comments and then Egyptologists can ignore it as just a myth; only artefacts from the ground may qualify as evidence.

Theories vary as to whether Menes was the same king as Narmer or was his son; or whether he is the should be identified with the Horus Aha, whose serekh were found in a First Dynasty tomb at Umm el-Qa'ab, Abydos, adjacent to a simpler tomb thought to be that of Narmer. Dreyer described this humble tomb as "completely predynastic" in style, quite unlike the mastaba architecture of its neighbours. [6] The assumption that Narmer was ever interred there is suggested primarily by the presence of his serekh in the adjacent tombs.

Horus Aha is believed to have built the temple of Neith at Saïs in the western delta. This conclusion comes from the Abydos Label discovered by Petrie in 1901; two fragmentary examples exist, showing the serekh of Horus Aha, together with the crossed-arrows of the goddess Neith (sometimes: *Neit, Net* or *Nit*) above a temple or shrine. The clearest example is that in the Penn Museum. Precisely what the scene records is again a matter of opinion and most citations refer back to Petrie's original interpretation. Equally it could recall a royal visit to Saïs, or to another Neith temple already in existence. However, it confirms that the cult of this goddess, whom the Greeks would later equate with their own Athene, was already flourishing before the First Dynasty. Radiocarbon dates would suggest that the higher ground of Saïs was settled as early as 4000 BC. [7]

The name of Horus Aha is also found in king lists on seal impressions discovered in the tombs of later First Dynasty kings Den and Qa'a. Both seals show the Narmer serekh for the founder of the dynasty, who was then followed by Horus Aha. An ivory label was found in the tomb of a queen *Neithhotep* who is thought to be his mother (and by inference the wife of Narmer); it shows the nebty-name interpreted as 'mn' alongside a serekh of Horus-Aha. This label seems to be the only connection, *from the artefacts*, to link these two names. [8] However, as with everything from this early period, specialist interpretations vary; and once this connection is made it leads to further supposition that Aha was Menes and the attributes of Menes can then be freely transferred over to him.

The seals showing both names would suggest that Aha succeeded Narmer. The only other early source is the Palermo Stone, a fragment of the Royal Annals dating from the Fifth Dynasty. [9] This gives a list of kings from the first to fourth dynasties but unfortunately the first two names are lost. The top line shows part of a list of kings all wearing the red crown; perhaps as many as 120 predynastic kings were originally listed there. The fragmentary Turin Canon dating from the reign of Rameses II (and thought to be closest to the source used by Manetho) has the name Menes (*mnj*) in place of Narmer and the following kings presumably have their birth-names in place of the Horus names. [10] By the era when Herodotus was given a tour of the temples, the priests remembered only King Min. One may conjecture that the oldest history was forgotten during the chaos of the First Intermediate Period. We cannot even be sure that Menes was anything but a legendary first-pharaoh from the predynastic era, who has simply been slotted into first place in the later king lists.

King List of Den
Showing the names of Narmer, Aha, Djer, Djet, Den and a name interpreted as that of a queen 'Merneith' preceded by the crossed-arrows symbol of the goddess Neith.
source: *https://pharaoh.se/other-king-lists*

King List of Qa'a
In this later list the name of Merneith is omitted but we see Narmer and Aha, here listed from right to left.

source: *https://pharaoh.se/other-king-lists*

From the excavations of Quibell at Hierakonpolis came other artefacts that still shape our view of the early dynastic period; among them the limestone macehead believed to belong to a king known as 'Scorpion'. Here again we see a king wearing the white crown of Upper Egypt, but with a scorpion symbol positioned in the same relationship as the serekh on the Narmer Palette. Quibell himself suggested that the scorpion was an additional title of the king, as it was later used to denote a nomarch, or regional governor of the south. Therefore, King Scorpion may be the same person as Narmer or Aha, rather than an unknown predynastic king. One whole side of the macehead is missing, leaving enough space for a lost second procession of a king in a red crown, as on the Narmer palette – but this can only be speculation. [11] The consensus is that King Scorpion was the immediate predecessor of Narmer and that the unification began during his reign or perhaps had been ongoing for generations. Once an eminent Egyptologist proposes a theory it grows wings and is cited over and over as if proven fact.
[* *see Note 1*]

In the 1990s the German expedition discovered a simple tomb (B50) at Um-el-Qaab, Abydos, containing various scorpion-decorated artefacts; among the grave goods were jars that had once held wine bearing the chemical signature of grapes, figs and spices from the Levant. This would appear to offer hard evidence that 'Scorpion', whoever he was, had strong trading links with the Levant during the predynastic era around 3150 BC. To date "thousands" of Protodynastic Egyptian artifacts have been found in Canaan, some with serekh of other supposed Protodynastic kings: *"Double Falcon", Ny-Hor, Iry-Hor and Ka*, as well as one serekh of Horus Aha; to date some twenty labels of Narmer are attested. The impression is of an early Egyptian hegemony in Canaan that was as complete as that found much later during the New Kingdom. [12]

These examples of the earliest writing allowed Egyptologists to propose a Dynasty 0, before Manetho's Dynasty I, comprising rulers whose existence is recognized only from these various serekh. This may otherwise be discussed as the *proto-dynastic period* (3200-3000 BC) before the first dynasty; also as Naqada III, the final phase of the Naqada Neolithic culture of the Nile valley. However, to follow these connections further here would be a digression. The king lists do not bring us any closer to a firm historical identification of Narmer and Aha nor offer a precise date for the reigns. There is no way to directly date a slate palette or a mace-head other than the archaeological context in which they are found; but such objects could have been valued icons, from an earlier generation. The radiocarbon dates from the tombs and artefacts remain around 100-150 years older than the historical dates (3100-3150 BC) that can be counted back via the king lists. [13] Much of this missing 'history' may be attributable to the omission of queens, co-regencies and usurpers. So what should we believe?

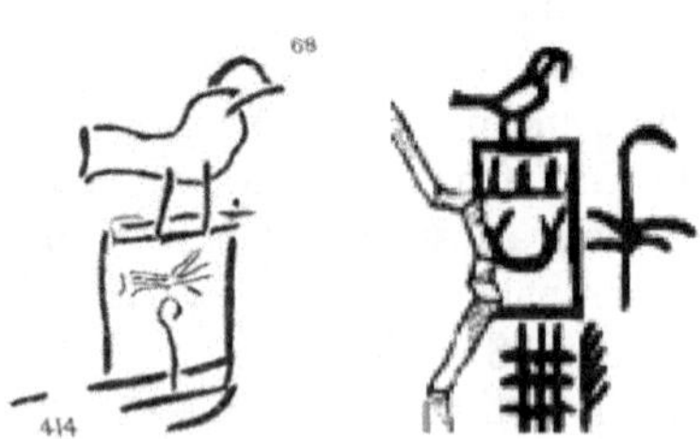

Examples of serekh of predynastic kings; 1) Narmer, from Tarkhan 2) Ka from Abydos

The reading of the earliest hieroglyphs in these various serekh are subject to specialist interpretation. They may be simple pictograms, for which the pronunciation was well-known to everyone; or they may be words and syllables conjoined, as in later hieroglyphs, to convey the sounds of the name. In later inscriptions, hieroglyphs were read from left-to-right or right-to-left depending on the direction that the symbols face, but when arranged in columns the convention is to read them top-down. However, we cannot be sure that these rules applied to the earliest pictograms in a serekh.

The Serekh of Cornwall!
That well-known British pharaoh who is often used to illustrate the principle of hieroglyphs; but should the pictogram instead be read downward as "wall-corn" (wl-crn)? The native-speaker does not need to be told which direction is the correct reading or what the missing vowels are. For similar reasons the interpretations of Egyptian serekh have to be treated with due caution.

The name *Narmer* is derived from its two parts, the catfish symbol *n'r* and the chisel *mr* read downwards as *n'r-mr* – Narmer. If read the other way then they give mr-n'r – mer-nar. Hieroglyphs give us no idea how the missing vowels were pronounced. Variants of the name may be found in discussion papers, according to the opinions of the Egyptologists. The alternative reading of the full name as *Horus Meri-nar,* I think, dates back to the Egyptologist Sir Alan Gardiner, in the 1950s – but the assumption of a king called 'Narmer' still dominates the literature. [14][15]

Why must it be assumed that the ruler depicted on the Narmer Palette was male? Later female rulers of Egypt represented themselves as kings on their monuments. The obvious parallel here is with the Eighteenth Dynasty queen Hatshepsut who presents as a king in her imagery even to the extent of wearing a false beard. The equality of women and matrilineal succession in ancient Egypt is difficult for Egyptologists to discuss, since of course, it is contrary to Islam. The assumption that Narmer was male lies deep in the literature, dating back to citations of the earliest excavators.

More examples of serekh of predynastic kings; 1) Double Falcon 2) Ny-Hor

If Narmer/Meri-nar were a ruling queen then we would expect to see a Neith-name, rather than a Horus-name. It may be that this custom began only *after* unification, when Neith's cult became established at Saïs. For kings during the First Dynasty the very legitimacy of their succession in the North came from their lineage via their queens, while Egypt remained two provinces, with separate administrations. We may look on it as something like the fragile Austro-Hungarian empire: two distinct nations united only under the same monarch. However, there seems to be little doubt that the legendary unifier known variously as Menes, Menas, or Min was indeed male.

The rule must be that if ever there be disagreement between the opinion of a modern specialist and that found in the oldest historical sources then we should always prefer the source closest to the events. We should only be convinced when historians and archaeologists agree on the same narrative.

A King or a Queen?

By contrast with all this Egyptology based on archaeological finds, we have a mythos preserved by Diodorus Siculus, of a Libyan queen named *Myrina*. Diodorus is our only source for the story of the Libyan Amazons. He tells us that Myrina, and her army of Amazon women-warriors swept through Egypt from Libya and came to an alliance with an Egyptian king who is here just named 'Horus'. Now this could refer to the Horus-name of any Egyptian king and so it does not help us to identify him. The Horus who met Myrina could be any of the Horus-kings from the predynastic onward, so it is necessary to seek other correspondences. The myth does not imply a conquest, as Diodorus simply writes of Myrina:

> *...she visited the larger part of Libya and passing over into Egypt she struck a treaty of friendship with Horus the son of Isis, who was king of Egypt at that time and then, after making war to the end upon the Arabians and slaying many of them, she subdued Syria.* [*Histories III. 54. 55*] [16]

Here, 'Arabia' would imply coastal Egypt east of the Nile along with Sinai; just as 'Libya' does not imply the bounds of the modern state but included all of the Mediterranean coast west of the Nile and as far into the desert as was habitable. Although the Levant (Canaan) is not specifically mentioned, Myrina must have passed through it in order to reach Syria and Anatolia. The mention of Horus and Isis here is usually sufficient for commentators to dismiss the entire Amazon campaign as an invented myth from the predynastic era. Once you confer the status of a myth upon an ancient story then the specialist is relieved of any responsibility to seek evidence of it as history.

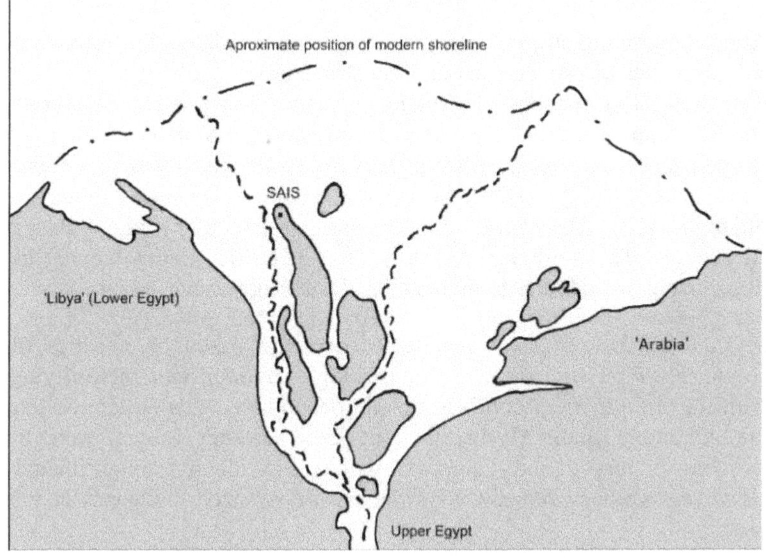

The Predynastic Nile Delta?

A summarised chart based on Butzer (1976) of the Nile Delta as it may have looked during the predynastic era. Older theories (still widely cited) regarding the unification of Upper and Lower Egypt, failed to acknowledge the changed climate and sea-level since that time. The delta regions that would be reclaimed as Lower Egypt during the Dynastic period lay below the shallow sea and the marshy estuary of the Nile. [17]

The full text and translation of Diodorus Siculus on the Amazons is now freely available online and so need only be summarised here. According to Diodorus the Amazons originated from an island, somewhere in the unknown west, called simply *Hespera*: 'west', which was near the marsh Tritonis. We cannot know precisely where this was, or when it was, from this timeless description. Diodorus didn't know where the island was either; he says it was of great size and held many fruit trees, birds and animals from which the natives obtained all their food. Significantly, he tells us that the use of grain for farming was then unknown; i.e. *they were pastoral farmers and hunter gatherers!* This simple statement is a 'fossil' and it tells us a lot about how old the story must be. One cannot imagine that Diodorus or Dionysius has taken this from a romanticised 'myth' – it is the kind of precise detail that only a competent historian would record. Another identifying feature is that the island held an active volcano. The only large island in the Mediterranean that fits such a description is Sicily; Diodorus fails to recognise his own home island because the description is of a much earlier time.

After dominating all the cities of their home island, the Amazons colonised the Marsh Tritonis and constructed a city of their own on a peninsula: "Cherronesus". In this lost ancient city arose Queen Myrina and her Amazons. Precisely where the city and the Marsh of Triton lay is open to debate, but they are usually set in the salt-lakes of Tunisia known at the Chott el Djerid – or perhaps somewhere now submerged offshore. [18] The River Triton was so-named by the visiting Argonauts. The region lies south of the fertile plains where the Phoenicians would later build the city of Carthage.

Myrina and her army of female warriors embarked on a series of conquests. First she turned west, making war upon and then allying with the *Atlantians*, a civilized people occupying lands as far west as the Atlantic Ocean. Myrina then attacked another Libyan tribe of women-warriors called *Gorgons*, whom she all but exterminated. However, we need not dwell further on the Amazon conquests in the west.

Myrina then turned her attention east. Passing through Egypt as previously described and subjugating the coast of the Levant, she then continued round the sweep of the eastern Mediterranean coast into Anatolia, through Cilicia, and on via Phrygia to the Aegean coast and its many islands. This conquest seems finally to have satisfied Myrina, who set a boundary at the Caicus River – the Bakırçay river in modern Turkey. However, she also seized the nearby island of Lesbos where she is said to have founded the city of Mytilene named after a sister who accompanied her on the campaign. The only other island mentioned is Samothrace, and it was on the nearby mainland that the Amazons were defeated by the Thracians and Queen Myrina was slain. The fighting, we are told, dragged-on for years, but ultimately, the surviving Amazons withdrew to Libya. However there is no mention of what happened to Myrina's earlier conquests. The impression left is of a brief campaign of empire-building, not unlike that of Alexander the Great in its duration and effect. Although Diodorus does not stress any ships, we can safely infer that *Myrina had a navy!* She seems to have been only interested in controlling the coastline of the eastern Mediterranean and was reluctant to venture too far inland.

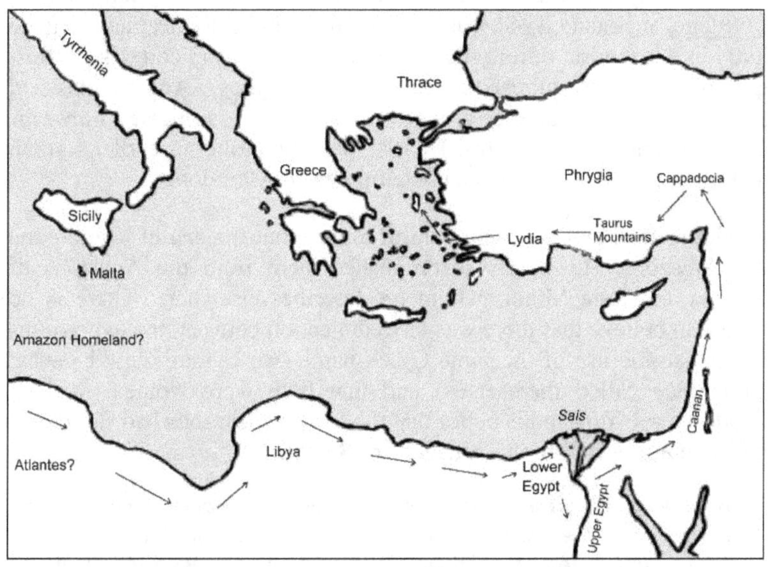

The Campaigns of Queen Myrina according to Diodorus Siculus

*We do not gain from Diodorus any idea of the ancient boundaries nor a precise era. It is clear that he considered the story to be very old; it is discussed along with other mythology that he attempts to place in a historical framework. The boundaries of the Amazon kingdom mention nothing between their homeland and Egypt. The Nile delta is not mentioned and everything east of it comprised simply 'Arabia'. *see Note 2*

Diodorus gives us some information as to the composition of Myrina's army. He says there were thirty thousand warriors of which only three thousand were cavalry. Translator Oldfather, for the Loeb editions, remarks that this is a very small number of cavalry – but that would matter little if the enemy had fewer or no cavalry at all. [19] Now we need not take this description too literally, as it may be contaminated with attributes of the later Amazons as will be discussed below. Egyptologists concur that horses and chariots were not known in Egypt and North Africa before the Second Intermediate Period (about 1700-1550 BC). The firing of arrows from horseback by the Scythian Amazons is often discussed along with the scorching of their breasts at birth, so that they should not hinder the archers in battle. It is important not to transfer this later imagery to the Libyan Amazons.

The ultimate source for the Libyan Amazons story is not Egyptian. Diodorus Siculus (himself an author much denigrated by classicists) is summarising an earlier mythographer or historian Dionysius of Mytilene, nicknamed 'Skytobrachion' from his false leather arm; he lived in Alexandria during the second century BC and composed a lost mythological encyclopaedia called the Kyklos. Again, classical scholars are disparaging of Dionysius and criticise him for romanticising ancient myths. He was perhaps citing an earlier Lydian historian: Xanthus who was a contemporary of Herodotus.

Diodorus does give us some helpful hints about the *era* of Myrina and her Amazons. He clearly distinguishes them from the Amazons of Scythia and Asia Minor, whom he describes elsewhere. There is no reason to believe that there was any connection between the two groups other than the use of the same Greek name (we cannot know by what name they called themselves) and that both were women-warriors. Diodorus was firm in his belief that the Libyan Amazons had flourished many centuries before the Amazons of Scythia.

> *But the truth is ... the Amazons of Libya were much earlier in point of time ... for since the race of these Amazons disappeared entirely many generations before the Trojan War, whereas the women about the Thermodon river were in their full vigour...* [*Histories III, 52, 1-3*]

However, this clear distinction has not prevented commentators on the subject of the Amazons from simply amalgamating all the references as if they applied to both groups. The statement: "many generations before the Trojan War" must push back the era of the Libyan Amazons into the third millennium BC; and there are good reasons for placing it even earlier.

The sources of Dionysius 'Skytobrachion' are themselves obscure. The fact that the story of Myrina occurs nowhere else tells us that his original sources were not Greek. The histories available to Dionysius in the Great Library of Alexandria were surely lost in the fires and earthquakes that destroyed the library in Roman times. The ultimate source was most likely Libyan or Egyptian; a historian working in Alexandria would need to be familiar with documents in many languages. North African history was most likely preserved in Carthage; itself burned and suppressed utterly by the Romans; and such history as remained was further silenced by later religious conversion.

We should also not rule out that Dionysius, who came from Mytilene, was evoking the history of his own region, relying upon local sources that recalled the ancient conquest by Queen Myrina. This would explain why there is so little detail of the Egyptian connection. In the earliest times the people of these Aegean coasts and islands were not Greeks, but a variety of non-Greek cultures: Lycians, Lydians, Luwians, Carians and others, all lying within the Cretan zone of influence – and of whose origins little is certain. Again we come up against the prejudice towards Dionysius by classical scholars, who see only fictional tales that fail to fit with more respected sources. So-much of ancient history may have been preserved in a more coherent form in these lost sources than in the jumbled-nonsense that is classical mythology. We should be prepared to trust that the best ancient historians knew the difference.

It is not quite true to say that Dionysius was our only source for these myths – Diodorus speaks of many poets and historians. The conflation of the Libyan Amazons with the later Amazons – which Diodorus attempted to correct – is not a modern error. It is also evident in the discussion of the Aegean coast given by the Roman geographer Strabo in deriving the names of various cities named after Myrina and her generals. He sets out to describe the campaign of the Amazons who fought in the Trojan war:

> *...and the naming of ancient cities after the Amazons attests this fact. And in the Trojan Plain there is a hill, which by men is called 'Batieia,' but by the immortals 'the tomb of the much-bounding Myrina', who, historians say, was one of the Amazons...* [*Strabo 12. 8. 5-8*]

Strabo goes on to derive the name *Myrina* from the speed that she drove her chariot; the mound, somewhere near Troy, is mentioned by Homer [*Iliad. 2.813*] as present in the time of the Trojan war. Overall, it becomes difficult to distinguish whether the later Amazons who dwelt around the Thermodon River should be equated with those of Scythia, or with the earlier incursion of Myrina. The founding of cites implies leaving behind colonies and evidently a longer occupation than the rapid campaign described by Diodorus; one at least as enduring as that of Alexander. The fact that some Anatolian tribes such as the Lycians and Carians practiced matrilinear or even matriarchal customs adds further coincidence. [*Herodotus I, 172-4*]. However, I shall not pursue this thread further.

The Real Amazons of Libya

From Herodotus we have a glimpse of the Libyan tribes during the mid-first-millennium BC: their customs, their religion and struggles with the ever-advancing desert. He offers us a summary of the ancient way of life that is free of any direct association with the Amazons. After describing the nomadic Libyans and the tribes closest to Egypt, Herodotus details the settled tribes living further west: the *Machlyes* and *Auses*. Further west still, as far as the Atlantic, he describes *Atlantes* and *Atarantes*, together with the nomadic *Garamantes* living further into the desert. Now to what degree these tribes may be equated to those described by Diodorus is another detour we need not pursue.

> *...along the coast are the Machlyes... Their country reaches to a great river called Triton, which issues into the great Tritonian lake, wherein is an island called Phla...* [*Herodotus, VI, 178*]

> *Next to these Machlyes are the Ausees; these and the Machlyes, divided by the Triton, dwell on the shores of the Tritonian lake...They make a yearly festival to Athene, whereat their maidens are parted into two bands and fight each other with stones and staves, thus (as they say) honouring after their people's manner that native goddess whom we call Athene. Maidens that die of their wounds are called false virgins. Before the girls are set fighting, the whole people choose ever the fairest maiden, and equip her with a Corinthian helmet and Greek panoply, to be then mounted on a chariot and drawn all along the lake shore...As for Athene, they say that she was daughter of Poseidon and the Tritonian lake, and that, being for some cause wroth with her father, she gave herself to Zeus, who made her his own daughter. Such is their tale. The intercourse of men and women there is promiscuous...When a woman's child is well grown, within three months thereafter the men assemble, and the child is adjudged to be that man's to whom it is most like.* [*Herodotus IV, 180*] [from the translation by A. D. Godley]

The island of Phla may be recognised as Djerba off the Tunisian coast: the island of the Lotus Eaters [*Polybius 1:39*]. The reference to *Athene* would imply the same goddess as Egyptian *Neith*. Herodotus comments disparagingly on the lack of formal marriages among the Libyan tribes. It may be that he simply did not understand their customs of matrilinear inheritance; his crude summary gives us a more realistic view of how the Libyan Amazon society may have functioned in an earlier time; a perspective that is free of contamination by the Greek myths of Amazons in Asia.

Rather than the usual view of the horse-mounted Amazons of the Bronze Age, we may see, for example from the motifs on the Narmer

Palette, that the weapons of war were much simpler in the pre-metal age. Egyptians fought with heavy stone maces (as seen in the smiting pose) together with long thrusting spears, slingshots and the bow-and-arrow. With such weaponry, and without the close individual combat that only evolved later along with bronze swords, we may see that women could more easily hold their own against stronger but similarly equipped male warriors – so long as they retained superiority of numbers and kept their enemy at a distance. Diodorus describes the later Libyans as fighting only with "three spears and stones in leather bags". [*Histories III.49*]

The account of Herodotus provides a further clue to the era when the Libyan Amazons flourished. The annual fighting-ritual between the girls of the Machlyes and Auses was likely a relic from the stone-age warfare of the Libyan tribes. It is another 'fossil' within the myths, coming from two independent sources, which suggests that the memory of the women-warriors of Libya is authentic. However, it should be apparent that any nation that routinely sends its young women off to perish in battle cannot endure through many generations, due to the lack or delay of child births to replenish the population. This cannot be a description of the long-term organisation of such a society, which would soon be numerically overwhelmed by its neighbours.

We may ponder how such a radical social structure could come into being? Matriarchy operates among hunter-gatherers, where the women are left to run the village along with the children and elders, while the young males are hunting or clashing with neighbouring tribes for limited resources. It would make sense for the girls to be armed and trained to defend themselves and their encampment. A small step from this allows us to see how a powerful queen might arise and hold onto political power with the acquiescence of the males; especially if boys were preferentially selected for infant sacrifice.

It is now generally accepted that the later Carthaginians performed child sacrifices at religious sites known as *tophets*. Although usually considered as a practice that came with the Phoenician colony, child sacrifice may also be seen as a ritual that began earlier among the native African inhabitants. [20] The onset of harsh desert conditions during the mid-Holocene gives a better explanation why the rulers of a state and its people might acquiesce in such a custom in conditions of famine. In Egyptian texts we similarly hear of the people eating their children in extreme circumstances. It is unreasonable to judge ancient people by modern standards, for sacrificing children to pitiless deities whom they believed would take them anyway, by hunger and disease.

A matriarchal system therefore confers long-term benefits when resources are limited, such as for an island society or perhaps for hunter-gatherers living around a desert oasis, where overpopulation could lead to total collapse and extinction. The delaying of childbirth then displays foresight. If the society has no customs of 'marriage' and interactions are restricted then the father of offspring would be uncertain. Therefore, the rules of inheritance can only operate through the female line. We may thus view the Libyan Amazons as a short-term aberration; an extreme evolution of a matriarchal society.

The spread of agriculture from the east during the Neolithic is another factor influencing population. Along with the planting of fields of corn comes an abundance of food allowing population growth, leading to more farming and taking of yet more land. The boys are now needed for the heavy work of clearing trees and planting fields. In such circumstances the hunter-gatherers were numerically overwhelmed. For a parallel we may look to how tribal cultures were so easily colonised by more recent European expansion.

Neit-Athene

A final clue that links the Libyan Amazons with Protodynastic Egypt is the religion of the war-goddess Neit-Athene. Typically, Neith would be depicted wearing the red crown of Lower Egypt, as on the Narmer palette, and with the crossed bow and arrow. In later imagery she became virtually indistinguishable from Isis and Hathor, but in the First Dynasty the crossed-arrows were used as her symbol in the serekh of queens. As discussed above in connection with the Abydos label, her temple at Saïs existed at least as early as the First Dynasty. Saïs briefly became the capital of Egypt when it enjoyed its final flourish of freedom from foreign rule under the twenty-sixth or 'Saite' dynasty (664–525 BC). The temple was visited by Solon around 590 BC but was sacked and then restored under Persian rule, before it was described by Herodotus. Sadly, very little survives on the ground to be excavated.

There seems little reason to doubt that Neith was the same deity as the Libyan goddess whom Herodotus equates with Athene; and likely the same deity as _Tanit_ who would become the principal goddess in later Carthage. [21] To Egyptians her very name suggested: "the land of Nit"? However, while it may be possible to associate matriarchy and priestesses with this goddess, it is less attested that any form of child sacrifice was associated with Egyptian Neith; and we know from Plato that the temple of Neith had male priests during the Saite Dynasty. [*Timaeus, 21-2*]

According to Plato, the priests of Saïs considered Neith to be their founding goddess. We may therefore conclude that Lower Egypt west of the Nile was strongly Libyan in outlook and customs at the time of the unification, when Horus Aha either constructed the temple, or perhaps restored and extended it. The significance of the temple to the queens of the First Dynasty cannot be doubted as may be seen from their serekh. Egyptologists find the names of the forgotten queens: *Neithhotep,* 'Neith is satisfied' and *Merneith,* 'Beloved of Neith'. However, the status of Neith seems to have declined after the Second Dynasty. The temple would only regain its pre-eminent status when the traditions of the early dynastic and the pyramid age were revived during the twenty-sixth Dynasty.

Egypt within the Mid-Holocene World

It may be informative to place the Protodynastic period of Egypt in its wider context and explore what was happening in other parts of the world at this remote era: five-thousand years ago (3200-3000 BC). For European archaeologists this marks the transition between the mid to late stone-age: the Neolithic. No history survives for the kings and queens who built the temples of Malta or the dolmens of Atlantic Europe at the close of the fourth millennium BC. For geologists and climate scientists this was the mid-Holocene climatic optimum; it takes us halfway back to the end of the ice age. The mid-Holocene was a time of climate transition in Europe and America, from warm and equable conditions to the cooler and wetter regime of today. In North Africa the savannah of the green Sahara, which had endured since the Pleistocene, began its rapid decline into the dry desert of today. This was also a time of worldwide sea-level changes, when Herodotus tells us that the Nile delta was not yet fully formed. Only from Egypt may we find written history and dynasties of named kings from this ancient time, imperfect though it may be.

Megalithic monuments, comparable to those of Atlantic Europe are also found along the North African coast. These sites were somewhat overlooked by European archaeologists in their syntheses on the megaliths of western Europe. A study by Iona Muscat in 2012 highlighted the neglected archaeology of the Maghreb region and how, for so long, it suffered from the academic bias toward Graeco-Roman classicism and Egyptology; pointing out that it comprised only 2.35% of articles in publication. [22] She summarises the work of Gabriel

Camps between 1960 and the 1980s, but at that time there were not enough radiocarbon dates to influence mainstream opinion; more recent studies have followed his hypothesis, but overall she prefers to see a local evolution among native North African peoples. However, this need not rule-out seaborne trading influence along the coast and elite-colonisation from across the Mediterranean. [23]

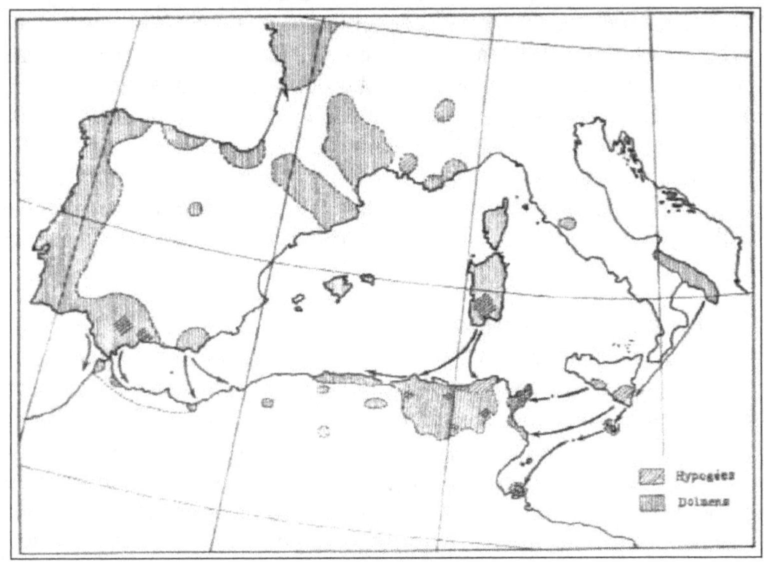

In a pioneering series of studies, Gabriel Camps sought to link the megalithic monuments of North Africa with those of southern Europe.

Camps highlighted that the Tunisian pottery and dolmens showed greatest similarity to those of Italy, Sicily and Malta. He proposed a new chronology based on carbon-14 dates, to replace the earlier pottery-based diffusion theories that held-back archaeology in the 1960s. [24]

[Source: G. Camps 1961: 151, fig. 45 as cited by Iona Muscat on p 348]

A more recent synthesis by João Zilhão would date the advent of farming into North African to earlier than 7000 cal BP. [25] He follows the trail of Pantellerian obsidian tools and would suggest that this culture arrived in phases from southern Europe via the shortest sea crossings: into Tunisia via Italy-Sicily-Malta and another via the Strait of Gibraltar. The civilization on Malta with its megalithic temples and underground hypogea dates from 3600 to 3200 BC. They demonstrate a more highly evolved civilisation than is evident in predynastic Egypt at that period. During the fourth millennium BC the western Mediterranean was at the apex of North African civilisation, rather than the Nile valley.

The late fourth millennia and early third millennia BC are also the era when modern DNA science highlights a population collapse-and-replacement in the west of Europe, with great migrations from east to west; [26] [27] together with the expansion of 'beaker people' from the Steppes into western Europe. [28] These followed an earlier migration of farmers from Anatolia a millennium before. In the Mesopotamian king lists this coincides with the time of the *Great Flood*; and Manetho (Africanus epitome) concluded that Menes was the first Egyptian king after the Flood. As far away as China we find the earliest evidence of farmers occupying the low-lying coastal plains and the beginning of the migrations by Polynesians from southern China into the Pacific. In India and Central America the years around 3100 BC were chosen as the year-zero of their calendars – an extraordinary coincidence that these should match so closely with the First Dynasty of Egypt? It may be seen that this was an era of synchronous remarkable events world-wide; the beginnings of recorded history before which everything dissolves into myth and legend.

In western Europe, the fourth millennium BC was the period when we find the building of the dolmens and portal tombs from Iberia to Denmark. In Ireland and Britain from around 3150 BC the astronomically aligned monuments such as Newgrange and Maes Howe are contemporary with Protodynastic Egypt; and the Orkney village of Skara Brae similarly dates from this time. From Ireland, we have named kings and legends of how they built the monuments, which should rightly be considered history every bit as authentic as from Egypt – except that they survive via dateable oral history rather than artefacts from the ground.

Why is the identification of events around 3200-3000 BC so important? The ancient historians give us two pegs on which to hang the events of myth and legend. One is the date of the Trojan War – still uncertain; the other peg is the king list of Egypt back to Menes, as recorded in their temples. If we could only tie some of these legends and myths to the archaeological record then we would be a long way towards knowing where to seek the hard evidence to verify them. For the history of Myrina and her Amazons we have a starting point of the Neolithic sites around the Tunisian chotts; and we have the place to look for her tomb – a mound opposite the gates of Troy. According to Diodorus Siculus, the Libyan Amazons were finally vanquished by (the second) Heracles on his way west to the Pillars that were named after him; so we may surmise that his era must be *later* than the Libyan Amazons. [*Histories III, 54, 55*] This would coincide well with the human migrations that DNA research is only now revealing.

The early dynastic period of Egypt potentially informs us about many other events that are only 'legendary' or 'mythical' in other regions. Incidental information about geography, climate and sea levels may be preserved within these stories. There is no longer any excuse for dismissing myths and legends as if they were the fiction of our 'primitive' ancestors. Myths and legends comprise garbled and muddled history. Even ancient fiction cannot exist in a vacuum; fossil details within it can tell us about the time and place of its setting. We should be more willing to trust the competence of ancient historians, such as Diodorus Siculus, Dionysius and Xanthus (who were closer to the events than us) to know the difference between jumbled history and fiction; they could consult older lost historical sources that were preserved by an even earlier generation of capable historians.

The picture now emerging from the archaeology and DNA would coincide well with the narrative that we that we are given by the ancient historians. If Diodorus had told us about a *king* Narmer rather than a *queen* Myrina; and of a *male* rather than a *female* army, would his semi-historical account be dismissed quite so readily? Archaeologists always disparage myths and legends unless they confirm their own theories; and the classicists have always taken little note of archaeology, preferring to discuss ancient authors as citing the 'ideas' of earlier writers. If the histories of Diodorus, Dionysius and others are to be regarded as invented fiction then we should ask how these ancient authors knew that their stories would correspond so well with the archaeologists' findings, two thousand years later?

Comparison Table – Narmer v Myrina

Narmer	***Myrina***
Horus name: Meri-nar	*Not applicable*
The father of Horus Aha?	*Alliance with a king: 'Horus son of Isis'*
Numerous Serekh found in the Levant	*Conquered Sinai, Canaan and Syria*
Unproven simple grave at Abydos (Umm el-Qa'ab tomb B17/B18)	*Not buried in Egypt*
Contemporary with the founding of Neit's temple at Saïs (c.3200-3100 BC)	*Neit-Athene was originally a Libyan goddess*

Conclusions

Once we look beyond the specialist opinions that have accumulated around the unification of ancient Egypt (some of which have stood for over a hundred years) then it is possible to propose an alternative interpretation, based on a cross-disciplinary pattern of historical clues and coincidences.

Matriarchal cultures prevailed in the Mediterranean region and Africa before the expansion of the Indo-European tribes from Anatolia and the Steppes. Populations were much smaller in the pre-farming era. This migration of farming cultures, which begun before 6000 BC, is supported by recent DNA studies and ultimately reached the coasts of the Maghreb. The principal reason why this picture was hidden for so long is that it suffered from a pre-radiocarbon archaeology based on out-of-Egypt 'diffusion' theories, some of which continue to be cited; together with the lack of excavations from further west.

We should also take a cautious view of the regional geography. During the Egyptian Protodynastic (3200-3100 BC) the Nile delta was not as we find it today; rather, as Herodotus records, the delta was then a shallow estuary, with only a few low islands showing above water on the raised 'koms' of the modern delta. The western desert retained many habitable oases and in patches, the grassy savannah of the green Sahara still survived. It is likely that the western delta and a few islands was all that then comprised 'lower' Egypt and it was culturally a part of Libya. This might explain why the Egyptologists find scant evidence of the kings of Lower Egypt, with whom Upper Egypt supposedly became unified under Menes; they did not exist!

The hypothesis proposed here is that the figure depicted on the 'Narmer' palette is not *King* Narmer, rather, it is *Queen* Meri-nar: the Queen *Myrina* of Diodorus. Originating from Sicily, the Libyan Amazons first colonised the coast of modern Tunisia and expanded as far west as the Atlantic Ocean, before Myrina turned her attention east. Rather than engage in open war with a strong Upper Egyptian kingdom, she favoured an alliance. One presumes that the king of Upper Egypt, Horus Aha, also gained something. He is the Horus-king shown on the other side of the palette and whose expedition into 'Arabia' in alliance with Myrina was recalled in the story of Menes and the legend of Scorpion; the Libyan queen herself being written-out of later history. This alliance is the ceremonial scene that is recorded on the so-called Narmer palette, to commemorate the foreign expedition of Horus Aha. He perhaps also gained a wife: *Neithhotep*, who may have been a close relative of Queen Myrina (and upon whose death became the rightful matriarchal queen of Lower Egypt and of Libya west of the Nile). Myrina however, had continued-on to conquer Canaan, Syria and beyond, as described by Diodorus. Later pharaohs could not tolerate the notion of a Libyan queen as the unifier of Egypt!

We know that Queen Myrina was not buried in Egypt but was killed when her Aegean conquests failed and the defeated Amazon survivors returned to Libya. One may suggest that Horus Aha then assumed control of both Egyptian kingdoms and of the conquered Levant; and that this marks the true unification of upper and lower Egypt. It would explain the presence of Egyptian serekh in the Levant, to assert authority over the region conquered by Myrina. However the Libyan Amazons' grip on the Mediterranean coast initially remained strong. To maintain unity throughout the First Dynasty, the male heir of Upper Egypt would marry the female heir of Lower Egypt (who would be a sister or cousin). From the Second Dynasty onwards, the alliance may have become merely symbolic since we find Manetho referring to the Libyans as "subjects". This may also explain why we find evidence of other ruling-queens during the First Dynasty, who are dropped from later king lists. Myrina too, was written out of Egyptian history but remembered elsewhere. The increasing desertification of North Africa would lead to the decline of Libya and the concentration of civilisation in the Nile valley.

It may be that the true history of early dynastic Egypt has been hiding in plain sight all the time, in the pages of the much-maligned Diodorus Siculus.

Notes and References

Note 1: As an example one need only read the summaries in the *Cambridge Ancient History* and some of the internet links offered herein to demonstrate how the opinions of eminent Egyptologists over the years have taken-on the status of proven fact. [15]

Note 2: This map is figure 1.2 on page 10 of *Towers of Atlantis* which further expands on the Libyan Atlantians of Diodorus.

Relevant hyperlinks

https://smarthistory.org/palette-of-king-narmer/

https://resources.saylor.org/wwwresources/archived/site/wp-content/uploads/2011/09/The-Narmer-Palette_1.pdf

http://www.ancient-egypt.org/history/early-dynastic-period/1st-dynasty/horus-narmer/narmer-artefacts/narmer-palette.html
http://egypt-grammar.rutgers.edu/Artifacts/Narmer%20Palette.pdf
https://www.livius.org/articles/concept/serekh/
https://www.ucl.ac.uk/museums-static/digitalegypt/ideology/kingname/horus.html
https://ancientegyptonline.co.uk/narmermacehead/
https://joyofmuseums.com/museums/united-kingdom-museums/ashmolean/narmer-macehead/
http://www.francescoraffaele.com/egypt/hesyra/labels/xxnarmer1.htm
https://ia800103.us.archive.org/0/items/Manetho/Manetho.pdf
http://www.ancient-egypt.org/history/early-dynastic-period/1st-dynasty/horus-aha/biography-of-horus-aha.html
http://www.ancient-egypt.org/monuments/abydos-sacred-centre-of/umm-el-qaab/index.html
https://www.ucl.ac.uk/museums-static/digitalegypt/abydos/abydoskingstombs.html
http://www.touregypt.net/featurestories/firstdynastysaqqara.htm
https://www.donsmaps.com/egypt2.html
https://www.worldhistory.org/Neith/
https://www.penn.museum/collections/object/122418
http://xoomer.virgilio.it/francescoraf/hesyra/merneith.html
http://www.ancient-egypt.org/history/early-dynastic-period/1st-dynasty/horus-narmer/narmer-artefacts/scorpion-macehead.html
https://ancientegyptonline.co.uk/scorpion/
https://www.businessinsider.com/scorpion-king-real-heres-what-this-explorer-found-tomb-rock-2017-6?r=US&IR=T
http://www.francescoraffaele.com/egypt/hesyra/dynasty0.htm
https://penelope.uchicago.edu/Thayer/E/Roman/Texts/Diodorus_Siculus/3D*.html
https://www.atlasobscura.com/places/chott-el-djerid
https://www.lesvos.com/history.html
http://www.perseus.tufts.edu/hopper/text?doc=Perseus:text:1999.04.0104:entry=dionysius-bio-38&highlight=scytobrachion
https://penelope.uchicago.edu/Thayer/E/Roman/Texts/Diodorus_Siculus/Vol2_Introduction*.html
http://www.perseus.tufts.edu/hopper/text?doc=Perseus%3Atext%3A1999.01.0126%3Abook%3D4%3Achapter%3D168
https://oxfordre.com/classics/view/10.1093/acrefore/9780199381135.001.0001/acrefore-9780199381135-e-6905
https://medomed.org/featured_item/djerba-island-cultural-landscape-tunisia/
https://www.ox.ac.uk/news/2014-01-23-ancient-carthaginians-really-

did-sacrifice-their-children
https://tannit-neith.firebaseapp.com/
http://www.ancient-egypt.org/history/early-dynastic-period/1st-dynasty/horus-den/biography-of-horus-den.html
http://www.ancient-egypt.org/history/early-dynastic-period/1st-dynasty/horus-qaa/biography-of-horus-qaa.html
https://www.jstor.org/stable/27925431
http://www.ancient-egypt.org/history/early-dynastic-period/1st-dynasty/horus-narmer/titulary-of-horus-narmer.html
https://www.ancientscribbles.com/2021/01/ruins-of-sais-and-temple-where-to-be-found.html
https://www.arabworldbooks.com/en/e-zine/the-sed-festival-heb-sed-renewal-of-the-kings-reign
http://www.hierakonpolis-online.org/index.php/history-of-exploration
http://www.etana.org/sites/default/files/coretexts/15249.pdf

References

1) Quibell, J.E. (1900). *Hierakonpolis*, Parts 1 & 2, Bernard Quaritch, London
2) Bolkashov, A.O. (1999) Royal Portraiture and Horus Name, in Ziegler, Christiane, ed. *L'art de L'Ancienne Empire, Egyptienne*, Paris: Musee du Louvre, pp 311-332 http://giza.fas.harvard.edu/pubdocs/948/full/
3) Dreyer, G. 2007 citing Kaplony 1963; see reference 10 below
4) Petrie, W.F. (1939) *The Making of Egypt*, Sheldon, London (see pages 78-79) https://archive.org/details/Petrie1939/mode/2up
5) Hoffman, Michael (1980) *Egypt before the Pharaohs*, Routledge, London, ISBN:0-7448-0020-X (*see page 322-3 citing Walter Emery (1961) p 47.*
6) Dreyer, G. 2007 see reference 10 below, final paragraph and his note 10
7) Wilson, Penelope (2006) Prehistoric Settlement in the Western Delta: A Regional and Local view from Sais (Sa El-Hagar), *Journal of Egyptian Archaeology*, Volume: 92, 1, pp 75-126, https://doi.org/10.1177/030751330609200102
8) Dreyer, see section 3 "Princes Seal" in reference 10 below
9) Hsu, Shih-Wei (2010) The Palermo Stone: the Earliest Royal Inscription from Ancient Egypt, *Altoriental Forsch.*, Akademie Verlag, 37, 1, 68–89
10) Dreyer, G. (2007), "Wer war Menes?", in Hawass, Z.A.; Richards, J. (eds.), *The archaeology and art of Ancient Egypt, Essays in honor of David B. O'Connor*, CASAE, 34, Cairo
11) "Predynastic Period." In *The Oxford Encyclopedia of Ancient Egypt*. Ed. Krzysztof M. Ciałowicz
12) Andelkovic, Branislav (2012) Hegemony for Beginners: Egyptian Activity in the Southern Levant during the Second Half of the Fourth Millennium B.C, *Issues in Ethnology and Anthropology*, n. s. Vol. 7. Is. 3.

https://www.academia.edu/6409058
13) Görsdorf, J., Dreyer, G., & Hartung, U. (1997). New 14C Dating of the Archaic Royal Necropolis Umm El-Qaab at Abydos (Egypt). *Radiocarbon, 40*(2), 641-647. doi:10.1017/S0033822200018579
14) Gardiner, Alan. (1961) Egypt of the Pharaohs., Oxford University Press
15) Edwards, I. E. S. (1971). "The early dynastic period in Egypt" in *The Cambridge Ancient History*, Cambridge: Cambridge University Press
16) Oldfather, C.H. (translator) (1935) *Diodorus Siculus, Library of History*, Vol 2, Loeb Classical Library, London, ISBN: 0-674-99334-9
17) Butzer KW (1976) Early Hydraulic Civilization in Egypt: A Study in Cultural Ecology, Univ of Chicago Press, Chicago, ISBN 0-226-08634-8
18) Monaco, Andrea et al (2020). Megalithic Structures of the northern Sahara (Chott el Jérid, Tunisia). 10.13125/caster/4078.
19) Oldfather C.H.; Comment 4 on page 253 of reference 16 above.
20) Schwartz, J., Houghton, F., Bondioli, L., & Macchiarelli, R. (2017). Two tales of one city: Data, inference and Carthaginian infant sacrifice. *Antiquity, 91*(356), 442-454. doi:10.15184/aqy.2016.270
21) Harden, D. B. (1927). Punic Urns from the Precinct of Tanit at Carthage. *American Journal of Archaeology*, *31*(3), 297–310. https://doi.org/10.2307/497821
22) Muscat, Iona (2012) University of Malta Thesis: Megalithism and Monumentality in Prehistoric North Africa https://www.academia.edu/6584373/Megalithism_and_monumentality_in_prehistoric_North_Africa
23) Zilhão, J. (2014). Early prehistoric navigation in the Western Mediterranean: Implications for the Neolithic transition in Iberia and the Maghreb. Eurasian Prehistory in Island Archaeology and the Origins of Seafaring in the Eastern Mediterranean, 11(1-2) 185-200.
24) Camps 1982 and 1961 as cited in ref 22 above
25) Zilhao, J., 2001. Radiocarbon evidence for maritime pioneer colonization at the origins of farming in west Mediterranean Europe. Proceedings of the National Academy of Sciences 98, 14180e14185
26) Fregel, Rosa et al (2018) Ancient genomes from North Africa evidence prehistoric migrations to the Maghreb from both the Levant and Europe, Proceedings of the National Academy of Sciences, Jun 2018, 115 (26) 6774-6779; DOI: 0.1073/pnas.1800851115
27) Hofmanová et al (2016) Early farmers from across Europe directly descended from Neolithic Aegeans, *PNAS* June 21, 2016 vol. 113, no. 25, 6889
28) Haak, Wet al. (2015). Massive migration from the steppe was a source for Indo-European languages in Europe. Nature, 522(7555), 207–211. https://doi.org/10.1038/nature14317

Other References:

Amiran, Ruth. "An Egyptian Jar Fragment with the Name of Narmer from Arad." *Israel Exploration Journal*, vol. 24, no. 1, 1974, pp. 4–12. *JSTOR*, www.jstor.org/stable/27925431

Emery, W. (1961) *Archaic Egypt*, Penguin Books, Harmondsworth

Gardiner, Sir Alan (1961) *Egypt of the Pharaohs*, Oxford Univ. Press, Oxford

9

Troy or Amarna? The Oldest Recorded Solar Eclipse

Summary: *A 2012 study by Göran Henriksson raised the possibility that a solar eclipse was described in the Iliad of Homer. If so then it would be one of the earliest dateable eclipses and of value to astronomers and geophysicists to determine the stability of the Earth's rotation back to the second millennium BC; and thereby confirm circumstances of other ancient eclipses. In 2005-6 I published my own research on the subject of eclipses visible from Amarna, Egypt during the Eighteenth Dynasty and from Anatolia, to investigate whether there was a non-linear change (a wobble or nutation) of the Earth's rotation ongoing at that era, residual from an earlier astronomical event. The possibility of another dateable eclipse observation allows an opportunity to revisit those concepts; together with its potential value in tying early-historical and legendary events to the Julian calendar.*

To begin, it may help to summarise some of the consensus theories, ancient and modern, about the date of the Trojan War. It was used by the Greeks as an epoch from which they would establish the date of other historical and legendary events both before and after the war. The date for the foundation of Rome also depends on it; and even the migration of the legendary eponymous Brutus to Britain is referred back to the Trojan War! We may therefore see how important an identification of its true calendar date could be for historians and archaeologists. This uncertainty is not modern; Various classical historians tried to back-calculate dates for the Trojan War with results ranging between 1135 BC and 1334 BC. Earlier Greek history from the Mycenaean era was lost during the so called Late Bronze Age collapse around 1200 BC; it is rather as if we could only date modern events by years before or since the Napoleonic War. However, the debate about the date of the Trojan war is an old minefield upon which I shall trespass no further. The focus here lies rather in the potential identification of a *dateable eclipse report* to verify the stability of the Earth's rotation as far back as possible.

Homer's Trojan war is now regarded as at least partly historical, since Schliemann's identification of Troy with the mound at Hissarlik near the Dardanelles. We may discard the interventions of the Greek gods and their influence on the participants; but our difficulty lies in where we should draw the line between the fiction and the reality upon which the story is based. The date of Homer's composition of the Iliad also remains vague but is typically placed around 850 BC; and so we can be confident that it was based on oral tradition in circulation for at least 300 years.

Archaeologists identify nine levels of occupation at Hissarlik. The oldest hill fort (Troy I) dates from 3000 BC or perhaps earlier. The level usually associated with Homer's Troy is the late bronze age layer of Troy VI; this shows clear evidence of burning and warfare that archaeologists date to c.1250 BC. However, even should we accept this destruction as the most likely date, we still cannot rule-out that events and characters of earlier or later conflicts have been conflated and woven into a fictional recreation. Such is the fate of oral history once its true chronology is lost.

Henriksson draws our attention to a possible reference to an eclipse within Homer's description of the final battle of the Trojan war:

...and you would have said that the sun and moon were no longer fixed in the sky, since a fog covered over all that part of the battle where the leading men had made their stand...But the rest... fought in the ease of a bright sky, with the sunlight spreading clear and sharp and no cloud to be seen...but those in the centre were suffering cruelly in the fog and the fighting...

[Iliad, 17, Martin Hammond Translation] [1]

You must decide for yourself whether you think this could be a reference to a solar eclipse.

Henriksson therefore posits that a solar eclipse of 1312 BC took place during the final battle of Troy, which can then be tied to events in the Hittite archives. The Hittite chronology is in turn dateable (according to Henriksson's summation) via another eclipse that occurred in 1335 BC, the tenth year of King Mursili II. [3] Dating of the Hittite chronology is itself dependent upon links back to Egyptian chronology via the Amarna letters; these would make Mursili II a contemporary of Akhenaten, Tutankhamun and the late Amarna period. However, as one might expect, there are many opinions as to the correct identification and others would prefer that the 1312 BC eclipse was itself the one referred-to in the Hittite text [4] As a proposed date for the Trojan War this is somewhat earlier than the 1250 BC consensus of the archaeologists and the median of the historical dates.

Following Henriksson, Papamarinopoulos and co-researchers preferred to date the battle much later via a partial annular eclipse of 1218 BC June 6 based on other potential astronomical references in the Iliad and Odyssey. [2] They would demolish Henriksson's links to the Egyptian chronology via the Hittite archives as too tenuous and prefer their own interpretation of Homer's epics. However, I shall not pursue their (primarily linguistic) arguments in detail here.

The circumstances of historical eclipses are now much easier for historians to study than when Henriksson first considered the matter in 1985, or even for myself 2000-6, due to the availability of retro-calculation software and various websites. The circumstances of these two eclipses according to the NASA website (2022) are slightly different from those originally cited by Henriksson:

1312 BC June 24 2 mins 48 seconds, total over Anatolia, partial over Egypt (Cat No: 01634)

1335 BC Mar 13 6 mins 36 seconds, annular/partial over Egypt and over Anatolia (Cat No: 01579)

The date and magnitude of an ancient eclipse can be retro calculated with confidence, however where the shadow fell on the Earth's surface is less easy to determine. This depends upon tidal slowing of the diurnal rotation (TDT - UT = ΔT) due to the pull of the Moon on the Earth's equatorial bulge. The discrepancy (Delta-T) between clock and calendar due to this tidal slowing amounts to about half a day since 1500 BC. [5] The fall of the shadow can be estimated within an uncertainty that would shift the path slightly east or west of expectation.

However the present author, being a *catastrophist*, could not trust any retro calculated eclipse tracks prior to mid-first millennium BC due to the possibility that non-linear 'events' could have changed the rotation in ancient times. Before the most recent of such events it would become impossible to determine historical dates in the absence of a contemporary historical chronology dateable by some other means. Such events would include 'glitches' in the length of day, due to variations in the figure and balance of the planet, causing the shadow of an eclipse to fall east or west of the retro calculated path; in addition, nutations of the axis and pole-shifts could also cause a north-south variation. These would arise if the axis of rotation were wobbling slightly, triggered by internal changes to the shape of the Earth (i.e. instances of the Chandler wobble of a magnitude greater than are experienced today) or even external astronomical forces that might trigger the core wobble.

To summarise my own earlier work as published in Under Ancient Skies in 2005; [6] and in a follow-up article, one such reset may have occurred during the Greek Dark Age that followed the Trojan War; [7] this being one of a series of such events coincident with earlier dark ages and climate-events. Coincidence is one thing – proving them empirically is quite another.

In order to verify ΔT for a particular date some precise information is needed and ancient reports are seldom so helpful. For accuracy, the specific time of day and the start or end point of the shadow on the ground are needed, together with a precise location where it was observed. [8] Professor F. Richard Stephenson, perhaps the foremost authority on these subjects, found no report of an eclipse that he was prepared to trust prior to that seen at ancient Ugarit (Syrian coast). [9] Originally, he had suggested that this was the eclipse of 3 May 1375 BC, later revised to 1223 BC, but the circumstances of the Ugarit text are better reproduced by the eclipse of 9 May 1012 BC. [8] The key aspect of this particular report is that it occurred just before sunset – a very conspicuous omen – thus offering both a precise location and time of day to confirm the path of the Moon's shadow. ***Note 1**

Stephenson also rejected a divination from a Shang Chinese oracle bone dated at 1302 BC because it appeared (inexplicably) to be a whole day out from the Chinese sexagenary cycle. [9] However, astronomers constantly update their calculations and this can be embarrassing for historical researchers who cite them! The NASA webpage no longer confidently suggests values for ΔT prior to 500 BC in the abbreviated table. [10] I should also mention at this point that Henriksson, in his 2012 paper, disputes some of the methods used by Stephenson to determine the path of ancient eclipses, declaring them: "completely useless for epochs before 700 BC". The earliest eclipse report currently suggested by historians would be that of 5 March 1223 BC. [11] However, for the reasons given herein, I would still prefer the 1012 BC eclipse as the earliest observation that can be reproduced.

The ancient historians, In their various opinions of the date for the final battle at Troy, cannot even agree upon the year or season of the year that it occurred, let alone give a precise time of day. At best it gives us a window of about six to eight hours of daylight. Set this alongside the vague location of the final battle and we may see that the circumstances of the 'Troy eclipse' would not provide the precise information needed by astronomers. Here and in the 2006 paper, I am attempting not so much to identify a historical report via retro-calculation, rather to find *an independently dateable event* that cannot be reproduced by uniformitarian retro-calculation methods alone.

In 2005 in *Under Ancient Skies* I proposed that the Atenist heresy of pharaoh Akhenaten was inspired by a statistically rare sequence of eclipses across Egypt during the Eighteenth Dynasty. [12] In parallel around the same time William McMurray independently published theories regarding the Amarna eclipses. [13] In a more recent paper Emil Khalisi [14] preferred to model earlier eclipses. As with Henriksson, these researchers follow *uniformitarian* assumptions that tidal slowing can be retro calculated indefinitely to estimate the eclipse paths.

My own proposal in 2005-6 was that the construction of Amarna by Akhenaten was inspired by the observation of a *dawn eclipse* from the site of the Aten temple on 30 December 1332 BC, which would fix year 5 of Akhenaten's reign according to inscriptions on one of the boundary stelae. The eclipse would have been observed from the Amarna temple site as the sun rose in in a cleft in the eastern mountains known as the Royal Wadi. [15] Such an identification (an eclipse occurring at dawn) would be of value not just for historical chronology but could fix both the location and time-of-day to a precision that would be more useful for astronomers. In 2005-6 I experimented with various values for ΔT to find one that would allow the start of the eclipse shadow to fall at Amarna; for this to be valid would require a non-linear step-change to ΔT of about 1500 seconds over a period of 300 years, since the 1012 BC observation. Such a change to the rate of rotation and the inevitable wobble that must follow it would have occurred during the Greek Dark Age (the Egyptian Third Intermediate Period) and therefore shortly *after* the Trojan War. It should also be coincident with other evidence of *climate and sea-level changes worldwide* consequent upon the wobble of the axis.

The 'evil reports' that inspired Akhenaten to build his new city were recorded on the boundary stelae. These give dates to the precise day within the king's reign – but unfortunately this does not help without a true calendar date for his accession.

The king declared that he would build the city in the place *chosen by the Aten himself* and that once established there he would never again leave its boundaries. In a proclamation of *year 8* of his reign, the king records that he came to Amarna in his *year 5* to formally celebrate the foundation of the city. The fragmented inscription was summarised by Egyptologist Cyril Aldred, citing the Amarna Boundary Stelae Project:

> *...as Father Aten lived, something had been said which was more evil than that which the king had heard in his Year 4...more evil than what he had heard in his year 1...more evil than what King (Amenhotep III?) had heard...more evil than what king Tuthmosis IV had heard...* [16]

To reappraise my own conclusions of 2005-6 the identification of the 'evil omens' as eclipses were based on an experimental ΔT *very loosely set at 33000 seconds* rather than the *31593 seconds* used for the 'standard' retro calculation of the 1332 BC eclipse. This would allow the dawn eclipse to commence at Amarna, giving the following evaluation:

- The evil of year 5 was a report of the 1332 BC 'dawn' eclipse
- The evil of year 4 was a report of the 1335 BC eclipse
- The evil of year 1 was a report of the 1338 BC eclipse
- The evil seen by Amenhotep III was the 1352 BC eclipse
- The evil seen by Tuthmosis IV was the 1375 BC eclipse (viewed from Syria)

Note that these are dates when the king received *reports* of the phenomena, rather than their true date of occurrence. It is not essential that the king actually saw the eclipses himself, but he may have experienced at least one of them, or their partial shadow as they crossed the Nile.

The author's crude drawing of a dawn eclipse as viewed from the temple at Tel-el-Amarna (click the photo for a link)

It seems likely that the annular eclipse of 1335 BC would also have been reported to Akhenaten and could also have been one of the evil omens – yet another ambiguity to add to the problem of pinning-down the precise dates for the reigns. Other possible reconstructions might perhaps prefer that the eclipse observed from the city of Akhetaten (Amarna) was one of the other dates: 1335 BC or 1338 BC – *but only the 1332 BC eclipse could correspond as the last-of-three reports in the king's proclamation.* So why should this third report be considered more evil than the others?

Some astronomical uncertainty must remain; the 1332 BC eclipse may have begun *just before* or *just after* dawn; the track would not have fallen precisely at the Amarna alignment at mid-winter, but to the south of it; or perhaps only a large partial eclipse was observed from the city itself? *Nevertheless the spectacle must have been sufficiently inspiring that Akhenaten took it to indicate that Aten wished him to build his new capital precisely at that place, which he called 'Akhetaten': "horizon of the Aten"*. The 'evils', as surviving on the boundary stelae, cannot be positively associated with eclipses. [17] We might wish for a more precise hieroglyph that Egyptologists would recognise as an eclipse rather than as a general reference to the sun-god. Unfortunately, the historical record is seldom so helpful. When Horemheb demolished the city to obliterate all memory of the Aten, he had the 'omens' on the stelae chiselled-out, so that we can no longer determine what Akhenaten actually saw.

When considering Egyptian king-lists, not only must we be sceptical of the precise start and end dates of the reigns, but also of their lengths, since overlapping co-reigns and regencies must complicate such estimates. In addition to the short reign of Smenkhkare (Nefertiti?) between Akhenaten and Tutankhamen, there was a co-regency of uncertain duration at the start of his reign, between Amenhotep IV/Akhenaten and his father Amenhotep III.

If 1332 BC were indeed year 5 of Akhenaten then it would refine the Egyptian chronology just 15 or 16 years *later* than current consensus, with knock-on effects for any other floating chronology that depends on it. Year 1 of Akhenaten would therefore fall *somewhere around* 1335 BC or 1336 BC. There is no point in trying to be more precise when there are so many uncertainties in the Egyptology as to the duration of the co-regnum with his father.

The current consensus historical dates for the Eighteenth Dynasty would place Akhenaten between 1352 BC and 1334 BC and for Tutankhamun between 1332 BC and 1323 BC. Between these reigns was a short reign of Smenkhkare or Nefertiti, about which Egyptologists hold disputed theories. Radiocarbon dates cannot help to pinpoint the dates either, as there remains a statistical uncertainty for all radiocarbon dates in the order of 100-200 years. Recent 'fine-tuning' attempts based on seeds from the tomb of Tutankhamun would tend to place his reign slightly later, between about 1320 BC and 1310 BC, adjusting Akhenaten's reign accordingly. [18]. However, a similar radiocarbon study of 2010 had indicated an earlier date. [19] So what are we to believe?

Again, the present author being a *catastrophist*, could never entirely trust radiocarbon dating either. The reasons for the ambiguity of carbon-14 at certain eras has never been convincingly explained by the specialists. It should be apparent that any abnormality of the Earth's rotation must also cause fluctuations in the magnetic field and the cosmic ray flux, thus destroying the assumptions upon which the rate of carbon-14 production in the atmosphere is based.

The proposed revision would then imply that, rather than the 1332 BC eclipse occurring (unrecorded) during the reign of Tutankhamun, it could have been the last in a series of total eclipses across Egypt that occurred during the lifetime of Akhenaten: 1352 BC, 1338 BC and 1332 BC. He may also have seen or heard reports of the annular "ring of fire" eclipse on 13 March 1335 BC. The circumstances of these eclipses according to NASA (Espinak 2021) were as follows:

1375 BC 03 May	2 mins 6 secs; a dawn eclipse at Syria & eastern Anatolia
1352 BC 15 August	3 mins 16 secs; total across southern Egypt, partial across Anatolia
1338 BC 14 May	6 mins 51 secs; total across Egypt, partial across Anatolia

1335 BC 13 March	6 mins 36 secs; annular across Egypt, partial over Anatolia
1332 BC 30 December	4 mins; a dawn eclipse commencing in western Egypt

The eclipse maps in the links above give the astronomical date number rather than the equivalent Gregorian date BC (or BCE) and have been refined slightly from those that I employed 2000-2006.

As for co-ordination with the Hittite chronology, we may well accept the conclusion of specialist Gary Beckman that the absolute dates for the Hittite chronology may never be known. [20] The "omen of the sun" mentioned in the Hittite text, *if the omen were indeed an eclipse*, could be that of 1335 BC or 1312 BC or perhaps one of the other eclipses above, which were partial over Anatolia. The dates for King Mursili II form a floating-chronology that depends crucially on links to Egypt via the *Amarna letters* (tablets in Akkadian cuneiform discovered at the Amarna site) together with archives from the Hittite capital Boğazköy.

Two letters are from a widowed Egyptian queen, begging King Suppiluliuma of Hatti, to send one of his sons to become her new husband. We may wonder whether this widowed-queen was Ankhesenamun, the sister-wife of Tutankhamun; or could the letter have been sent by Nefertiti upon the death of Akhenaten? Conventional Egyptology prefers that the letter was written by Ankhesenamun. However, little is known about Nefertiti; she also had no sons of her own and she too, rapidly disappears from the historical record. The identification depends crucially upon the linguists' preferred identification of *Bibhuria* or *Nibphuria* as the Babylonian rendering of Tutankhamun's birth-name rather than that of Akhenaten: *Naphurria*; yet another uncertainly to add to the list. Egyptology researcher Russell Jacquet-Acea has re-analysed this issue and suggested a revised chronology that favours Nefertiti as the widowed queen; and that it was the long eclipse of 1338 BC that inspired the building of Amarna. [21] However, such an identification would neglect the two later eclipses; it would not explain the three evil omens, or why the city had to be built at that precise location.

It should be stressed for the benefit of non-astronomers that the fixed-points in time provided by astronomical events remain invariable. An adjustment of the regnal dates in the king lists by 15 or 16 years would relocate the eclipse of 1335 BC within the Hittite chronology, with knock-on effects for other reigns – and therefore for synchronisms to the Trojan War. This becomes a chain of too many 'ifs' that makes it fruitless to project eclipse correspondences with any validity. The debate is another minefield. Hence I shall not pursue the Hittite chronology further here; with so many uncertainties it is perhaps best to keep the arguments simple.

From the motivation of my own investigations into *possible catastrophic events* during the Bronze Age and in earlier millennia, my previous conclusions would stand with only slight adjustment due to the refinement of the eclipse data since 2006. If we could once prove that a glitch or nutation has occurred at some point in the past then all retro calculation and historical date assumptions *prior to that event* become unreliable. We can no longer estimate where the eclipse shadows fell. However, acceptance of such an event would open minds to discussion that might prove the validity of other catastrophes earlier in Earth history.

One cannot expect specialist Egyptologists and other academics to cite or even read the work of non-specialist authors such as myself; or to cite catastrophist theories that are published in books aimed at the popular mass-market. Over the years there has been so much nonsense put out by followers of the 1950s pseudohistory of Velikovsky, that it became almost impossible to publish sensible research on the subject of catastrophism in prehistory. Even the more-restrained authors such as Graham

Phillips - who sought to link the 'omens' of Akhenaten with the Thera eruption, or the revised chronology of Egyptologist David Rohl that would place Akhenaten's reign 300 years later – both well argued – do not help to establish credibility. [22] [23] So muddied has the water become! *Note 2

Conclusions

The statistically rare concentration of eclipses crossing Egypt during the Eighteenth Dynasty would fit well with the 'evils' reported to Akhenaten, which inspired him to establish his new solar religion. However, to adopt the dates proposed here would require Egyptologists to abandon the uniformitarian Delta-T constraints and accept a step-change event that affected the diurnal rotation at some point between the 1012 BC and 1302 BC eclipses. The actual change is likely to have been quite modest amounting to less than half-an-hour over 300 years, shifting the fall of the shadow to the west. It should then be possible to apply standard formulae to extrapolate the most likely paths of eclipses before and after the new fixed point. However, this still tells us nothing about any variation due to wobble or pole-shift resulting from the same event.

This brings us back to the possible identification of an eclipse during the final battle of the Trojan War. I recall my own experience of the 1999 eclipse viewed beneath thin cloud as it passed over Cornwall. The sky darkened rapidly; sea gulls flew towards the light and then a few minutes later, as the shadow passed over, the screeching birds flew back the other way. The darkening of the sky through cloud was only significant during the few minutes of actual totality and quite unremarkable during the thin crescent of partial sunlight. This convinces me that the description given in the Iliad was not an eclipse under cloud; and an eclipse certainly would not produce fog at ground level over half the battlefield, with bright sunlight (not eclipsed) over the rest of the plain.

The eclipse of 1312 BC (on any retro calculation) was total for just over two-and-a-half minutes but, as Henriksson accepted, only partial at Troy. Appreciable darkening – such as would be so conspicuous as to be noticed in the heat of battle – could only have lasted for a few minutes. It could not explain a darkening that persisted throughout a long battle, even allowing for the fact that the poet was recording a degraded oral memory. Overall it seems more likely that the mist, *in the very centre of the battle*, was a local weather phenomenon. Regrettably, the description in the Iliad is not sufficiently concise to be trusted as a report of an ancient eclipse, much as a historical researcher might dearly wish it were so.

Homer's description of the fighting would however fulfil my own definition of a 'mythological fossil' as the poet or his source had no need to include a weather references within a fictional account of a battle. It gives us confidence that he based his poetry on oral recollections of a real historical conflict. The date of the battle, however, remains uncertain. Hopefully, the discussion and references here will serve to assist future researchers who can approach the subject with an open mind.

Note 1: The retro calculation by Mitchell of the 1012 BC eclipse, as cited by Egyptologist David Rohl in his book: *A Test of Time* could no longer be found in 2021 to re-assess for this article. However I did reproduce this eclipse as Figure 6.1 of my 2005 book. While I did not and do not accept the revised chronology, the circumstances of the Ugarit sunset eclipse can indeed be reproduced in retro-calculation software and via the NASA website much better than for 1223 BC. It is an interesting aside that close to the eclipsed sun would have been – as Rohl remarked – a first-magnitude red giant star that exploded to form the Crab Nebula in AD 1054.

Note 2: Muddy Waters! In 2006 I did attempt to publish an article on these eclipses in a specialist journal to complete the research of my earlier book, but the mere mention of 'catastrophism' led to a dismissive rejection by that journal's referee who assumed that it was inspired by Velikovsky's ideas; and another journal that supposedly publishes alternative chronology suppressed a revised version because it would *not* support Velikovsky's chronology! The revised article was therefore left in abeyance until I included it in *Prehistory Papers* in

2020. However, it was made available on request as unpublished to a small number of interested researchers who commented on the earlier book.

****

Relevant Hyperlinks

https://www.history.com/news/bronze-age-collapse-causes
https://www.researchgate.net/publication/44963755_Hittite_Chronology
http://www.touregypt.net/featurestories/letters.htm
https://eclipse.gsfc.nasa.gov/SEhelp/deltat2004.html
https://eclipse.gsfc.nasa.gov/SEhelp/uncertainty2004.html
https://eclipse.gsfc.nasa.gov/SEhelp/deltaT.html
https://eclipse.gsfc.nasa.gov/SEcat5/SE-1399--1300.html
https://eclipse.gsfc.nasa.gov/5MCSEmap/-1399--1300/-1301-06-05.gif
https://eclipse.gsfc.nasa.gov/5MCSEmap/-1399--1300/-1311-06-24.gif
https://eclipse.gsfc.nasa.gov/5MCSEmap/-1399--1300/-1331-12-30.gif
https://eclipse.gsfc.nasa.gov/5MCSEmap/-1399--1300/-1334-03-13.gif
https://eclipse.gsfc.nasa.gov/5MCSEmap/-1399--1300/-1337-05-14.gif
https://eclipse.gsfc.nasa.gov/5MCSEmap/-1399--1300/-1351-08-15.gif
https://eclipse.gsfc.nasa.gov/SEhistory/SEplot/SE-1374May03T.pdf
http://www.michaelmandeville.com/earthmonitor/polarmotion/plots/chandler_wobble_plots.htm
https://earth-planets-space.springeropen.com/articles/10.1186/s40623-018-0971-9
https://eos.org/science-updates/earths-wobbly-path-gives-clues-to-its-core
https://www.third-millennium.co.uk/under-ancient-skies
https://f7e94415-3a55-48d9-ba14-ed235f05a65f.filesusr.com/ugd/e5604c_b2b136af2b8f4a05b72ea1c0b6bf9797.pdf?index=true
http://www.egyptologyforum.org/EMP/DAPE.pdf
http://www.touregypt.net/featurestories/amarna.htm
https://www.archaeometry.org/helios.htm
https://pharaoh.se/dynasty-XVIII
https://www.sciencedaily.com/releases/2018/06/180605112057.htm
http://www.thehistoryblog.com/archives/29044#:~:text=Since%20Amenhotep%20ruled%20for%20approximately,for%20at%20least%20eight%20years.
https://www.smb.museum/en/museums-institutions/aegyptisches-museum-und-papyrussammlung/collection-research/bust-of-nefertiti/the-queen/
https://www.researchgate.net/figure/The-Akhet-hieroglyph-Cf-Frischers-zone-3-figure-6_fig19_317647684/download
https://keisan.casio.com/exec/system/1227757509

References

1) Hammond, Martin (1987) *The Iliad, A New Prose Translation*, Penguin, Harmondsworth, London
2) Papamarinopoulos, S. et al (2013) A new astronomical dating of the Trojan war's end, *Mediterranean Archaeology and Archaeometry*, Vol. 14, No. 1, pp. 93-102 https://www.academia.edu/7806255/A_NEW_ASTRONOMICAL_DATING_OF_THE_TROJAN_WARS_END
3) Henriksson, G. (2012) The Trojan War Dated By Two Solar Eclipses, *Mediterranean Archaeology and Archaeometry*, Vol. 12, No 1, pp. 63-76
4) Jacquet-Acea, Russell (2020) The Solar Eclipses of Mursili II, independent.academia.edu https://www.academia.edu/15591950/The_Solar_Eclipses_of_Mursili_II
5) Morrison, S.L. & Stephenson, F.R. (2004) Historical values of the Earth's clock error ΔT and the calculation of eclipses, *JHA*, Vol. 35, Part 3, No. 120, p. 327 – 336 (ISSN 0021-8286)
6) Dunbavin, P. (2005) *Under Ancient Skies: Ancient Astronomy and Terrestrial Catastrophism*, Third Millennium Publishing, Nottingham; ISBN:0-9525029-2-5
7) Dunbavin, Paul (2020) Akhenaten and Eclipses, in *Prehistory Papers*, pp 85-97, Third Millennium Publishing, Beverley; ISBN: 978-0-9525029-4-4 https://www.third-millennium.co.uk/features
8) Mitchell 1990 as cited by Rohl (see ref 23 below and Note 1)
9) Stephenson, F.R. (2008) How Reliable Are Archaic Records of Large Solar Eclipses? *JHA*, 39, 2, No. 135, p. 229 – 250 (ISSN 0021-8286) - see pp241-2
10) https://eclipse.gsfc.nasa.gov/SEhelp/deltat2004.html
11) Pardee, D & Swerdlow, N. (1993) Not the Earliest Solar Eclipse, *Nature*, 363, p 406
12) See Ref 6 above, chapter 6
13) Mc Murray, W. (2003) Dating the Amarna Period in Egypt: Did a Solar Eclipse Inspire Akhenaten? www.egyptologyforum.org/EMP/DAPE.pdf
14) Khalisi, Emil (2004) The Solar Eclipses of the Pharaoh Akhenaten, *arXiv*: 2004.12952 [physics.hist-ph]
15) Aldred, C., (1988) *Akhenaten, King of Egypt*, Thames & Hudson, London ISBN: 0-500-27621-8, (chapter 3 pp 27-43)
16) ibid, chapter 4 (*pp 47-51 summarising the Amarna Boundary Stelae Project)*
17) Murnane, W.J. & van Siclen III, C.C. (1993). *The Boundary Stelae of Akhenaten*, Kegan Paul International, London and New York:
18) Manning et al., (2010) Mediterranean radiocarbon offsets and calendar dates for prehistory, *Sci. Adv. 2020; 6*: eaaz1096, 18 March 2020
19) Ramsey, C.B. et al. (2010) Radiocarbon-Based Chronology for Dynastic Egypt, Science 328, 1554
20) Beckman, G. (2000) Hittite Chronology, *Akkadica*, pp 19-32
21) Jacquet-Acea, Russell (2019) The True Length of Reign of Pharaoh Horemheb. Independent.academia.edu www.academia.edu/15119537/The_True_Length_of_Reign_of_Pharaoh_Horemheb

22) Philips, Graham. (1998) Act of God, Sidgewick & Jackson, London; ISBN: 0-283-06314-9

23) Rohl, D. (1995), *A Test of Time*, Century, London; ISBN: 0-7126-5913-7

Other References

Walker, C. (1989) Eclipse seen at Ancient Ugarit, *Nature*, 338, pp 204-5

De Jong, T. & Van Soldt, W.H. (1989) The earliest known solar eclipse redated, *Nature*, 338, pp 238-9

Stephenson FR. The earliest known record of a solar eclipse. *Nature.* 1970 Nov 14;228(5272):651-2. DOI: 10.1038/228651a0. PMID: 16058640.

Stephenson F.R. and Holden M.A. (1986) *Atlas of Historical Eclipse maps,* Cambridge University Press

Bryan, Betsy M. (1991) *The Reign of Thutmose IV,* John Hopkins Press, Baltimore, ISBN 0-8018-4202-6

10

Dismissing The Venerable Bede!

Summary

A critique and update of the author's previous research into Pictish origins since the publication of Picts and Ancient Britons in 1998. Older theories that the Pictish tribes and their lost language were 'Celtic' no longer stand scrutiny alongside the historical sources or more recent DNA evidence that throws doubt upon the continental Celtic origin of the British people. This article follows instead the evidence from the various historical sources, including Bede and the Picts' own books, that they were 'Scythians' who arrived in ships from the Baltic coast.

A linguistic theory that Finno-Ugrian languages and people were formerly more widespread in the west of Europe has been promoted by Andres Pääbo, a Canadian of Estonian descent. [1] He would suggest that the various *Vene*-names found in western Europe were Finnic-speaking (Estonian) maritime traders originating from the Baltic coast. This group would include the Baltic *Venedi*, the *Veneti* of Brittany, the Adriatic *Veneti* (where modern Venice lies) and also the Picts of Scotland, where he includes Ptolemy's tribal names: *Venicon(t)es* and Irish *Vennicnii* in the same group; the name *Venedi*, he suggests, would mean something like 'of the boats'. More details of his theories will be explored later. A Baltic point of origin for the Picts is certainly not a new suggestion – it goes back to our oldest historical sources, the most respected among these being the Venerable Bede.

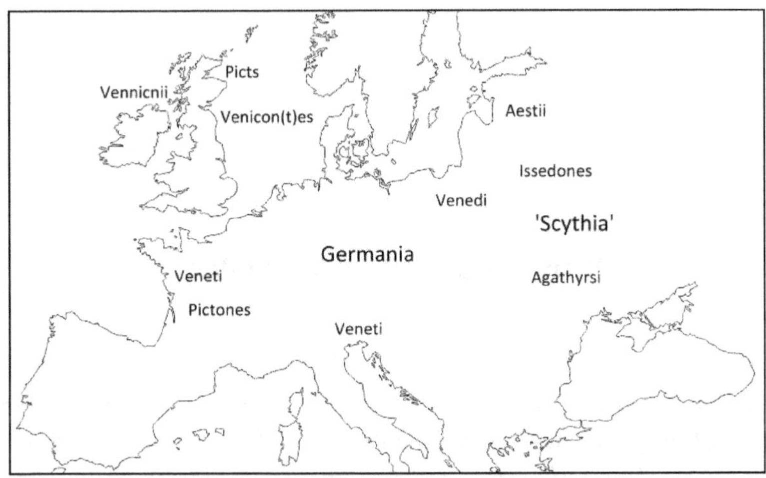

The Northumbrian monk Bede, who lived and worked at the monastery at Jarrow, is widely recognised as the father of English history. Without his book: *'The Ecclesiastical History of the English people'*, written in 731, we would know far less about early Anglo-Saxon history. However, historians and archaeologists have always liked to pick and choose which parts of his history they rely on. Nowhere is this more apparent than in the treatment of his passing references to the Picts. Bede repeats the Pictish origin story, saying in his introduction, that '*Picts from Scythia*' had arrived in ships and settled in the north; and also that their language was distinct from those of the Scots and Britons. We are not told precisely when this colonisation occurred, and we should not lose sight here that there must have been native tribes already present when the Picts arrived.

Bede was contemporary with the Pictish king Nechtan, writing his history some 46 years after the Battle of Nectansmere (near modern Forfar) in 685 when the southern Picts recovered their independence after an interlude of Northumbrian rule. During this period the Northumbrian Bishop of the Picts occupied the monastery at *Abercorn* on the River Forth until he was forced to take flight. Bede also wrote a biography of Saint Cuthbert and describes Cuthbert's visit to the Picts during this period of Northumbrian hegemony. Therefore, we may be certain that the monks of Northumbria knew much more about the Picts than we are told in our surviving sources.

For Bede to suggest that the Picts were colonists from 'Scythia', does not tell us to which ethnic or linguistic group they may have belonged. The name was used loosely by Greek and Roman writers to denote the entire region that we might today refer-to as Russia, or the former Soviet-Union. [2] Over this vast area, from the Baltic to the Caspian Sea the various tribes were tributary to the nomadic Scythian (Iranian) horseman who ranged freely across the Steppes. We do know however, that tattooing of the body was a characteristic of many tribes in the 'Scythian' region. The fact that sea voyages may have commenced from the Baltic coast therefore would not rule-out an origin from further inland [See Note 2].

For my 1998 book <u>Picts and Ancient Britons</u> I therefore attempted to collect all the sources in translation that might inform us about the pre-historical Pictish period up to 565 AD and which might tell us more about the origins of the proto-Pictish tribes. [3] This cut-off date was chosen to exclude later influences from Gaelic and Brittonic that specialists think they see in the Pictish ogham inscriptions, particularly following Christian conversion. The later sources, such as the symbol stones and oghams, tend to crowd-out the meagre evidence about earlier periods. The later language would certainly have been pervaded by Celtic loan words and culture during the historical period; however this can prove nothing about their origins hundreds of years before.

You might expect all the relevant literary sources to be easily available in a Scottish library, but no (at least not back in pre-internet 1990s). Indeed some books were so rare, or in such poor condition that the various libraries would not inter-lend. I had to visit libraries from Wales to Paris; and often make hand-written notes because I was not allowed to photocopy the fragile book. In tracing back various research papers, it became apparent that the writer of a particular research paper might know the primary reference that they were discussing yet would rely on a modern citation for others; and following that one back still might not lead to an original source text!

Historical references to the early Picts are few and no ancient writer leaves us a true history. Typically the sources are Roman, Irish or Welsh, non-contemporary with the events, or mere context to the main topic – as with Bede, who is writing about the English church. Only about thirty possible Pictish words are known, most of these being names on Ptolemy's second-century map of Britain.

It was this very scarcity of evidence that led to the 1955 symposium and subsequent report known as: *The Problem of the Picts*, which offered a series of papers by the various specialists. [4] Among these were Kenneth Jackson, a specialist Celtic linguist; and the archaeologist and editor Frederick Wainwright. Jackson subsequently published translations of Gaelic and Pictish texts and was undoubtedly the foremost authority of his day, being widely cited. His opinion, having reviewed the earlier studies such as Skene, MacBain, Watson and others, was that many of the Pictish words could not be recognized as 'clearly or probably Celtic'. Despite this, the editor concluded overall that the Picts were Celts, probably speaking a p-Celtic language, but distinct from Welsh. In the closing summary he acknowledged Bede's legend that the Picts originated from Scythia to be a tradition current among the Picts and the Irish, but lacking supporting evidence, concluding:

> *"...the story must be dismissed as legend or literary invention".*

I found this statement quite astonishing; for any modern scholar to assert that they might know more about an ancient people than they knew about their own history seemed to me the height of arrogance.

This influential symposium set the pattern for the next half-century. Others would press forward by citing Jackson as their authority that Picts were Celts, particularly the linguists. They would take the meagre Pictish vocabulary as a list of Celtic-Pictish words, which they would then use in comparative studies, to establish Pictish as a branch of Continental Celtic, terming it *Prittenic*. [5] However, in his later work, Jackson seems to have had enough of all this and in 1977 declared, based on an ogham inscription, that he no longer believed the Pictish language to be Celtic.[6] Too late; it had already entered the textbooks as a proven fact.

Therefore it seemed to me as an outsider coming to the problem from a wider focus, that the various specialists were finding Celtic-Picts simply because they wanted to; and because it was the right thing to say. For modern Scots, Celtic identity is tied up with anti-English sentiment and nationalism; they simply *wanted* the Picts to be Celts.

The Celticists therefore had to remove the obstacle that the Picts' ancestors supposedly came from 'Scythia'. We first see this in nineteenth century investigators such as Skene and MacBain. William Skene was convinced that Pictish was a form of Gaelic and simply brushed aside the Irish additions to Nennius and Solinus, which suggested various 'Scythian' origins for the Pictish colonists; this despite the assertion that the stories came from the Picts own books. Unfortunately, we do not have these first-hand sources. Skene's research of the Irish and Welsh texts was so extensive that subsequent scholars used his books as a source of translations, even though his Gaelic hypothesis was not favoured. In dismissing Skene's Gaelic conclusions, later specialists also threw-out any serious consideration of what the Picts lost books might have said.

Those Irish monks have a lot to answer-for! How dare they attempt to preserve lost history for us by writing in the margins of historical texts? As an (amateur) historian I can assert that no historian who takes the trouble to study such sources would ever deliberately introduce false history. We should respect these ancient scholars and listen to what they tried to tell us. As I have said in other contexts: if ever there be a clash between an ancient source and a modern academic then we should always prefer the source closest to the events.

The logic is clear. Celtic languages were not spoken in the Scythian region. Therefore if Picts came from there they could not be 'Celts'. Rather than pursuing which languages were actually spoken in Baltic Scythia, the specialists preferred to ignore the aberrant historical sources. Celtic scholars and linguists were taught for over a century that Picts were Celts and that some earlier expert had proved it. As long as they cited the chain of references then their work would be accepted; to suggest otherwise became heresy. Bede was indeed 'dismissed'. Instead of going back to source, the various modern academics cited each-other.

Linguistics is not a science; perhaps more than any other discipline it sits on a base of eminent opinion citing earlier opinion. It may work fine for languages where a large vocabulary is available, but less so when you have only some thirty disputed words and no idea of the grammar. New archaeology can always challenge older finds, but you can't put a linguistic theory in a test-tube and watch it change colour! Since 1950, when *The Problem of the Picts* symposium was published, the archaeology surrounding Celts and Picts has been forcibly revised by the advent of radiocarbon dating; then again by tree-ring calibration. Yet through all this the linguistic theories about Celts and Celtic languages sailed-on, little affected. It is only since the new science of DNA ancestry that the linguists have been forced to go back to the sources and think again.

In 2015 the first complete DNA study of Britain was published followed by a more comprehensive study for Britain and Ireland in 2017. [See note 1] and it would overturn everything that archaeologists thought they knew about the origins of the British population. Studies as early as 2003 had shown the persistence of 'Celtic' populations within England; however, the correspondence of the DNA to the known tribal areas, as shown in the full study, seems to have come as a complete surprise to scholars. However it was no surprise to those of us who had taken the trouble to go back to the historical sources. The DNA study showed that there was no single 'Celtic' genetic group; indeed differences between the so-called Celtic populations were greater than those with groups in England. The DNA evidence has prompted a complete revision of thinking about the origin of languages and the old notion of a Celtic 'invasion' of Britain has been shown to be quite simply – wrong.

Following the revised understanding of origins, historians and archaeologists have become more guarded in their usage of these terms. By way of illustration, I quote here from an archived (2018) internet blog '*Ask Historians*' [7] in case it should be subsequently taken down, as is common with such ephemeral sources. The historian replies:

> *To expand a bit on what has been said, the ancient people of Britain and Ireland were never really called 'Celts' by an ancient source. That association only came about at the turn of the 18th century after it has been established that the Pre-Germanic languages spoken in the islands like Irish and Welsh were related to that of the ancient Gauls, who the Romans also termed 'Celts'. There is a growing consensus, especially amongst archaeologists of Britain and Ireland that the word 'Celtic' is problematic because it subscribes to and perpetuates erroneous ideas which equate language and art style as markers of ethnicity or 'nationhood'. In the past two decades, you'll see the word 'Celtic' being increasingly avoided or in inverted commas when used at all.*
>
> ...

The classification most people are familiar with, which divided the Celtic branch into a 'Q-Celtic' and a 'P-Celtic' family is now obsolete and most scholars talk about 'Insular' and 'Continental Celtic' instead.

...

While it has fallen out of favour amongst archaeologists, it still remains a linguistic term, that is, Celtic, nowadays refers to a language family rather than an ethnic group or culture...

This all corresponds quite closely with my own published views back in the 1990s which attracted venomous comment at the time, while the old Celtic dogma still held sway. For example, in a 1999 review by a Pictish specialist of the time:

[The author] *is no professional academic, but this book resembles books by scholars. Half of it contains translated extracts of ancient sources...*

And concludes:

Dr ... is a specialist in the Picts, and is based in Glasgow [8]

Is he reviewing here the content or its author? We see a typical example of a single-subject specialist trapped in his box, unable to challenge his own thinking. It would surely be unacceptable prejudice today to imply: It's very good but you can't take it seriously because the author is black, or a Jew, or homosexual or, its written by a woman, etc.; however it would seem that academic snobbery remains acceptable for publication in a refereed journal. As for any specialist being an expert, there is no such thing. Anyone who holds themselves up as an expert immediately shows a lack of competence to be one. Someone else may declare you an expert but they would still be wrong! We all remain mere students until we die.

The subject of the Pictish language is an old minefield! It is complicated by the fact that we have the later Pictish inscriptions using the Irish ogham script. Various specialists have claimed to find recognisable Celtic words embedded in these otherwise indecipherable inscriptions. A Polish linguist in a 2012 review of theories about the Pictish language (just a few years preceding the DNA revolution) would be another example of an academic, confidently citing modern opinion, just as I was finding back in the 1990s. [9] Everything in the content as regards a Finnic-Pictish can be found in the one-page review by the self-appointed expert; with no indication that the author has traced back the cited sources to a translation or original text. This is even more important today, because modern papers published on academic platforms can rank higher in internet search-engines than the older sources that they cite.

The suggestion of a root similar to Finnish 'venekunta' for Ptolemy's tribal name *venicon(t)es* is rubbished as 'not the way we do linguistics today'. Yet this is a dictionary word meaning 'a boats crew', consisting of two acknowledged ancient roots; and no-one can say how old its usage is. To suggest that the place name *peanfahel* might share some affinity with the Finnish word for a 'pilgrimage' is similarly trashed; this was the Picts' own name for the monastery at Abercorn, where Pictish Christian converts would have converged during the period when the southern Picts were tributary to the Northumbrian Angles. Bede would have known all about this mission and probably knew priests who had worked with Pictish Christians. Can we doubt therefore that the monks of Jarrow knew more about the Pictish language than anyone alive today? The Celtic explanation for the name *peanfahel* is that it consists of a continental-Celtic root 'penn-', joined with an insular-Celtic root 'fáil'. I don't hear the linguists saying that this unlikely juxtaposition from two different languages is not how they do linguistics today. Yet if you trace back the various papers through the chain of citations then this old-thinking lies at the base of the assertions about 'Celtic' Picts. The same linguist again dismisses Bede, saying:

If a monk comments on a language spoken by certain people, his account deserves at least a thought.

Bede was much more than a monk – he was a historian – who actually drafted letters to a living Pictish king while Pictish was still a spoken language. Perhaps then, he might have known more about them than any modern linguist?

The arguments in favour of a Baltic 'Scythian' origin for the Picts are primarily *historical* rather than linguistic – one may find other non-linguistic coincidences in the sources. These historical references have to be massaged-away before the linguists can bring-in their Celtic assertions. The above-mentioned linguist, for example would say, again citing earlier academics, '*There is no evidence for the Pictish or Celtic tribes using body painting or tattooing between the 5th and 9th century...*' This is immaterial as the custom died-out upon Christian conversion along with other pagan traditions, whereas in fact the use of tattooing during the Roman period is recorded in various sources, such as: Dio Cassius, Herodian, Solinus, Claudian, Isidore and the *Pictish Chronicle*.

Bede is not the only basis for the tradition that Picts (or at least their dominant tribe) originated from 'Scythia'. We also find it in Geoffrey of Monmouth's history; whatever you may think of that, its inspiration came from a Welsh source not a Scottish one. It is also found in additions to Irish versions of Nennius made by the monk Gilcaemhin and states that it came from the Picts own books. [10] This version says that the Irish Picts (Cruthneach) were *Agathyrsi*, who migrated west via Gaul. He also tells us that they tattooed their skins. We find these Agathyrsi among the tribes listed by Herodotus some five hundred years earlier and who had resisted the Scythian invasion (see note 2); they occupied the region of western Ukraine around the Transylvanian mountains. Therefore, as with recent European colonisation of America, there was probably more than one expedition and more than one migration route from the east; with only the first voyage being remembered. The constant pressure from the Scythians would give ample reason why these subject peoples might wish to flee their homeland.

Perhaps the most frustrating of the passing historical references to Picts are those by Tacitus. [11] Not only does he leave us a frustratingly vague account of the northern tribes that faced Agricola in 80-84 AD, but also in his *Germania*, he describes tribes in the east whom he does not know how to classify, whether as Germans or as Scythians. Among these are Venedi and Aestii on the Baltic coast. He describes the Aestii language as being: *'more like that of the Britons'*. [12]

Here again, the Caledonian tribes are not the primary subject for Tacitus. He clearly knows that the northern tribes spoke a different language to the Britons of the Roman province, but he does not bother to tell us whether he compares the Aestii language to the northern or the southern Britons; he was writing about Germans not the Britons or the Scythians! It would be wonderful if Tacitus had told us all that he knew about the Caledonians – but he doesn't; it would be wonderful if the Venerable Bede had told us all that he knew about the Picts – but he doesn't. We are left to argue about the meaning of these fragments of knowledge.

It is important to note that not-one of the stories of Pictish origin would bring them as continental 'Celts' from Gaul. Yes, we do find migrations to Ireland and southern Britain suggested in the sources, but where these refer to the Picts then they are merely passing-through from further east onward to Britain and Ireland. There is nothing that would make them continental 'Celts' in the long-traditional sense. So why for so long did the concept of Celtic-Picts prevail over the historical accounts that they came from 'Scythia'? It all goes back to the entrenched nineteenth-century dogma about an Iron Age invasion of Britain by Celts from Gaul. Now that we have clear DNA evidence that this invasion never happened, we may see more clearly that the history and the linguistics do not meet in the middle.

It is interesting to follow how much the debate has moved on since the 1990s. In 1999 another Canadian author, Farley Mowat, introduced the concept of a maritime race that he called: *Albans*, whom he suggested were the Gaulish Veneti and Pictones. [13] These seafarers, he argued, were 'Celts' fleeing the Roman occupation; and who had invaded Ireland and Scotland before continuing their voyaging across the Atlantic to Canada to join the native American tribes. Now, a professional author may recognise here a 'mid-Atlantic' book; a marketing concept pitched to a publisher to sell both in Europe and the lucrative American market. The 'Albans' are a fictionalisation on a base of miscellaneous facts. Here again we find Bede's references to Picts from Scythia incorporated within the Alban concept; 'Scythia' is rationalised as a reference to 'Scilly' and the Albans therefore must have migrated from Brittany, via the Isles of Scilly – well it does start with the same two letters! None of this would convince a critical historian but it certainly sold books; the author has to be admired for his craft. A very similar theory was (I think first) suggested in 1954 by Lethbridge in *The Painted Men* citing the Irish sources [14]

This brings us back again to the theories of Andres Pääbo. These are more soundly based than Mowat's Farfarers and cite a trail of plausible linguistic evidence. In his analysis, the influence comes from Estonian rather than Finnish or other Finno-Ugrian languages. Indeed, he would abandon the accepted evolutionary tree for the Finno-Ugrian languages, preferring a continuous evolution among the Baltic amber traders as they voyaged between their coastal colonies. He would see Estonian roots among the language of the Veneti (Venetic) including inscriptions from northern Italy. He would also see an evolution of Estonian roots among Ptolemy's tribes and place names. As a native Finnic-speaker who is prepared to go against the prevailing wind he should receive a proper hearing. He points out that the name *Picti* is rendered in Estonian as *püükide* meaning 'of the [fish] catches'; so perhaps this was the ancient root of that name rather than the accepted Latin derivation? However, historical sources say that the Pictish tribes did not eat fish, treating them as somehow, sacred. [15] Read Pääbo's theories yourself and form your own opinion rather than reading dismissive reviews by 'experts'. Another interesting modern internet discussion about the Venedi and the Baltic Wends is available here in a 'history file'. [16]

Rather like Mowat before him, Pääbo would see the ancient Venetic-Estonians as an arctic maritime culture that roamed the northern seas in their skin-boats, from the Baltic to the Atlantic coasts, as far back as the Ice Age. He too would suggest that they crossed the Atlantic on the edge of the retreating ice, mingling with the tribes of the Canadian arctic. This is by no means implausible, as we do have respected sources such as Plutarch, who tell us about ancient voyages into the Atlantic made by seafarers from the Scottish islands during the first-century AD. [17]

However, Pääbo too, sometimes selectively employs the historical sources, incorporating Bede and Tacitus but excluding Irish sources that might not quite fit. Yet, if he is even half-right, then it is a challenge to those linguists who think they can see a Celtic language from Belgic Gaul in northern Britain. They may simply be comparing a few words of a Finnic-Pictish with a Gaulish language that was replete with Finnic loan words from the maritime Veneti who had lived there since the Neolithic.

Ultimately, it is the DNA evidence, not linguistics, which will determine where the northern British tribes originated and whether any of these boat-people crossed the Atlantic in ancient times. The linguistics will then have to follow and the historical fragments will then fall into their proper place as supporting evidence. Researchers can now find the latest DNA research much more easily via internet searches – a luxury that was not available to earlier generations! Research is so easy now that it can leave no excuses for those specialists who continue to dismiss the Venerable Bede.

Note 1 - DNA

Anyone who wishes to research the chain of DNA references for Britain, Ireland and France may find the following introduction useful and save time in tracing the sources.

On the rethink of language origins
https://www.nature.com/news/polopoly_fs/1.16935!/menu/main/topColumns/topLeftColumn/pdf/518284a.pdf

On 'Celtic' DNA in England
https://www.nature.com/articles/news030616-15

The first fine-scale genetic map of the British Isles
https://www.ucl.ac.uk/news/2015/mar/first-fine-scale-genetic-map-british-isles

The fine-scale genetic structure of the British population
https://www.nature.com/articles/nature14230
Leslie, S. *et al.* The fine-scale population structure of the British population. *Nature* **519**, 309–14 (2015).

DNA map for UK
https://www.nature.com/news/uk-mapped-out-by-genetic-ancestry-1.17136
doi:10.1038/nature.2015.17136

DNA map for Ireland
https://www.nature.com/articles/s41598-017-17124-4

DNA map for Western France
Karakachoff, M. *et al.* Fine-scale human genetic structure in Western France. *Eur J Hum Genet* **23**(6), 831–6 (2015).
https://www.nature.com/articles/ejhg2014175

Eurasian DNA in Native Americans
https://www.nature.com/news/americas-natives-have-european-roots-1.14213

Note 2 - Tattooing

A discussion of tattooing on the preserved body of a Scythian princess from the Altai Mountains is available to follow here:

https://siberiantimes.com/culture/others/features/siberian-princess-reveals-her-2500-year-old-tattoos/

We may compare the styles of Scythian animal figures to the symbols found on the Pictish symbol stones, although we cannot be sure precisely what the Picts tattooed on their own bodies. Tattooing must be seen as a much older custom of many tribes in the east, not just of the Scythians themselves. As a non-linguistic clue to origins this custom has long been overlooked. [18] Another correspondence comes with the Pictish inheritance via the female line and the free social customs as found in Dio Cassius and Solinus; these may be compared to similar descriptions of various 'Scythian' tribes 'sharing their women in common' (or suchlike wording) in the ancient sources. These were not customs of the continental 'Celts'. Another coincidence comes in the practice of the Agathyrsi, to paint their hair and bodies blue and the similar practice among the Britons who painted their bodies in blue woad. I recall in the 1990s finding one older academic paper that did manage to smuggle this idea past an academic referee, by referring to body-art as a custom that Celts must have learned by contact with the Scythians in the East. Such has been the dominance of Celtic dogma over the years that these non-linguistic clues were never given weight compared to the linguistic arguments.

References

1) Pääbo, Andres, *The expansion of northwest Eurasian boat peoples at the end of the ice age*. (2002-2018) http://www.paabo.ca/uirala/contents.html;

2) Herodotus, Book IV, 100-120

3) Dunbavin, Paul (1998) *Picts and Ancient Britons, an Exploration of Pictish Origins*, Third Millennium Publishing, Nottingham; ISBN: 0952502917.

4) Wainwright, F.T. (ed) (1955) *The Problem of the Picts*, Nelson Press, Edinburgh

5) Koch, J.T. (1983) "The Loss of Final Syllables and Loss of Declension in Brittonic" in *Bulletin of the Board of Celtic Studies*, 30, 201-33

6) Jackson, Kenneth. (1977) "The ogham inscription on the spindle whorl from Buckquoy, Orkney", *Proceedings of the Society of Antiquities of Scotland* 108. Edinburgh: National Museum of Antiquities of Scotland. 221–222.

7) Ask Historians; Thread posted Jan 11, 2018 (archived) https://www.reddit.com/r/AskHistorians/comments/7pkof3/did_the_celtic_peoples_arrive_in_britain_or_did/

8) Samson, Ross. (1999) *Claiming Finnish origins for Picts*, S. Denison (ed.) *British Archaeology*, 43 York: Council for British Archaeology.

9) Zajączkowska, Agnieszka (2012) *A study of chosen theories about the genetic classification of the Pictish language*, Poznan.

10) Gilla Cómáin mac Gilla Samthainde; the reader is referred to William Skene (1867) for translations of these Irish additions to Nennius, for which there are abridged extracts in my *Picts and Ancient Britons*.

11) Tacitus, *Agricola*, 10-38

12) Tacitus, *Germania*, 38-46

13) Mowat Farley (1999) *The Alban Quest, The Search for a Lost Tribe*, Wiedenfeld & Nicholson, London.

14) Lethbridge T. C. (1954) *The Painted Men*, Andrew Melrose, London.

15) Dio Cassius, Roman History, LXXVII, 12, 1-4.

16) https://www.historyfiles.co.uk/KingListsEurope/BarbarianVeneti.htm

17) Plutarch, Moralia; The Face on the Moon, 941.

18) Mayor, Adrienne (2016) *The Amazons: Lives and Legends of Warrior Women across the Ancient World*, Princeton Univ. Press.

11

A Pictish Miscellany

Summary: *A collection of the author's smaller articles and web-pages (2017-2021) on the subject of the Picts of Scotland. For the most part, they complete or build-upon the research of the author's 1998 book: Picts and Ancient Britons. The individual articles collected here are:*

1) *A Crocodile in Loch Ness? – the first report by St Columba that started it all*
2) *Ptolemy's Map of Scotland – an Alternative Exploration*
3) *Three Pictures of Picts – and a new one recently discovered in Fife*
4) *The Problem of the Picts – overcoming text-book prejudices about origins*

****

1) A Crocodile in Loch Ness?

An interesting aside to any study of the Picts of Scotland is to read Adamnan's Life of Saint Columba. Among other things it describes the progress of the Irish saint through the Pictish regions around 565 AD. We hear of his exchanges with the pagan Pictish Druids (shamans) and how he would regularly perform miracles and exorcise demons as he sought to convert the locals to Christianity. In one example, he drove out a Demon that supposedly dwelt in a milk-pail; and another time, he purified a poisonous fountain, which the locals were worshipping as a god. And he also encountered the Loch Ness Monster!

It is unfortunate that, wherever it has gone, conversion to Christianity has blurred or destroyed the older beliefs and the information about earlier history that accompanies it. We are left with only snippets of useful information – such as the fact that Columba, himself a Gaelic speaker, had to converse with the Picts through an interpreter. For further information on this topic, see my: *Picts and Ancient Britons*.

One day as Columba was crossing the River Ness near modern Inverness, we are told of how he vanquished an 'aquatic creature' that was attacking a local man.

> *...when the blessed man was living for some days in the province of the Picts, he was obliged to cross the river Nesa (the Ness); and when he reached the bank of the river, he saw some of the inhabitants burying an unfortunate man, who, according to the account of those who were burying him, was a short time before seized, as he was swimming, and bitten most severely by a monster that lived in the water...*

Perhaps disbelieving this, Columba instructed one of his companions to swim across the river to fetch a boat, with the inevitable result:

> *But the monster, which so far from being satiated, was only roused for more prey, was lying at the bottom of the stream, and when it felt the water disturbed above by the man swimming, suddenly rushed out, and giving an awful roar, darted after him, with its mouth wide open, as the man swam in the middle of the stream.*
> [Chapter XXVIII of Adamnan's Life Saint Columba in William Reeves translation of 1874]

We are told how Columba simply raised his hand and told the monster to go back; at which point it fled, seemingly terrified; and the watching Picts were amazed by the power of the Christian god.

Now, this description of a creature attacking 'with its mouth wide-open', if it were it to occur anywhere else, would be instantly recognisable to us as the typical attack of a crocodile or an alligator! But: a crocodile in Loch Ness? How could that be?

Most rationalisations of the Loch Ness Monster myth look no further than the influence of modern hoaxers, such as the 1933 Surgeon's Photograph, and their influence on the twentieth-century mind. This neglects the older folklore about a monster in the loch. However, Adamnan's description does not describe some huge monster, rather a normal-sized predator; and it was in the River Ness, not in Loch Ness itself.

It is possible that a crocodile could have been imported into the region as a baby, perhaps by a traveller, or as part of a circus menagerie. People in northern Scotland would never have seen such an exotic creature. It may have become too large for its captors and escaped or was simply released. As a lone animal living in Loch Ness it could have survived for many years and grown to full size; thus starting all the legends that have persisted ever-since of a 'monster' in the loch.

Coincidences like this in legends should always catch our attention. Adamnan could not have known that twentieth-century hoaxers would start a monster-myth in precisely this place. If he had wanted to create a fictitious miracle to enhance his story then he could just as easily have placed it in Dornoch Firth or the River Dee. Such coincidences are always a pointer that a core of truth underlies an ancient story. We should then ask: in what circumstances might this be true? Could the Loch Ness Monster myth really be so simple after all, as just one lost crocodile?

2) Ptolemy's Map of Scotland – an Alternative Interpretation

In the geography of Claudius Ptolemy, dating from the second century AD we are offered a curious map of Britain. The map shows the Roman province of Britannia with the unconquered areas of Scotland apparently rotated west-east through a right angle; but here, I shall refer to the north of Britain at this era as Caledonia rather than as Scotland.

Ptolemy is believed to have taken his northern geography from an earlier map made by Marinus of Tyre (c. AD 100-120), who is thought to have obtained his details of Caledonia from a quite different source to that of the Roman province to the south. The absence of any mention of Hadrian's Wall tells us that the source predates the Stanegate frontier and may therefore offer us a snapshot of Caledonia dating from the earlier period of the Flavian expedition around AD 80-84.

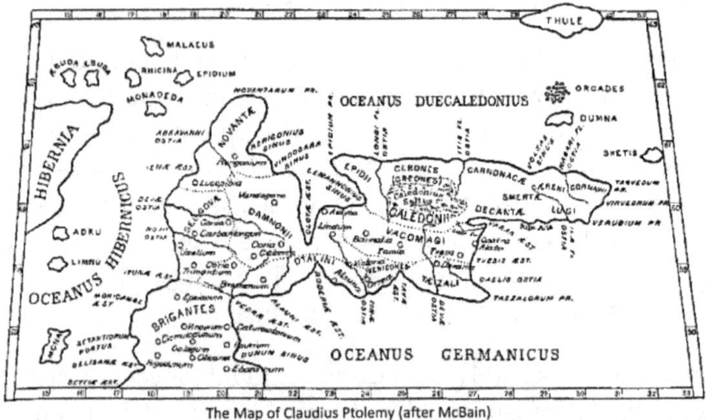

The Map of Claudius Ptolemy (after McBain)

Most of our meagre list Pictish words are names taken from Ptolemy's geography. [1] In *Picts and Ancient Britons* I explored the possibility that *Pictish*, the language spoken in the North before the Scottish kingdom absorbed the Picts, may have been a Finnic language closely related to Finnish and Estonian. This would be in line with the Picts own traditions of origin, but at odds with the view that specialists have held for so many years.

Modern DNA evidence now contradicts the old doctrine that the northern tribes were Celts. If the names on Ptolemy's map of Caledonia were indeed Finnic then it would make Ptolemy's names the oldest written form of any Finnic language. [See: Note 1]

An alternative explanation that I left unexplored in the 1998 book was that the map used by Marinus was actually made by Rome's northern proto-Pictish allies; and that Marinus may have mistaken the disposition of the Roman and allied forces to be tribal names. This possibility can only be seen by analogy with a Finnic vocabulary.

Our knowledge of Agricola's expedition to the North-East comes only from the writings of Tacitus. He does not acknowledge that Rome had any client kingdoms or allies in the region; although this would have been normal diplomatic practice as with the Brigantes further south. He does however tell us that Agricola left his troops over winter in the territory of a tribe named the 'Boresti'; a name unknown from any other source. [2] The accepted explanation is that it simply means: 'a northern tribe'.

The earliest clue that we have comes from Cicero (54 BC). He ventures in a letter that the only economic justification for a conquest of Britain might be the acquisition of slaves. [3] From Saint Patrick we know that the later Picts traded in slaves. [4] A non-contemporary account by Eutropius (AD 360) contradicts Tacitus, saying that the Orkney Islands had submitted to Rome in AD 43 as soon as the Claudian conquest began. [5] May we suppose then that the Orcadians were Rome's allies in the North? The possibility that the Orcadian-Picts were slave-traders is suggested by the name 'Orrea' as a city that was situated somewhere near the River Tay. The Finnish word *Orja* means: 'a slave'.

We find two further names on the map that may have been misinterpreted. The first of these is the name 'Venicones' (or perhaps 'Venecontes' – a manuscript variant) supposedly a tribe occupying the Fife peninsula. Again in Finnish we find *Venekunta* which means 'a boat's crew'; therefore one may suggest a meaning: 'sailors' or 'marines'. Perhaps Fife was the base of the Roman or allied navy? It must have been there somewhere to support Agricola; and we are told that it circumnavigated the north of Britain while the army wintered with the Boresti. [6]

In the Grampian triangle we find the 'Taexali', a name that has never been convincingly explained as p-Celtic. The nearest equivalent in Finnish is *Taistelija*. This word means: 'a fighter' or a 'combatant' (verb: *taistella*: 'to fight a battle') hence perhaps an interpretation: 'soldiers' or 'warriors' may be appropriate. One may suggest that this is showing us the disposition of the Roman legion, which fought the battle at Mons Graupius somewhere in this region.

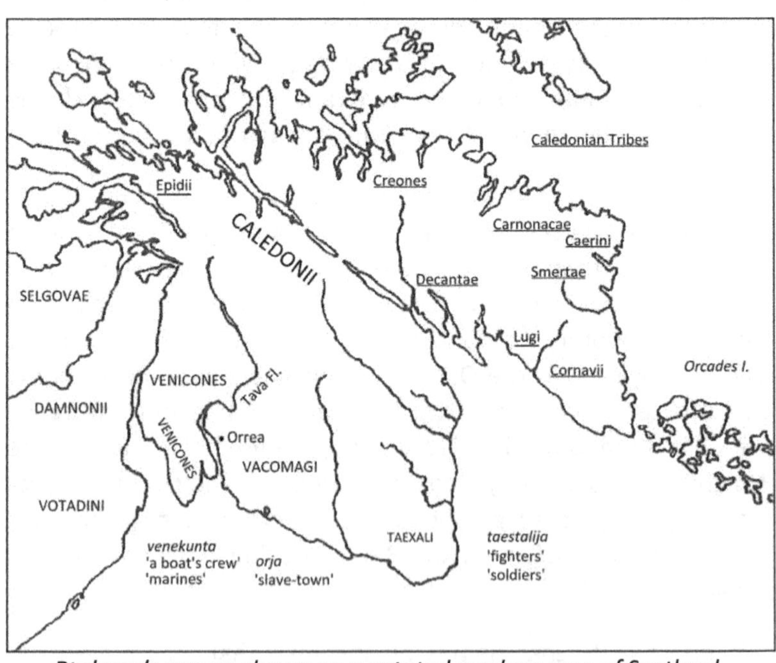

Ptolemy's names shown on a rotated modern map of Scotland (other places and rivers omitted)

These three coincidences are indicative taken alone. However, other words from the map and later sources also show strong cognates. It may be that either a Pict or perhaps a Roman has rendered the various Pictish words and names phonetically into the Latin alphabet, which fortunately is the same one as used today for most European languages, including Finnish.

It may be that the other tribal names in the interior and west coast are just a list of regional Caledonian tribes; as distinct from the 'proto-Pictish' tribes of Orkney and the east coast. This would concur with the situation later around AD 208 when we find Severus now opposed by just two northern tribes named as Caledonii and Maeatae. [7]

This name 'Maeatae' would further support a Finnic interpretation as, in Finnish, the word *miehetaa* means simply: 'the men'. This would concur with the Picts own myth of origin as given in various sources, of which the best known is Bede. [8] He tells us that the Pictish invaders came from Scythia (which here implies the Baltic coast region of Russia); also that they were all-male and they obtained wives from the Irish.

This interpretation would suggest that, during the Flavian conquest, the Romans were able to penetrate so far to the north only with the acquiescence of their Orcadian allies; but sometime in the early second century this alliance collapsed. In later centuries we find Caledonians and Maeatae as unified opponents of Rome under the general name of Picts. The tribes of the west coast and islands seem to have remained unhindered by Rome until as late as the fourth century when we find them as Attacotti and Scots, raiding the ailing province of Britannia alongside the Picts. [9]

Further investigation of all the sources may be found in *Picts and Ancient Britons* and the various etymologies may now be investigated via any good online translator (*see Note 1 Below). Sceptics may say that such linguistic coincidences could be found with any language, to which I say: try it and see; you will only find these correspondences with Finnic languages.

Note 1:
Although lay-persons may make their own comparisons with modern languages; it should be noted that all the suggested Finnic derivations here and in the 1998 book were based on the ancient native Finnish vocabulary as defined by Lauri Hakulinen in "The Structure and Development of the Finnish language" (1961). [10] These root words he defined as deriving from the proto-Finnic language as it was spoken in the region of the Gulf of Finland in the years around the beginning of the Christian era (with some dating from the earlier Finno-Ugrian period). This would be contemporary with the supposed Pictish invasion as described in the various sources. I add this note to forestall the inevitable criticisms of certain Celtic linguists and others who defend the p-Celtic derivations.

References
1. Based on MacBain (1891-2) 'Ptolemy's Geography of Scotland', *Transactions of the Gaelic Society of Inverness*, 21, pp 191-214
2. Tacitus, Agricola, 38
3. Cicero, Ad Familiaris, VII,16,7 (letter to Trebatius)
4. Saint Patrick, Epistola 15
5. Eutropius, Roman History, VII,13,3
6. Tacitus, Agricola, 38
7. Dio Cassius, Roman History, LXXVII, 12, 1-4
8. Bede, Ecclesiastical History, 1,1
9. Ammianus Marcellinus, Library of History, XXVII, 8, 5
10. Hakulinen, Lauri, *The Structure and Development of the Finnish Language*, translated by John Atkinson, Indiana University Press, Bloomington, Indiana (1961)

****

3) Three Pictures of Picts - What did the Picts look like?

Three pictures from the symbol stones of Northeast Scotland give an indication of how the people viewed themselves during the historical Pictish era and in the proto-Pictish tribal era that preceded it.

The three carvings featured here (there are others) are the *Rhynie Man,* now on display in Aberdeen; the *Collessie Man* on a standing stone in Fife; and the 'mother and child' shown on the *Inchbraoch Stone*, which was used as a cover illustration for my 1998 book: *Picts and Ancient Britons.* *

The Rhynie Man

on a stone found on a farm near Rhynie, Buchan, shows a quite unique view of an older man in a tunic carrying a ceremonial axe. The age of the monument is uncertain, but it is assumed to be AD 500-700.

The proportions of the Rhynie figure are significant. The head takes up a quarter of the figure rather than a seventh part as most modern artists are taught to draw the human form. His head clearly shows a long beard, a hooked nose and prominent eyebrows. He has a bald (or perhaps shaven) head; and his ears and teeth are visible. It is not clear whether he has long hair or is wearing some kind of head-dress. It has been suggested that he is a miner, or perhaps a tonsured monk.

The 'hooked' nose can be observed among many modern people in the north-east triangle.

The Collessie Man

A much-worn figure on a standing stone set in the middle of a field near the village of Collessie, Fife.

It depicts a naked warrior carrying a shield and spear with an 'apple' on the shaft. It matches the description of Dio Cassius (third century AD) and may represent a soldier of the Maetae (Miathi) or the Venicones.

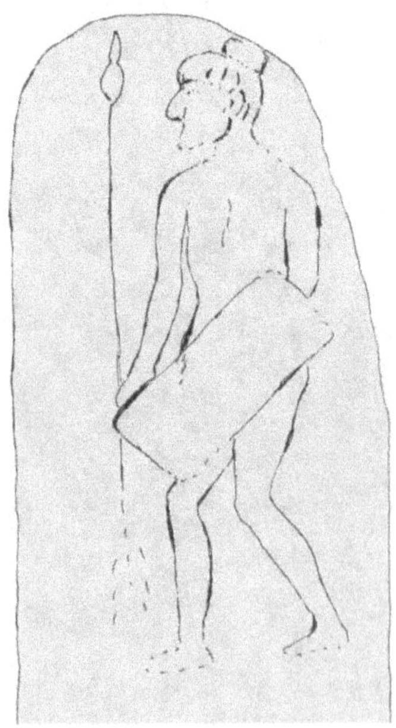

http://www.brand-dd.com/stones/fife/collessie.html

Again the proportions of the figure and his short legs are evident, as is the prominent nose. He too has long hair; but tied-up in a top-knot. Tacitus describes a similar hairstyle among the Suebian Germans, to give the impression of height.

The Inchbraoch Stone

The relief carvings on the Inchbraoch stone show us what appears to be a woman, styling the hair of a young child. However, we should avoid the assumption that the stylized figures are female.

As with the other two figures discussed above, both exhibit short legs (or a long body) and again with long hair in the process of being tied-up. The nose is again given prominence although both figures are cartoon in nature. A stocky build with broad muscular legs was remarked-upon by the Roman historian Tacitus as a characteristic of the Caledonian tribes who faced Agricola in the first century AD and whom he likened to the Suebian Germans.

In 2017 another stone depicting a naked Pictish warrior was discovered during construction of the new A9/A85 road junction in Perth and Kinross. Although the face is somewhat damaged we can just about make-out again the top-knotted hair, together with a spear reminiscent of the Collessie Man. Of more significance again are the proportions and the thickset limbs of the warrior.

An excavation report and illustration is available at:

https://www.thenational.scot/news/15629182.workers-discover-significant-pictish-artefact-while-constructing-road/

It is interesting that none of the figures offer any evidence of tattooing. Fashions of hair-style or body art are cultural and could have entered the region with an immigrant population; however, morphology is genetic. The short thickset build can be observed in many modern Scots and less frequently further south. It will be interesting to see whether geneticists can one-day associate such characteristics with a native 'Pictish gene' or whether it can be traced to immigrants from Baltic Scythia as the legends suggest. Some of the native tribes named by Ptolemy may have occupied northern Britain since the Ice Age and strictly, they would be neither Picts, nor Scots, rather we should consider them native Caledonians.

****

4) The Problem of the Picts

In the 1980's and 1990's I lived in Northeast Scotland and, as an Englishman out-of-place I was struck by how different the locals were from other Scots. It seemed obvious to me that the reason for this is that most are not Scots, but Picts! So I decided to investigate further, resulting in the book that I wrote in 1998.

Anyone who studies the ethnography of the Picts will find that very little is known about their history. Therefore in 1955 the various historians, linguists and archaeologists got together in a symposium and published their papers in a report called 'The Problem of the Picts'. The conclusion of the editor F.T. Wainwright regarding Bede's story of the Scythian origins of the Picts is memorable:

"At best it represents a tradition current among the Picts; but no concrete evidence has yet been produced to support the suggestion that the Picts came from Scythia and the story must be dismissed as legend or literary invention"

This 'dismissive' attitude towards traditional evidence is sadly typical; I encounter it again and again as I study other myths and legends. Quite incredible: for a modern academic to assert that they know better than the Picts knew about their own history, or better than historians who were contemporary with them.

Another hangover from this landmark study was the linguistic review given by Kenneth Jackson, which summarised all the earlier commentators. He reviewed the prevailing opinion that Pictish was a p-Celtic language related to Welsh and concluded "there the matter rests". However if you read his words carefully he was himself far from convinced that many of the words in the meagre vocabulary available were 'clearly or probably Celtic'. Nevertheless the editor summarised the prevailing opinion and henceforth the Picts became Celts.

The difficulty is that once such ideas become embedded in the textbooks it becomes almost impossible to challenge them. We may find later researchers doing comparative studies of Celtic languages including all the Pictish words as proven Celtic and citing these earlier references. My own opinion of most of the comparative linguistics that I have read could be summed up by an English word beginning with 'b'. This kind of linguistic study is unsafe when you have only 30 or so words of variable provenance (mostly names from Ptolemy's map) that can be claimed as Pictish. If some future researcher possessed only 30 random words of English then 60% of them would be of French origin. They would likely conclude that English was a Romance language.

New Deer

I am indebted to Mrs Jean Pearce of Insch, Aberdeenshire, who wrote to me after reading *Picts and Ancient Britons* to offer an insight that I had not considered. She suggested that the Picts called *Niduari* by Bede in his Life of Saint Cuthbert (or *Niuduera* in another source) might recall a visit by the saint to the monastery at *New Deer* in Buchan. Although believed to date from 1219, notes in the Book of Deer claim that the first monastery was actually founded by Saint Columba and has its origins in the Pictish period. The etymology of the place-name *Deer* is obscure (see Kenneth Jackson, *Gaelic Notes in the Book of Deer*, p 39) and so the name New Deer could be an anglicised form, of a Gaelic form, of an original Pictish word. Note that there is also a village called Old Deer a few miles away! Mrs Pearce also drew my attention to the hill of *Dunnideer*, the vitrified fort near Bennachie.

One of the suggestions in my book was that this word *Niduari* is an example of a Finnic-Pictish word related to the modern Finnish word *Noita*, implying a shaman, a witch or a warlock, i.e. a Druid. Perhaps Cuthbert was merely stating that he had visited the converted Christian priests of the Picts, who continued to call themselves by their pagan Pictish name. The lady's suggestion that the saint visited Deer is therefore quite reasonable; and the name *Dunnideer* would mean something like 'hill of the Druids'; a venerated pagan holy site.

Pictish DNA?

Since *Picts and Ancient Britons* was published in 1998 the science of DNA analysis has advanced beyond all expectations. In 2017 a study of British DNA was published that includes results for Scotland. In the triangle of north-east Scotland the results show overlapping populations that are termed Northeast Scotland 1 & 2. This corresponds to the two tribes on Ptolemy's map, the *Taexali* and the *Vacomagi*. The overlap would suggest an older population overridden by later immigrants.

For the Orkney Islands a complex picture emerges; and for southern and western Scotland the populations are more homogeneous and show overlap with Ireland. This has raised again the question that there was an identifiable 'Pictish gene', unrelated to the 'Celtic' populations further south and west – if indeed these people were themselves ethnically Celtic. This entire question is now opened-up for further study.

It should not surprise us that 10% of Scots may carry a unique gene related to the Basques of Spain. After all, the historical Scots came from Ireland and all the Irish legends of origin bring the Irish invaders over from Spain. The legends of Pictish origin say they were all-male and came from Baltic Scythia - but they took Irish wives. Therefore, half the people of Pictish origin and all of the western Scots should have Irish DNA. But there were people already in Scotland before these invaders came, so there is much more to this story.

Not to be taken too seriously!

In the 1990's I attempted to publish an article in a Scottish magazine, about the Scythian origin of the Picts as it is related by Bede. It was heavy with the usual references to Jackson, Watson, Wainwright, etc., that are expected. The editor came back that unfortunately they couldn't publish because (I paraphrase from memory) this sort of 'Biblical who-begat-whom style' does not make very interesting reading.

So, I toned it down a bit and instead tried sending the revised article to a journal that publishes more scholarly papers on Scottish history, who responded that it would indeed be the right place to publish. As expected he submitted it to a suitable referee for an opinion. Back came the reply: '*clearly he has not read the works of Jackson, Watson, etc. ... he seems to be suggesting that there were no Celtic Picts*'. There is no use saying that it's only what the Picts themselves believed; and also the venerable Bede, who actually corresponded with living Picts. You can't argue with a judge in court and you can't argue with an academic referee!

* Longer extracts of all the literary sources discussed here are given in:

Dunbavin, Paul (1998) *Picts and Ancient Britons*, Third Millennium Publishing, ISBN: 978-0-9525029-1-7

****

INDEX

C

D

G

H

I

J

K

L

N

O

R

S

T

U

V

W

X

Y

Z

ABOUT THE AUTHOR

Paul Dunbavin was born in 1954 in Derbyshire; educated in physics and computing. From 1974 to 1999 he pursued a career in computing and subsequently ran a business transfer agency in Yorkshire. He is broadly self-taught across the arts and sciences and was a former Mensa local secretary in Aberdeen. His interest for over 35 years has been cross-disciplinary research into prehistory, which he has occasionally published in his books and various articles and papers. His work is well known among enthusiasts and academics and receives a mixture of both positive and negative reaction. He contributed to a History Channel television series called *Puzzles of the Past* in the 1990s and has also had several magazine articles published.

Being largely self-taught and broadly educated across the arts and sciences, he has always preferred to consider himself as a researcher first and an author second. In authorship his primary interests are astronomy, ancient history, mythology and catastrophism with a side interest in the ethnography of Scotland and the British Isles.

His first book *The Atlantis Researches* was published in 1995 and republished in second edition by Constable in 2002 as *Atlantis of the West*. This was followed by *Picts and Ancient Britons* in 1998 and *Under Ancient Skies* in 2005. He has also written a number of research papers and articles on related subjects. Although for some years out of physical print these books were made available again in 2017 in Kindle editions. A new book: *Towers of Atlantis* was published in 2017.

As an author, of non-fiction Paul Dunbavin prefers to write 'real books' rather than publishers' formula pap. He prefers to present evidence in an interesting way but with fully referenced source bibliography in the academic style. The reader can expect to find original theories and conclusions unique to the author within every chapter, yet all are entirely based upon source evidence and current standard textbook science. The author offers an alternative theory of catastrophism in prehistory that owes nothing to Velikovsky.

www.third-millennium.co.uk

www.ingramcontent.com/pod-product-compliance
Lightning Source LLC
LaVergne TN
LVHW012048160826
845678LV00014B/2749

* 9 7 8 0 9 5 2 5 0 2 9 5 1 *